RUNNING WITH THE BUFFALOES

RUNNING WITH THE BUFFALOES

A Season Inside
with Mark Wetmore, Adam Goucher,
and the University of Colorado
Men's Cross Country Team

Chris Lear

THE LYONS PRESS
Guilford, Connecticut
An Imprint of The Globe Pequot Press

The Lyons Press is an imprint of the The Globe Pequot Press

Printed in The United States of America

10 9 8 7 6 5

ISBN 1-58574-804-8

The Library of Congress Cataloging-in-Publication Data is available on file.

Acknowledgments

RUNNING WITH THE BUFFALOES would not have been possible without the help of many people. First, Mark Wetmore. He granted me total access to everything and anyone in his program. This book exists because of him. Second, the men of the University of Colorado cross country team. They welcomed me into their lives, and they remain a special part of my life. Special thanks to Adam Goucher and Adam Batliner, whose help and candor have incalculably enriched this work.

Thanks also to my editors: Tom Coogan, Tom Kloss, Tim Lear and Andrew Goldstein. In particular, my gratitude goes to Andrew, who edited the manuscript so adeptly and inspired me to finish when the task appeared daunting.

Thanks to Shawn Feeney, for continual support throughout the project. Thanks to Kristen Coogan for her original cover design, and Adam Batliner for the original cover photo. Thanks to Colleen Reilly and the CU athletic department for their help and cooperation.

Finally, thanks to my family, Tim, Freddy, Mom and Pop, for giving me the courage to follow my bliss.

In Loving Memory

Yvonne Tock
May 22, 1922–July 13, 1999

Christopher Severy
June 22, 1976–October 12, 1998

Foreword

I got to know Chris Lear in 1996 on an eighteen-mile run through the Big Basin Redwood Forest. He had this crazy idea to follow a Division I cross country team through their season. He wanted to write a book about the trials and triumphs the team would encounter. As we ran through the towering redwoods, we talked about how much fun and interesting it would be to actually do it.

A year and a half went by before I heard from Chris again. This time, though, he was in Boulder preparing to do exactly what he had discussed with me while running through that redwood forest. He was in Boulder to document three months of our training, the University of Colorado Cross Country team. Little did he know that within those three months he would be documenting one of the most trying years in CU history. Chris was there through it all; every step of every run. He witnessed each moment of pain, distress, excitement, and happiness with every workout. Almost instantly, his presence among the team became natural, he fit in, and he became one of us.

Looking back, I can see how Chris helped me through my last collegiate season. At the time he was recovering from foot surgery, and wasn't able to run with us. Instead, he would bike alongside us. Typically, at that point in my career at CU, I ran the majority of my workouts alone, and I looked at Chris as somewhat of a training partner. There were many times when he would ride along with me and help me maintain the pace I desired. He brought an element of competitiveness that kept me from settling, and gave me the perfect edge of the intended workout. Some people would say that I was racing, and there were times that this was somewhat true (mainly on a 22-miler in 2:03 out at the Boulder Reservoir). But I was in the process of taking the next step, and Chris was there helping me. He became one of my closest friends, someone I could confide in, someone I respected tremendously, and someone I could hang out with!

Through a season that commanded the courage of every CU runner, through the good times and definitely the bad, Chris was there every moment, *living* it with us, and he, too, was just as much a part of it as we were.

Adam Goucher

Contents

The 1998 University of Colorado Cross Country Team

Adam Batliner   *Senior*
Lakewood, Colorado (Green Mountain)

Wetmore: "Adam should be one of the best cross country runners in the nation this year. He has as good a reason as anyone to win the national championship. He's definitely among the top eight or ten runners in the country, and the other seven or nine will be dreaming of a national title. He might as well also."

1997: 26th at the NCAA Cross Country Championships. He ran a 7:58 for 3000 meters indoors and a finished third in the steeplechase at the Outdoor NCAA's.

Wes Berkshire   *Junior*
Aurora, Colorado (Smoky Hill)

Wetmore: "Wes is one of the hardest workers in our program. He could surprise some people and make our [Varsity] team.

1997: Redshirt. Did not compete.

Aaron Blondeau   *Sophomore*
Salida, Colorado (Salida)

Wetmore: "Aaron had a good freshman year in cross and was disappointed with a left shin stress fracture during the outdoor season. He's been training full speed all summer and I predict that he will be much improved. I expect him to be a top-25 runner at Nationals this year."

1997: CU's top freshman. 101st at the NCAA Cross Country Championships.

Zach Crandall   *Freshman*
                          Fort Collins, Colorado (Rocky Mountain)

Walk-on seeks to make the roster.

1997: All-State performer in Colorado.

Jason Drake   *Assistant Coach*
                          Gillette, Wyoming (Campbell County)

First Wyoming prep to run under 4:20 in the 1600m. A 1994 CU graduate, he had a disappointing collegiate career until he made great strides
under Wetmore in Wetmore's first two seasons with the Buffaloes. He
is Wetmore's right hand man.

Matt Elmuccio   *Freshman*
                          Westfield, New Jersey (Westfield)

Wetmore: "Matt has an outside shot of making our varsity this season."

1997: Redshirt. Did not compete.

Mike Friedberg   *Sophomore*
                          Columbia, Maryland (The Park School)

Wetmore: "Mike will be an unknown guy on the national scene this year.
He would make any other varsity team in the United States, and will
probably make ours. People are going to wonder where he came from.
While Goucher, Batliner, and Reese have been getting all of the attention,
he's been putting dollars in the bank and waiting his turn. He'll be a surprise in November."

1997: Redshirt. Did not compete.

Adam Goucher   *Senior*
                          Colorado Springs, Colorado (Doherty)

Wetmore: "Adam has wanted to win an NCAA title in cross country
since two and a half minutes after finishing second his freshman year. He's
been snakebit by interruptions the last three years and he feels that he
has something to prove this season. He will be the Boulder favorite, but
there will be seven or eight different favorites all over the country."

1997: An undefeated fall ends in disappointment with a fourth-place finish at the NCAA Cross Country Championships. Goucher subsequently

won the NCAA Indoor 3000 meter title in a collegiate record 7:46.03 and the NCAA Outdoor 5000 meter title.

Cameron Harrison *Freshman*
Colorado Springs, Colorado (Doherty)

Walk-on from Goucher's alma mater seeks to make the roster.

Jay Johnson *Senior*
Castle Rock, Colorado (Douglas County)

Enters the season hoping to end career on a positive note. A disappointing spring track season in 1998 followed by a case of mono places Johnson at the bottom of the heap starting his senior campaign.

1997: 84th at Pre-Nationals.

Adam Loomis *Sophomore*
Highlands Ranch, Colorado (Highlands Ranch/Portland)

Walk-on seeks to make roster.

Matt Napier *Senior*
Socorro, New Mexico (Socorro)

Wetmore: "Napier had a breakthrough last fall when he became an All-American. He is one of the great blue-collar success stories of CU running. He's in the best shape of his life, but he will most likely redshirt."

1997: The former walk-on follows second-place performance at the Mountain Regional with a 39th-place finish at NCAA's.

John O'Mara *Sophomore*
Northboro, Massachusetts (St. John's/Providence)

8:24 3000 meter runner is an unknown heading into the 1998 season.

Oscar Ponce *Junior*
Denver, Colorado (Denver North)

Wetmore: "Oscar was a varsity runner until we had to go from nine to seven runners at the end of last season. He definitely wants to be in the seven that go to the NCAA championship. The only road he knows is the hard road. If he can survive 105 to 110 miles per week, he might get there."

1997: 32nd at Big Cross Country Championships.

Tom Reese *Senior*
Golden, Colorado (Wheat Ridge)

Wetmore: "As was planned, Tommy redshirted last spring to balance his eligibility. His recovery from arthroscopic surgery in May has been slow. If rehab on his left knee goes the way we think, he will be among the varsity seven and be an All-American again this year. He's too good a runner not to make it back."

1997: 33rd-place finish at NCAA's earns Reese All-American honors.

Jason Robbie *Junior*
Boulder, Colorado (Alexander Dawson/Vermont)

Wetmore: "Robbie was the most impressive guy at the Varsity Time Trial last year. But since the day he made the team, his training has been interrupted. A lot of guys have run more than him this summer."

1997: Fourteenth at the Ft. Hays State Tiger Invitational.

Lorie Moreno-Roch *Assistant Coach*

She attended Adams State College (Alamosa, Colorado) from 1982 to 1984 before graduating from Western State College (Gunnison, Colorado) in 1988. Between the two schools, she was an eight-time all-American in the mile, 5k, 10k, and distance medley relay. Roch was a member of the U.S. national team at the World Relay Championships in 1994, and she was coached by Wetmore in the spring of 1995. She adds her vast national and international racing experience to the staff.

Ronald Roybal *Junior*
Pojoaque, New Mexico (Pojoaque)

Wetmore: "Ron pulled our tails out of the fire for us a year ago with a great race at the NCAA championships. He helped us to stay in third place. He's been training well this summer and if he takes the next logical step, he will be a top-30 finisher and a First Team All-American at Nationals."

1997: 45th at the NCAA Cross Country Championships.

Matt Ruhl   *Freshman*
                            Runnemade, New Jersey (Triton Regional)

9:28 high school 3200-meter runner seeks to make the roster.

Chris Schafer   *Sophomore*
                            Yakima, Washington (Eisenhower)

Colorado Indoor 800 meter Record Holder (1:49.37) is a long shot to make the varsity.

1997: 26th at the Fort Hays State Tiger Invitational.

Chris Severy   *Senior*
                            Aspen, Colorado (Aspen)

Wetmore: "Chris battled mono a year ago, but he's back training. He's a little behind his normal summer, but he is completely healed. He finished 17th two years ago at the NCAA championships and hopes to improve."

1997: Redshirt. Did not compete.

Steve Slattery   *Freshman*
                            Flanders, New Jersey (Mt. Olive)

Wetmore: "He is a big talent. But most likely, he will redshirt."

1997: New Jersey state champion in cross country. Fourth at the Foot Locker National Championship.

Sean Smith   *Sophomore*
                            Montrose, Colorado (Montrose)

Triathlete seeks to make the roster.

1997: Did not compete.

Brock Tessman   *Graduate/Transfer*
                            Danville, California (Monte Vista/Brown)

Wetmore: "A Brown transfer, Brock still has a cross country and an outdoor season of eligibility left. He's a national caliber 1500-meter runner, the fastest guy in the country who didn't qualify for the NCAA Championships last year. His success will depend on how he adapts to our system, but I'm pretty sure he will be a Varsity-caliber runner for us. I wouldn't be surprised if he finished in the top 30 or better in Lawrence."

1997: 14th at the Heptagonals (Ivy League Championships).

Chris Valenti   *Sophomore*
                                      Littleton, Colorado (Littleton)

Sophomore walk-on seeks to make the roster.

1997: 26th at the Fort Hays State Tiger Invitational.

Mark Wetmore   *Head Coach*
                                 Bernardsville, New Jersey (Bernards)

A Bernardsville, New Jersey, native, Wetmore graduated from Rutgers University with a degree in English education in 1978. In 1988 he earned his master's in movement sciences from Columbia University. A middle-distance runner at Rutgers, he began his coaching career as coach of the Edge City Track Club in 1972. He then spent fourteen years as an assistant to his high school mentor, Ed Mather, at Bernards. In 1991, after a four-year stint as the distance coach at Seton Hall University, he emigrated to Colorado. He was named men's distance coach at the University of Colorado in 1992, and his cross country teams have finished no lower than fifth in the NCAA Men's Cross Country National Championships since 1993. On November 6, 1995, Wetmore was named head cross country and track and field coach for both the men's and women's programs.

Wetmore enters the 1998 season with his best team ever, having only lost two-time All-American Clint Wells from the 1997 team that finished third at the NCAA championships. Wetmore seeks nothing less from Adam Goucher and the Buffaloes than their first national titles.

RUNNING WITH THE BUFFALOES

Introduction

The team stretches in silence, finishing their pre-race preparation before ambling off, one by one, to the starting line. Adam Goucher is the last one to leave. Finished tying his spikes, he stands nervously and stares into the distance. Coach Mark Wetmore calms him with some final words. "You're fine, Adam. You're fine. Trust it, Adam. Trust all your work."

His voice terse, Adam responds, "I know." With that, he turns away from Wetmore, and departs to meet his teammates at the starting line.

Goucher is now ten minutes from a moment he has worked toward since late November 1994. As a precocious freshman he finished second to the University of Arizona's Martin Keino at the NCAA championships in Fayetteville, Arkansas (in the process becoming the highest freshman finisher in the NCAA championships since Indiana yearling Bob Kennedy took home the title in 1988). Goucher moves with confidence.

Goucher is not alone. Oscar Ponce, Mike Friedberg, Ronald Roybal, Tom Reese, Adam Batliner, and Jay Johnson, each with aspirations of his own, also ready themselves to join Goucher in the battle to establish collegiate distance-running supremacy.

On August 18th, the 23 men of the University of Colorado cross country team dreamt of being here. In the ensuing 94 days, these seven demonstrated that they indeed possessed the right stuff. After myriad trials, they emerged: leaner, meaner, wiser, and ready.

Ponce readies for start.

At campuses across the country, from Princeton, New Jersey, to Palo Alto, California, similar rites of passage have taken place. Now 31 teams have converged to find out which team—and which person—can lay claim to the title of National Champion.

The Buffaloes are in starting box fourteen, right toward the middle of the 31-team field. Mountain District rivals Northern Arizona University ready themselves in box thirteen, to the left of the Buffaloes. Individual qualifiers (including a man familiar to all the Buffaloes after training with them last summer, Columbia's Tom Kloos) are to their right in box fifteen. Oregon, their primary rival, is at the far end of the line to their right.

Ronald Roybal stands at ease, snaps his arms backwards, and takes in the sight of the 250 foot soldiers, a battalion awaiting the bugle's call, that surround him. Wetmore says that last year the Pojoague, New Mexico, native "swooped up and saved our ass" at NCAA's, finishing a remarkable 45th after only running to an 80th-place finish at the Mountain Regional. "Ronald had one good day of running all fall," Wetmore recalls, "when we needed it." Without his breakthrough performance, CU would not have finished third in the team competition. They need him today. And, unlike last year, his training has progressed sufficiently enough so that Wetmore now expects him to gain All-American honors.

Oscar Ponce, the diminutive Mexican from inner-city Denver North High School, has had a dream season. Having finally made it to his first national championship competition, he stands on the precipice of reaching his dream: to inspire others, for whom mere survival is a struggle, to reach for the stars by becoming the first All-American ever to graduate from Denver North. On October 3rd he finished seventh at the Rocky Mountain Shootout, two spots ahead of his buddy Roybal. They hugged and celebrated afterward, thinking of their progress, and how fit they would be, come today, if all went well. In the last three weeks, shin pain has threatened to unceremoniously dash his dream. Unbowed by the development, he stands at the ready, prepared to fight again.

Team Captain Tommy Reese shakes out his limbs and stares blankly into space as he takes his position on the line. An All-American a year ago after finishing 33rd at NCAA's, the fifth-year senior accelerated his return from surgery to repair a cracked femur in order to lead his team in its quest for a national title. But his path to this point has been full of interruptions. Two weeks ago his knee swelled to the size of an orange after running repeat miles. "Right then," he said, "I knew three things. One, there's blood in the joints again. Two, the cracking and clicking tells me there is loose, cracked cartilage. That all hurts and affects the bending of the knee. But the cracked femur is what I can totally feel, and that's what stops me. It doesn't feel at all stable when I land. The pain shoots, and it feels like my leg is going to go backward." He has had the knee drained, and now he is convinced he is a top-thirty guy. But with everything he has endured, is this possible?

Tired and wanting to yawn, legs feeling just a smidge lethargic, Adam Batliner knows it is time to go. Another fifth-year senior, he, too, earned All-American status last year with a 26th-place finish at NCAA's. He capped an outstanding year with a third-place finish in the steeplechase at the NCAA's last spring despite only training intermittently because of a stress fracture in his fibula. He built upon those accomplishments with the best summer of training in his life. When practice started in late August, finishing in the top ten today looked realistic. But like Reese, his training has suffered from numerous setbacks. Now a top-ten finish will require a miracle, and he lines up with only the vaguest idea of what is possible. He will need to summon all of his savvy to repeat last year's All-American performance.

Goucher adjusts his necklace of shrunken skulls, symbols of his prey, determined to add more scalps on this day. Julius Mwangi, a Kenyan running for Butler University, handed Goucher his only loss of the season on this course on October 10th. As Mwangi crossed the finish line, he raised his hands in exultation, celebrating, in Goucher's opinion, "like he's the national champ. I'm not worried," he said then of the loss, "I'll destroy him when I'm ready."

But since then Goucher has also suffered setbacks in his preparation. By now, though, he is no stranger to untimely misfortune sabotaging his season. Since his freshman year he has been poised to win the NCAA championship, but each time illness or injury has debilitated him when it mattered most. Just last year he seemed indomitable as he marched through the season undefeated. But a cold felled him the week of the NCAA's, and a beleaguered Goucher could only manage a fourth-place finish.

He would not have to wait long for a chance at redemption. Just four months later, he electrified the crowd at the NCAA Indoor Track and Field Championships by running away from Bernard Lagat of Washington State University to win the 3000 meters and set a new collegiate record of 7:46.03 in the process. He complemented that championship with a victory in the 5000 meters at the NCAA Outdoor Track and Field Championships in Buffalo, New York, for his third career NCAA championship (he also won the NCAA 3000 meter title in 1997). Yet, the one title running enthusiasts thought he would already have, the one title he should already possess, has eluded him. It is a title he covets so much that he elected to postpone his professional career for one final opportunity to claim it as his own. Rightly or wrongly, his season and his collegiate career will be judged by how he performs today. Ready or not, showtime is about to begin.

As 250 men bounce, fiddle, and stretch, hoping, by God, just to get this thing started, Wetmore barks final instructions to his runners. "Gentlemen, you'll hear no splits, and you won't see any mile markers. You're running by feel. Pay attention to your sensory data."

No splits? This angers the Buffaloes, particularly Mike Friedberg. "I was pissed," he recalls. "I just knew they weren't going to be able to give splits because that's the way things were run out there." Hearing this now rattles him nonetheless. With only five minutes until the start, Friedberg is losing his shit. Nicknamed "the Iceberg" by Wetmore early in the season for his unflappable temperament under pressure, his fears are getting the best of him.

Jay Johnson, another fifth-year senior, senses Friedberg's anxiety, and he tries to settle his nerves. "Don't worry about this," he says. "This is fake. Everyone's full of shit. What's real is Magnolia Road, what's real is milers out on the course." No one has traveled as long a road as Johnson to get to this moment. A veteran of two prior NCAA cross country championships, he never expected to race in another. He has run the last eight weeks thinking each race would be his last; but he performed just well enough in each instance to prolong his season. Like the others, he has endured under the most trying of circumstances, and because of this, he is able to put the race into perspective for Friedberg when he needs it most.

Friedberg internalizes Johnson's counsel, and to a certain extent, it works. But still, doubt lingers. Just a year ago he was a Junior Varsity runner, a walk-on nobody from the Park School in Baltimore, Maryland—hardly a recruiting hotbed. Now he is being counted on to be up at the front, contending for All-American honors.

It's go time. They nod and slap hands with one another, wordlessly expressing their hopes, their prayers, and their brotherhood. Ninety-four days and thousands of miles since they convened at Kitt Field on an 88-degree afternoon, they await the starter's call. All that remains is thirty minutes to "man up" and take the pain, one last time. They are not afraid . . .

Tuesday, August 18, 1998
Balch Field House
3:15 p.m.

94 Days to Lawrence

The CU cross country team gathers for the first official practice of the year. The men and women form a large circle in Balch Field house, while fifth-year senior Tommy Reese, last year's cross country captain, leads the team in stretching. Matt Elmuccio, a sophomore miler from New Jersey, is back on campus for the first time. He has had the best summer training of his life in his hometown of Westfield. He has sprouted a robust red goatee during the summer. Coupled with his thick auburn hair and two-foot-long rat's tail, his is a distinct appearance. He is tan and fit, and his calm demeanor as he stretches suggests he is ready to work.

Opposite Elmuccio, Adam Goucher stretches quietly. While many of his teammates spent the summer training together in Boulder, he elected to spend the summer in his hometown of Colorado Springs. He performed odd jobs at the United States Olympic Training Center in Colorado Springs and worked at a dog track in order to make enough money to pay his bills this semester. In spite of the fifty-hour workweeks, he trained *arduously*. Rising most days at 6:30 a.m. to run, he increased his volume quickly and steadily. Last Friday, in Colorado Springs at an elevation of 7500 feet, he comfortably ran a five-mile AT (anaerobic threshold) in 25:43, in the midst of a week in which he ran 95 miles *in singles!** His training is right on schedule.

That same Friday afternoon at Potts Field (the University of Colorado outdoor track), CU teammates Chris Severy, Oscar Ponce, Brock Tessman, and Chris Schafer also ran a five-mile AT. They were joined by Steve Slattery, a hot-shot freshman who just rolled into town with his family from New Jersey. Sporting a sleeveless Mt. Olive T-shirt, a fresh tattoo of the cartoon character The Flash was visible on his right shoulder.

After passing two miles in 10:40, Slattery pulled off the track. Hunched over with his hands grasping his shorts, he looked up and said, "I feel like crap. I thought I was in shape, but that was tough!"

Welcome to high altitude, young man.

The others pressed on. Severy and Friedberg ran 26:30, and the others

---

* "In singles" is a common term in Wetmorespeak. He is not overly concerned with volume. Wetmore places greater value in how much mileage you do running once a day. A Lydiard disciple, he stresses the greater physiological benefit of running, for example, 70 minutes in one run as opposed to two runs that total 70 minutes. Goucher and his teammates all set out to meet their summer volume goals running once a day.

filed in ten seconds later. After a long summer of distance runs up and down Boulder's trails, they too showed they were ready to get to work.

Inside Balch, the mood is calm and relaxed as Wetmore strides around the inside of the circle, checking to see if the runners received their equipment and have had their physicals. MaryBeth, the team's equipment manager and assistant throws coach, enters the circle to have a quick word with Wetmore. As she approaches, Wetmore introduces her, and jokingly tells the squad, "Be real nice to MaryBeth 'cause she's in charge of all the stuff."

It is a lot of stuff. The university has a contract with Nike, and each runner receives a pair of Terra Humma training shoes, cross country racing flats, track flats, shorts, long and short sleeve T-shirts, sweatpants, sweatshirts, and even wristbands and a headband. It is a far cry from Wetmore's undergraduate running days at Rutgers University in New Jersey, when in the fall of his freshman year, the equipment manager gave him used training shoes that formerly belonged to another member of the squad.

Everything is in place. All of the runners have received their equipment and their physicals. The only glitch is with Wetmore's personal order. Nike has mistakenly sent him soccer shoes for the third year in a row. This inconvenience does not bother Wetmore, and will not affect his running in the least. He has not missed a day of running in over *nineteen years*.

The stretching circle is fairly divided in half, with the men on one side and the women on the other. As they stretch they talk quietly among themselves in groups of two to four, catching up on their summers and such. All are dressed in running shorts and T-shirts, with the exception of freshman Steve Slattery, who wears his old red and yellow Mt. Olive T-shirt with cutoff sleeves and basketball shorts that extend to his knees with boxers poking over the waistband. Various upperclassmen are already placing bets on how long it will be before Wetmore starts ribbing him about the shorts, and when he will start wearing running shorts. Asked the previous Sunday by Jay Johnson, "Steve, you run in boxers?!" Slattery shrugged and nonchalantly replied, "Yeah, my whole team did in high school." Reese shook his head and said, "Damn, even with my little junk, I still need some grippers to hold my shit together!"

Done stretching, the team departs the gym and jogs for two miles down to Kittredge Field (Kitt), a flat, grass athletic field with a half-mile circumference. The runners gather and stretch lightly again while Wetmore divides them into three groups for the day's athletics. The men are doing anywhere from ten to sixteen loops of Kitt with a 200-meter pickup at "cross country race pace" on each lap. The women's workout is identical, the only variable being the number of repetitions. The runners do this workout by feel rather than time, and none of them check their watches to monitor their pace. Assistant coaches Jason Drake (referred to as JD by all) and Lorie Roch set out cones to demarcate the 200-meter segment where they will do their pickups.

All the runners take off at once, and immediately Goucher grabs the lead, heading around the first corner. The first two groups of men pass the mile in 5:40, and everyone looks good. This is Wetmore's first opportunity to see the fruits of summer training. He eyes his runners carefully as they circle the field, noting who is running easily and who is laboring excessively.

Slattery runs next to Elmuccio, his predecessor as King of New Jersey prep running. While obviously laboring as his chest heaves in search of oxygen, Slattery still captures Wetmore's attention. "Look at him," he says with the admiration of a veteran horse trainer admiring the gallop of a promising colt. "He's got a big, powerful stride!" Slattery gobbles up ground as he runs, taking one stride for Elmuccio's two. Despite their Jersey roots, the two are a study in contrasts. From Elmuccio's short, clipped stride and reticent demeanor to Slattery's gallop and brash countenance, the two are polar opposites. What they do share is an intense rivalry born in their prep days, and this first workout is just a prelude for the battles to be waged between the two throughout the fall.

Ten minutes in, the first group is rolling, with Goucher, Batliner, and Friedberg up front. Wetmore leans in as they pass. "Careful what you're doing, Flagstaff tomorrow." The comment is aimed at Friedberg, a Junior Varsity runner a year ago who is determined to run with the big boys, and it is in reference to Wednesday's thirteen-mile run up and over Flagstaff Mountain. In the agonizing first 30 minutes from Balch gym to the trail summit on Flagstaff Mountain, the runners will climb over 1400 feet. Wetmore's words help keep their ambition in check, and the workout from escalating out of control.

Six loops in, Wetmore pulls Slattery and junior Ronald Roybal. Running his first 65-mile week in over a year, Roybal is healthy, but not fit. To Slattery, Wetmore says, "Enough for today. Welcome to 5000 feet." Slattery catches his breath before responding, "I got this funny taste in my mouth." Wetmore smiles and says, "Does it taste like pennies? Hemingway says that's the taste of death."

The others keep running around the perimeter. Although laboring more than his compatriots, Friedberg hangs tough with Batliner and Goucher up front. His summer of training appears to be paying dividends, and at this early juncture, he appears a lock to make the squad. Nevertheless, it is a long road to Nationals. Looking to pull in the reins once more, Wetmore says as they come around again, "We got ninety-four days to go. We don't need to show off."

All the runners are done after fourteen circuits except for Goucher and Batliner. They continue on for two more. That Batliner runs with Goucher is no surprise. He is in arguably the best shape of his life. This past Sunday he ran an eighteen-mile run, wrapping up a 94-mile week that was the culmination of eight weeks of great base training. Like Goucher, Batliner is shooting to win the NCAA individual title.

Goucher picks up the cones on the last circuit, and he and Batliner jog in comfortably, chatting. They have run 43:10 for eight miles, an average of 5:24 per mile. They have accomplished the day's objective; a highly aerobic effort without compromising tomorrow's run up Flagstaff.

Reese finishes shortly after Goucher and Batliner, having run easy for 45 minutes while his mates were put through their paces. His summer training began only a week ago due to spring surgery to repair a cracked femur. At Wetmore's urging, Reese jumps in for a 200-meter pickup and also does two 150s. Many runners in Reese's shoes would pack it in for the season, having been unable to get in a full summer's worth of training, but Reese is undaunted. Two years ago, he did not begin running until September 23rd due to injury. He finished the season 60th at NCAA's, having run a maximum of 40 miles a week. A fifth-year senior, this is his last shot at collegiate cross country. Therefore, Wetmore has developed an ambitious plan for Reese. If all goes perfectly, Reese will have seven 85-mile weeks under his belt before NCAA's this year. With that volume, and his talent, a top-twenty finish is not unrealistic. Informed of Goucher and Batliner's time, he shakes his head. "Don't tell me that . . . I don't want to know. I know I have seven weeks to the [Colorado] Shootout. I want Nordberg [his nickname for Friedberg]. But don't get me wrong," he continues, "I want Nordberg to do well, top five at NCAA's. I just want to be one step ahead."

Meanwhile, as most of the runners were finishing and warming down back to Balch, Roybal was finishing his run down on the Boulder Creek Path. He bumped into Jay Johnson, a fifth-year graduate student in exercise physiology who aspires to once again make the Varsity in his last collegiate cross country season. They decide to sit in the creek and soak their legs for a while. After an outdoor season where he was overweight and never "fully invested" in track, as Wetmore would say, Johnson was hoping to bang out a good summer of training. Unfortunately, a bout of mononucleosis did him in, and he is woefully out of shape. Johnson lagged even behind Roybal in the run today, but he is not discouraged. Like Roybal, Johnson has had success in the past. Most notable was his 3:49, 14:20 1500 meter/ 5000 meter double at Mt. SAC two years ago. Today, they decide to take things one day at a time. Johnson says to Roybal, "You know what, we have experience. We have to be calm, and we'll run better, even if it takes to indoors." But each wants to be on the squad that toes the line in Lawrence. They have 94 days.

Like Ten Pounds of Shit in a Five-Pound Bag

Those runners who failed to heed Wetmore's advice to stay controlled yesterday are now in for an even more painful task. The men and the women are going to be running from Balch gym up to Chautauqua Park, where they will climb a single-track trail towards the summit of Flagstaff Mountain. From the time they exit the gym until they approach the trail's apex roughly four miles later, they will not run a single step on flat land. In the roughly 30-minute climb to this point the run cruelly ascends over 1400 feet at a slightly ever-increasing grade. The first fourteen minutes of the climb leading up to the trailhead are not overly strenuous, but once one sets foot on the trail itself, it switchbacks hard and fast up the mountain. The rapid ascent almost instantaneously puts a runner in oxygen debt. The worst is yet to come.

As the summit is approached the trail steepens so much that the runners must scamper, bound, or, if the will is broken, walk over increasingly high steps that tax your lungs and make your quads burn and quiver. Of the climb, Batliner steadfastly says, "You're hurting. If you are doing more than walking, you're hurting." Such is the notoriety of the run's climb that US Army runner Sam Wilbur says frequent runs up Flagstaff will transform the meekest of runners into "Quadzilla."

Once the summit of Flagstaff is reached (so named because of a flagstaff visible from the mountain's base), the run levels out for a quarter mile, allowing the runners' respiration to return to normal before they descend a fire trail that switchbacks for several miles around the other side of the mountain. The descent offers magnificent views of the surrounding aspen- and pine tree–covered peaks. The trail terminates in the parking lot of the Red Lion Inn off Canyon Road. In all, the run is thirteen miles long. Says Batliner, "The thirteen feels like eight because after you work your ass off, you coast back home." But for the less fit, the downhill run on the creek path is little more than a dead-legged dawdle back home.

While they stretch before heading off, Wetmore instructs them that the run is to be easy and conversational. As he says this, some of the veterans, such as Berkshire and Batliner, lower their heads and chuckle, no doubt pondering the remote possibility of *ever* holding a conversation at *any* pace while climbing Flagstaff.

This is not exactly encouraging news for transfers John O'Mara and Brock Tessman, who are preparing for their first run up the mountain. Tessman appears anxious before the climb. Before embarking on the run he says, "Usually the guys downplay the runs, but none of the guys are downplaying Flagstaff. They all say it's tough." Their first Flagstaff run is a memorable one.

The top nine guys head out together while O'Mara and Tessman team with junior Jason Robbie. The trio quickly loses sight of the Goucher-led main pack. Unfortunately for O'Mara and Tessman, Robbie's IT (ilio tibial) band begins aching and he is forced to turn around for home. Without Robbie's trailblazing, they miss the turn onto the fire trail down the mountain. They are forced to retrace their steps after losing their way—ending back on campus an hour and forty-five minutes after their departure.

The main pack runs Flagstaff in 1:21 before tacking on a loop around campus to make the run a full 90 minutes. Oscar Ponce is in high spirits after the run. He was dropped handily yesterday, but today he beat his previous Flagstaff best by a minute, without the effort required during his record run. Others are not so upbeat. Wes Berkshire exclaims that he "feels like ten pounds of shit in a five-pound bag." He felt fine until they added on when they arrived back on campus, at which point, "I felt like I was punched in the face. I died a thousand horrible deaths, but that's the way it goes, I guess."

The underclassmen stretch before heading home to get ready for tomorrow morning's departure for fall camp. Chris Valenti, a sophomore who ran on Goucher's heels during the run, will be staying home, as will Jason Robbie. Wetmore says, "Valenti always looks heroic in practice," and he has looked great thus far. He is running with the top guys, and his long lean torso appears fit. For a walk-on like Valenti, judgment day is seventeen days away when he will try to earn his spot on the roster in the Varsity time trial. Valenti was on the squad a year ago, but each year all walk-ons must earn their spot on the roster. If they do not run competitively in the time trial—and this is a subjective decision on Wetmore's part—they are done. Wetmore will be looking for Valenti to shine as he does in practice, and if he runs the way he has the past two days, he will be difficult to beat.

Jason Robbie faces a greater challenge. He is injured and demoralized. Despite making the squad a year ago, he too is guaranteed nothing. He must also regain his spot on the roster in the time trial. He is quite upset about having to make the squad again, but Wetmore does not budge. Like Valenti, he will have to perform on September 5th. Otherwise, his journey will reach an all too premature conclusion.

After the rest of their teammates have left Balch for home, seniors Goucher, Reese, and Batliner join women's team members Heather Burroughs, Carrie Messner, and Jen Gruia to set an agenda for a team-only closed-door meeting at camp. The team-only powwow is a yearly tradition that they have all participated in in the past. Nevertheless, they have been unable to come to a consensus on the meeting's agenda, so this is their third discussion on the task. Coaches Wetmore and Drake relax in Wetmore's office, marveling at the seniors' indecision. "So much for democracy," says Wetmore, and they both break up laughing.

Camp this year will be held in Buena Vista, Colorado. Those hoping for a little alcohol-induced mayhem will be in for a surprise. There will be no booze, no panty raids, and no respite from the training. It will be especially difficult for Slattery and Elmuccio, who are just becoming acquainted with Boulder's 5500-foot elevation, for the town of Buena Vista is situated at an unforgiving elevation of over 7000 feet.

The Unspoken Agreement

Most of the men's and women's teams arrive in Buena Vista, Colorado, for their annual preseason training camp. Slattery, Tessman, and O'Mara are making their first trip to camp. Among those missing are the walk-ons who have yet to make the squad, including junior Jason Robbie. A Boulder native and University of Vermont transfer, Wetmore debated bringing Robbie with the squad. As Wetmore explains, he is "an inner circle guy," well-liked by all of the team's members. He was the most impressive man at the time trial last fall, yet he spent most of the year unable to compete because of injury, and now, still battling a sore IT band, he is not assured of a spot on the squad. Also missing is senior Matt Napier, a likely redshirt senior who is the only married member of the team. He is staying in Boulder with his wife and two children.

According to Wetmore, the weekend "provides an opportunity for interpersonal intimacy few and far between once we're in our normal routine." The training camp presents him with the opportunity to better understand his charges, to "sit with Bat and talk about books, or to sit with Jay Johnson and talk of hiking in the Northern Cascades."

Wetmore views camp as his opportunity to create a rapport between the staff and the athletes that will make work and trust easier down the road. More important, Wetmore sees the trip as the opportunity to start creating a *synergy* among the members. If successful, at season's end, the sum of the parts will be greater than the whole.

O'Mara, Johnson, Schafer, Severy, Batliner, and Tessman chat and finish stretching.

Wetmore also looks to camp to set the tone for the season. "This is when everyone looks each other in the eye and realizes we're all here to do one thing in common: to train and be righteous. This is where they'll make this unspoken agreement."

Having arrived and checked into their rooms at the Buena Vista Inn, the runners load up the team vans and head four miles out of town for a relaxed run of 60 to 90 minutes. Coaches Wetmore and Drake found the trails the team will be running this weekend when they went to Buena Vista on two separate occasions last month to explore the area. As the runners stretch before heading out, Wetmore only half-jokingly exhorts them to pair up, because "we're in serious mountain lion country." He then reminds them to take it easy and run relaxed. "We're running in two groups today, men and women. Take it easy, we're running hard in fifteen hours."

At 3:30 the runners head south on one of the loose dirt trails that roll gently in every direction. It is an overcast day, and the air is pleasant. To the west are the "collegiate peaks." Though overcast, the barren tops of Harvard, Princeton, and Yale are still visible. These are three of Colorado's fifty-four 14,000 foot peaks, and their presence is majestic. There are miles and miles of trails, twisting between short juniper trees and rolling cactus. The runners chat amicably and run together at a leisurely pace. Goucher sets the pace up front. No one challenges his authority. Despite the relaxed tempo, the run is still arduous. At an altitude of over 7000 feet, a molehill feels like a mountain.

One runner accustomed to the area's endless dirt trails is sophomore Aaron Blondeau. Blondeau grew up and attended Salida High School in the neighboring town of Salida. He smiles easily, and shaggy blond hair frames his blue eyes and face. He is a man of few words, and he runs silently and contentedly in the back of the pack. A devout Christian, he sports a W.W.J.D. (What Would Jesus Do) bracelet on his wrist.

As a senior in high school he finished twelfth in the Foot Locker National High School Championships. He considered Princeton and Stanford before deciding on Colorado. Unlike most of his teammates, the intensely academic computer science major is living this year in a single room in the dorms. There are mandatory quiet hours every evening on his floor, a deciding factor in his decision to live there. Having excelled in the classroom last year with a 4.0 G.P.A., he stands poised to inherit Chris Severy's mantle next year as the academic star of the squad.

As a freshman, he also excelled over hill and dale. He was the only freshman to make Colorado's top seven and compete at the NCAA's. Blondeau finished 101st there, and followed that performance with a fine seventh-place finish at the US Junior championships. The latter performance earned him a spot on the US Junior National team competing at the

World Championships in March. After a successful indoor season in which he lowered his 5000-meter PR (personal record) to 14:42, he was poised to represent the U.S. before illness struck. A stress fracture in his shin stopped him cold the week before departing, and he was forced to miss the World Junior Championships in Morocco.

After recuperating and redshirting the spring track season, he returned to Salida this summer, working at a local Holiday Inn and running the nearby trails. A question mark heading into camp, he has shown Wetmore that he is ready to go. Blondeau has been running 65 miles a week, and he will be looked upon to make a big jump this year if Colorado is to contend for the national title.

The loose dirt turns to sand at points as the runners scramble on trails through the short pinion pines and scrubby little bushes that populate this arid climate. They finish with dirt in their teeth, ready to work hard tomorrow at seven a.m.

But first, there is other business to attend to. After showering, the men and women gather together for the team-only meeting in the hotel's conference room. It is understood by the captains that they are to discuss and set the season's objectives.

As everyone files in, seniors Reese, Goucher, and Batliner join women's team seniors Burroughs, Gruia, and Messner in the front of the room. When everyone is settled in their seats, Reese begins the meeting by offering a quote: "If you're not enjoying the journey, you probably won't enjoy the destination."

The mood is very understated and relaxed, and the seniors proceed to alternately take turns adding their input about the purpose of camp, and the goals for the season. Reese adds, "We want to make sure that we are all on the same page, that we are all fully invested." More to the point, Burroughs says, "Mark wants to know what our priorities are."

What is interesting is the element of choice. It is

Slattery, Reese, and Roybal lead Blondeau, Johnson, and Elmuccio.

ingenious of Wetmore that he does not dictate what they will be shooting for, but that he lets them decide what they hope to achieve. It is their choice. Once they elect to aim high, they are effectively empowering Wetmore to train them as hard as he sees fit to take them to that level. If they complain, he has but to remind them that they are the ones who decided they wanted to excel, he is merely following their prerogative. Goucher understands this, and he will try to convey this to the underclassmen during the meeting. Later, after they have adjourned, he adds:

> *Mark gives us the decision. Hey, if you want to go out on Saturday night and party and drink, fine, practice is at 8 a.m. Most people here want to be the best at what we do. We've chosen. We don't want to live a lifestyle of partying. Maybe that's why we fit so well with Mark. He doesn't want to party either. He encourages us to make our own decisions in running and in life . . . That's why this team is so righteous outside of running.*

The decision to sacrifice for running is not Goucher's alone. It is a collective decision. The road ahead will be tough, and they understand that they will need to lean on each other to get through the season. Creating and cementing the relationships that will enable them to survive is why they have camp. Batliner says, "We're not here for training, we're here to hang out and be friends, because friendship is the foundation of our team. When the foundation is friendship, it makes it a hell of a lot easier to get through the season."

Taking this cue from Batliner, Roybal jokingly yells from the crowd, "Heeyyyy! Let's get some beer!" Everyone laughs, and Jay Johnson returns to the task at hand. "When we come together as a group," he says, "we'll be way stronger than as individuals. But get to know the personalities of the guys, because we're individuals, we're not carbon copies of each other; we're neat."

Inevitably there will be some personality conflicts during the season, but Johnson says, "Still, you don't have to hang out, as long as you're serious two hours a day." The conversation continues in this vein before Goucher speaks for the first time:

> *We're in a unique position. It's my fifth year. Incoming freshmen, if you have any questions, come talk to us, we know what's going on and we're not above you or whatever . . . There's such good talent in here, we're there if we bring everyone together for that national number-one team, if that's what you want to do. I think most people in here want that.*

Batliner sarcastically responds, "Who doesn't?" Already, the unspoken agreement is there; they are committed to doing what it takes to win the national title. Sensing this, Reese brings closure to the meeting after only ten minutes. "This meeting is for the coaches," he says. "It doesn't show how dedicated we are." Wetmore would be the first to concur with Reese. They will do their talking with their feet . . .

Later that evening, Tessman and O'Mara relax in their hotel room. The succinct meeting is a welcome change for both. Burroughs says of the gathering, "We didn't want to set a tone that was artificial or insincere." The seniors achieved their objective. Says Tessman, "It didn't feel like empty rhetoric. It's cool to talk of winning NC's matter-of-factly. It's gonna happen." O'Mara adds, "At Providence, Ray [Treacy, the Providence College coach] would say, 'Don't fuck it up!' Not very inspirational. Here, we want to get over the hump of being top five. Until we win once, it's kind of elusive . . . but you're expected to do well at NCAA's. It's just a question of one, two, or three on the podium. Excellence is expected."

Excellence indeed. Since Wetmore started coaching the Varsity men's cross country team in 1993, Colorado has finished no worse than fifth at NCAA's (fifth in 1996, fourth in 1993 and '95, third in 1997, and second in 1994). Both transfers are thrilled to be a part of such a successful program, but Tessman has a greater sense of urgency than O'Mara. This is his last season, so he wants to win NOW! While never much of a cross country runner at Brown, Tessman is coming off of a breakthrough year after what he calls "three years of crap." Last winter he made the transition from half-miler to miler with great success. He PR'ed in four consecutive races going from 4:15 to 4:11. But Tessman was just getting started. He continued his remarkable senior year outdoors with an opening 3:54 in the season's first 1500-meter race. He quickly dropped his PR to 3:50, before having his breakthrough race at the Princeton Invitational. There, he surprised the field and finished a close second to Princeton alum and perennial national championship finalist Scott "Slicko" Anderson in 3:44. Anderson recalls that, "I had no idea who he was. I knew [Brown miler] Neville Davey [also in the race] was legitimate, but I didn't know who this other Brown character was. With 150 to go I was expecting them both to fade, especially this guy. But with 100 to go he made a move to grasp the lead, and I started to panic. I moved out to lane two and had to give it all I had to beat him down the stretch. This guy clearly had made a jump from being inconsequential to being a dominant force in the conference. He definitely has a chance to make a splash on the national scene."

With this effort, Tessman provisionally qualified for NCAA's. Knowing he was on the bubble, he skipped his graduation weekend to run a last-chance meet in Atlanta. Again, he ran 3:44. Heartbreakingly, he was the first non-qualifier for the NCAA's. The last qualifying spot is burned into his memory: Chuck Sloan, Oklahoma State, 3:43.76. He is still salty about the experience, but he says, "It made me do what I'm doing this year."

He chose Brown for its academics. He flatly admits he knew absolutely nothing about the political science program in which he enrolled before matriculating to the University of Colorado. He is here because of Wetmore. He is here to "dedicate myself one hundred percent to running," because he is convinced he is going to "do real well and have a great year if [he] trains with these guys."

He knows only seven men will represent Colorado at the NCAA's, and despite having finished a mere fourteenth last season at the Heptagonal (Ivy League and Navy) cross country championships, his spring track season has given him reason to believe he can take one of the spots. Although he has been in town training with the guys for but a few weeks, his new teammates have made him feel welcome. He says, "I've gotten a great reception from the guys on the team . . . I get the feeling they're excited that I'm here, I'm appreciated. I feel no animosity towards me because I have a shot at one of the top seven spots. There's respect there."

After having been on a Brown team that never won a conference title, let alone a national crown, Tessman is eager to do anything to taste victory. "My goal for the fall is to help these guys win a national championship any way I can. If I can score as the fifth guy, or be seventh and displace someone, I'll be jacked. I feel I have one year to be as much a part of this team as I can."

With his age and experience, he adds veteran leadership to an already senior-laden squad. And, he brings an outsider's perspective—an appreciation of Wetmore and how excellent the program really is. "At Brown," he says, "we never won Heps, so there was this undercurrent that we weren't winners." Colorado won the inaugural Big 12 title in 1996 and defended that title last year. Tessman knows that another Big 12 title is likely this year. Moreover, he knows what the track community thinks of CU's chances of winning Nationals. "I hope everyone here thinks we can win it, because on the outside everyone thinks we can." And according to Tessman, there is one leader steering the ship. "Here," he says, "there is no negativity about Wetmore. Everyone takes Wetmore's word as law."

If there is one runner who takes Wetmore's word as law more than any other, it is Goucher. Wetmore says of his star, "This guy is absolutely the most loyal team-oriented guy I've ever had." Goucher explains:

He has molded me and helped me become the person I am from day one. This guy has been everything from my coach to a father figure to my best friend. He's done it not by imposing his ideas on me, which he does, but he

words it or puts it in a manner of letting me make my own decisions . . .
[For example] you could go into his office one hundred percent sure you
want to cut your miles. Then you'll talk about it, and somehow when you're
in there he'll convince you that you need to run more miles instead of less.
When you walk out you say what the hell happened! But you feel good
about it.

It is a symbiotic relationship in which each enhances the success of
the other. Goucher follows Wetmore's instructions unequivocally and
improves. Meanwhile, every success Goucher has is another validation of
Wetmore's methods. Tessman knows the success Goucher has had with
Wetmore, and he derives a tremendous amount of confidence from
doing the same workouts as the champ. "To see Goucher, the top dog,
working with me, I know I'm going to run well. There's no reason not to
run well." The logic is hard to beat: *if Goucher does it, and he is a three-time*
national champion on the track, I better do it too.

O'Mara has also observed CU's success the past few years, and he
came to CU to train under Wetmore. Nevertheless, transferring to CU
was the most difficult decision he has ever made. "My best friend back
home just transferred to PC [Providence College]," he says, "so when I
made the decision to transfer here, it was tough for me. But running is
important to me, so I had to make that change to realize my potential."

A former footballer in high school in Northboro Massachusetts, he
has lost 30 pounds to get down to a still less than svelte 150 pounds. He
has trained over 80 miles per week this summer in preparation for the
fall season, yet his goals remain long-term oriented. He says, "I want to
adapt to the new training load, stay injury free, and by outdoors there's
an opportunity to race well. I set myself up for disappointment when I
went to PC because of the adjustment needed (to succeed as a collegiate
runner). It's not the same adjustment now, but it's an adjustment
nonetheless. I've got time. There's no rush to contribute now."

Despite his lessened sense of urgency, O'Mara is convinced of the efficacy of Wetmore's system. "Mark is very methodical, and he knows exercise physiology," he says. "I'm a convert to his Lydiard system."

Wetmore' system is based on the training principles of New Zealand
coaching great Arthur Lydiard. It is a high-mileage program that emphasizes
the development of his runner's aerobic capacity or endurance. Much has
been alleged about Colorado's training regimen. The coming weeks will
separate the myth from the reality of the Colorado program. Whether
focusing on the impending season or one on the horizon, Tessman and
O'Mara will join their new teammates and do their talking with their legs.

At 10:30 p.m. not a soul walks the halls.

The Day of Truth

Every year, the penultimate stage of the Tour de France is a cruel, pun-ishing time trial that the French refer to as the "race of truth." Here, it is said, champions impose their will on their competitors. Today's workout is one that Wetmore will later refer to as "the day of truth."

As the runners trained through the summer, some, such as Adam Batliner, entertained thoughts of grappling with Goucher, and perhaps even defeating him. Others, such as Oscar Ponce, emboldened by their newfound strength, entertained thoughts of closing the gap. Today, Goucher proves that this day is a long time coming.

The men are doing a fartlek run today; they will do one and a half minutes at "AT pace," with three and a half minute "steady" between in-tervals. This means that they will run 1:30 at the pace that they could currently sustain for five miles before running 3:30 at an even pace that allows them to recover for the 1:30 segments. Goucher, Friedberg, Ponce, Batliner, and Severy are assigned 40 minutes (eight AT runs); Tess-man, Schafer, O'Mara, Blondeau, O'Mara, Elmuccio, and Berkshire 31:30 (seven AT runs); and Roybal, Reese, and Slattery 26:30 (six AT runs).

When drawing up the plan for the upcoming season two months ago, Wetmore determined that today's effort was going to be a high-level aerobic workout. He did not know the specifics of the workout until he and JD scouted out the roads a month ago. Once he uncovered River Road—a dirt road with a very slight grade that winds along the river—the workout took shape. It starts and finishes at aptly named Elephant Rock; when the runners approach the rock on the return it resembles an enor-mous elephant ambling off into the distance.

On the warm-up Goucher immediately separates himself from the pack. And though his comrades try to gain on him, it is in vain. Once out front and in control, his lead increases. On the AT segments, he runs be-tween eleven and twelve miles per hour. He settles into a six-minute mile pace on the recovery—a taxing pace at this elevation. He runs like a prizefighter, punching the air with his fists. His shoulders roll slightly as he moves, and his right arm rises a touch more than his left. A tad bow-legged, he lands on an even plane on the outside part of his foot, before rolling in. Mouth agape, he grimaces intermittently as he flies along the road, alone. Remarkably, his stride appears no different on the fast seg-ments than on the recovery.

Farther back, the front pack moves on. Batliner has caught the group after having to make a pit stop en route. He appears no more fatigued than the others despite having had to run hard to catch the pack. He runs with an uncanny efficiency, resembling a cat ready to pounce. He bounds from toe to toe, upper body motionless, head completely still, eyes forward. On the pickups he extends his stride, all the while looking smooth and effortless.

Severy, however, is laboring. He runs with shoulders hunched and a high arm carriage, and his skin turns ever brighter hues of crimson as the exertion rises. As they turn for home and Goucher runs out of sight in the distance, Bat complains about the effort. Friedberg responds, "I'd rather see the glass as half full." Without missing a beat, Sev turns to Friedberg and says, "Your glass may be half full, but I already drank mine!" The guys are too tired to laugh. It is downhill from here, and the pack maintains its cadence until the 40 minutes are completed. They then jog easily to the rock.

Wetmore is completing a run of his own, as he is wont to do while his runners are out for a long effort, when Goucher runs past alone. While he pulled away with ease, his teammates should not be discouraged. His work rate is phenomenal. An unfazed Wetmore says as he passes, "He's not even warmed up. Dan Browne [five U.S. titles, 1998], Marc Davis [1996 U.S. Olympic finalist, steeplechase], on a good day they can only manage to annoy him."

Later in the afternoon, many of the runners head to the Mt. Princeton Hot Springs. The springs themselves are something of a disappointment. A pool is built next to the springs and water is piped into the pool, so it hardly differs from a regular swimming pool. No matter, the runners whoop it up and everyone mixes freely together. The Colorado runners are joined by a number of other lean and tawny folks in the pool. The runners are from Malone College, and one of their guys boasts to Reese that they have two awesome Kenyans. It is enough to rile Goucher, who says as Reese points them out, "Let's race. I'll race 'em tomorrow!"

In the evening the runners hit a small park down the street from the hotel for burgers and

Elmuccio, Johnson, Batliner, and Severy.

games. The men and women relax, chat, and play volleyball with one another. Goucher and Reese continually end up on losing teams, which proves frustrating to both. Needless to say, the volleyball coach will not come knocking on either of their doors anytime soon.

Showers prematurely end the barbecue. The runners gradually disperse from the canopy that sheltered them as the rain lets up, but Elmuccio, Johnson, Severy, and Batliner linger. Johnson recounts to Elmuccio how in the old days when Wetmore was but a volunteer assistant coach, the team used to have mandatory lifting sessions at 6:30 in the morning. Wetmore would rant, "no one is working harder than you guys," and blare The Doors' "The End" as they worked through a circuit. Now, with all the administrative battles that he has to fight, Johnson feels Wetmore is not as accessible as he was in the past when he would sit around for hours bullshitting with the guys.

Due to the inclement weather, Wetmore chooses to postpone his annual speech detailing the whys and hows of the season's training. In previous years this speech has proven to be wildly popular among the guys. Reese recalls Wetmore's speech at camp his freshman year as "the most memorable speech in all my five years here."

It recent years, the speech has been more or less exclusive to freshmen, but in 1994, in Wetmore's first fall as the established distance coach for the men, the whole team was there. The meeting started on a whim, when Wetmore called everyone in their hotel rooms and asked them to meet him outside under a covered picnic area. Alan Culpepper was there, coming off a year where he garnered three All-American certificates under Wetmore's tutelage. The others were primarily unestablished Junior Varsity runners like walk-ons Jay Cleckler and Jon Cooper. Also among the group that day were the core of this year's team: Goucher, Batliner, Severy, Johnson, and Reese. Wetmore started by giving the team some information about his training methodology before he rather abruptly started talking about his plans for establishing "a new era" in CU distance running. In the process, Reese says, "He gave us a little insight into his character."

According to Reese, his speech was something like the following:

Look, this is what I am. This [coaching] is my main job [he held other part-time jobs at the time]. I don't play golf. I don't have many hobbies. I don't have a wife. The bottom line is I'm here to make you guys run fast. When I go to sleep at night, my mind's churning, thinking of ways to make you fast . . .

I want you guys to be businesslike in your approach; think like Clint Eastwood. We work every day, and when we go to town, we tie up the horse, spit on the dog, and we leave without a word. We do our talking with our legs.

But what Reese remembers more than words is the emotional chord Wetmore touched. "He mesmerized us right away. It pumped us up so much to think that someone cared that much about us. I'm telling you, if you were there you would have felt the aura." Reese pauses, seemingly brought back to that day before he finishes. "He won everyone over right then."

Wetmore re-earns their loyalty every day. He demonstrates his commitment to his athletes. In turn, they seek to match his commitment to them. Says Goucher, "We work hard for ourselves, but we also work hard for him because he works so hard for us. I don't know any other coaches who would sacrifice like he does. He's in his office every day, even in the summertime. He's always at work. He conveys a work ethic that everyone feeds off of. It's just unspoken."

When he does address them, it is usually in a calm, understated manner. Former CU runner Shawn Found remarks, "Part of his quirkiness is that he's known for how he can speak under a crowd, not over one. In a race you'll hear him say 'You're fine,' in a conversational tone, and you'll hear that."

The speech ends up being the day's only casualty. Wetmore will never recite it this season. At 10:15 the halls again are quiet and empty. Practice resumes at 7 a.m.

Saturday, August 22, 1998
Shields Gulch Trailhead, Buena Vista, Colorado
7 a.m.

Fuck This Shit

It is another warm morning in Buena Vista. Fortunately, Wetmore has planned an easy run along an old railroad bed in the San Isabel National Forest outside Buena Vista. It is hard to fathom from the desolation of the trail that there was ever anything of consequence here, but the trailhead at run's end describes this as the site of the infamous "April Fool's Tragedy" of April 1, 1908. However, the CU runners will be too spent by that time to give a rat's ass about the details of that tragedy after a journey gone awry of their own.

The men depart from Shield's Gulch Trailhead with instructions to climb the short switchback to the deserted railway bed and follow that to the run's end. The run climbs slowly yet steadily for the first 25 minutes without incident. Drained from yesterday's practice, they chat and run at a leisurely pace—except for Goucher and young Slattery.

After trailing at the back of the pack in every run thus far, Slattery looks great as he lopes alongside Goucher 100 feet in front of the pack. Perhaps today Slattery will run like the guy who finished fourth at the Foot Locker National High School Cross Country championships a year ago.

Twenty minutes in, the runners reach a fork in the path, and Goucher and Slattery head off to the left. The trail has never relented its steady

ascent, and now they start to really climb. Ten minutes later, the pack catches a flagging Slattery. He mutters a thought that has most certainly occurred to all the harriers, "Fuck this shit!" and starts to walk.

This is definitely not the recovery day Wetmore has planned. Reese is also strug-

Goucher and Slattery
lead the Buffs.

gling. He runs alone in back of the pack. He has been battling to run at least parts of the workouts with his teammates, and today he runs with a noticeable limp. When healthy he runs with a giddy-up in his stride reminiscent of Mark Everett, the great American half-miler. His right arm swings smoothly back and forth, but his left arm swings in a clockwise circular motion. He dips his left shoulder as his left knee rises, and his left forearm swings out and down away from his body. It pauses there for the briefest instant before whipping up and around as his right knee thrusts forward. Coupled with the limp from his knee injury, he is a picture of instability, rocking back and forth, all elbows and knees as he moves.

Goucher, alone up front, knows something is amiss. The trail has narrowed considerably, and 45 minutes in, they have yet to level off. Several minutes later, he reaches a short fence that must be climbed to continue on the trail. He turns back.

One by one the runners turn around after Goucher passes them. In all they have climbed over 2000 feet in 50 minutes. The sun is bearing down, and by the looks on their faces, no one is even remotely enjoying the run, least of all Tommy Reese. He makes it back with the others in 1:17. His knee was aggravating him early in the run and getting lost only exacerbated his troubles. He had no intention of running more than 50 minutes today.

Slattery also looks weary. He says afterwards, "That's the farthest, or the second farthest I've ever run in my life." Batliner chuckles and says, "Well, you'll beat that tomorrow."

Tomorrow they will be back in the friendlier 5300-foot elevation of Boulder. But that is of little solace to the men for they will be running at an elevation of 8000 feet on a course that defines the Wetmore era at CU: Magnolia Road.

THE PLAN

The fundamental principle of training is to develop enough stamina to enable you to maintain the necessary speed over the full distance at which you plan to compete. Many runners throughout the world are capable of running the 400 meters in 46 seconds or faster. But remarkably few of them have sufficient stamina to run 800 meters in 1:44, or 52 seconds for each 400. That clearly shows the vital part stamina plays in middle- and long-distance racing. Consider those relative times again. It will help you realize what could be achieved by fast runners if they concentrated on endurance development and shifted their attention to longer distances.

Peter Snell was basically the slowest runner in the 800-meter final at both the Rome and Tokyo Olympic Games. But he had the stamina to carry him through the heats and then sprint the last 100 meters of the finals

*faster than any of his rivals. By then they were too tired to use their supe-
rior speed. Snell was trained to be capable of running a fine marathon, but
I doubt that his rivals could. This was the advantage that enabled him to
succeed; it's also the advantage you can give yourself.*

Arthur Lydiard
Running the Lydiard Way

As much as today's misadventure was not planned, Wetmore's training schedule is already complete. The plan has five stages, beginning with
Period A, when his athletes ascend to full volume over the summer after
taking a break following spring track, and culminating with Period E,
anaerobic speed, two weeks prior to the NCAA championships.

While the phases themselves and the length of time they comprise
are relatively static, the specific workouts in Wetmore's plan may change
year to year. The rate of change from one season to the next is directly
correlated with the barometer he uses to gauge a successful season: did
his team run their best at NCAA's? If successful, the plan will not vary
significantly the following year. But, even if everything goes perfectly, his
team can expect a new wrinkle or two in the following year's plan. This
is because Wetmore sees a danger in not changing and becoming, as he
sees it, "old and curmudgeonly." Therefore, he constantly refines the
recipe that has brought him success his entire coaching career.

In creating the plan he works backwards from the NCAA's to the
summer base period. Each runner receives a copy of the plan, with most
of the season's workouts in place, in the summer. Sharing the plan with
them at this early date ensures that they will know *why* they are doing
what they are doing, and in turn, his athletes tend to buy into it.

The principles of aerobic development and periodization that he in-
corporates in his "recipe," as he calls it, are lessons learned from New
Zealand coaching great Arthur Lydiard. What Lydiard discovered through
trial and error over 30 years ago—that the development of one's aerobic
capacity is almost limitless (and almost universally underdeveloped by
today's coaches)—continues to be proven by exercise physiologists today.
Wetmore's system is modified Lydiardism; he compromises Lydiard's
method to meet the unique demands of collegiate athletes looking to peak
three times a year for NCAA's. (In training Olympic champions like Peter
Snell, Lydiard's athletes competed in *one* 6–8 week season a year with a
long-term goal of peaking in an Olympic year.) Wetmore has adapted Lydiard's teachings to enable his athletes to race at a high level nine months
a year. In the process, he is establishing a coaching legacy of his own.

Wetmore was introduced to Lydiard methods when he read his
book *Running the Lydiard Way*. He refers to it as a "foundational work"

whose principles "on many levels, are sound to this day." Lydiard's emphasis on long-term development with marathon training, coupled with his relentless development of an aerobic foundation, and his system of periodization are all concepts that Wetmore employs in designing his plan. Lydiard taught Wetmore two principal ideas:

1. Anaerobic and interval training is overrated.
2. You must continuously develop your aerobic capacity—and pick a time to run well.

This is Wetmore's plan:

Period A: Ascending to Full Volume

The period lasts roughly six weeks, beginning when they resume training after taking a break at the end of outdoor track and lasting until the end of July. Each runner has a different goal volume depending on what he has done in the past. Wetmore recommends "no more than a ten percent increase from his last successful maximum volume." In a letter he sent to the squad on June 24th, he wrote of this first period, "For the time being don't attempt any hard workouts. No intervals; no ATs [Tempo runs]; no fartlek; no *races*. Just steady medium-distance runs and a weekly long run that is 20 percent of your total week. Get your bodies ready for the sustained volume of September and thereafter."

Period B: Aerobic Short Specificity

This phase lasts five weeks and is characterized by work done at task pace (be that mile pace for milers during track season or 10k pace during cross country since that is the distance run at NCAA's) that is not anaerobic. This means that another interval is not started until the athlete is fully recovered from the previous one. An example of a workout in this period is a fartlek with one minute on, four minutes off. There is a complete recovery between each hard effort so that no significant oxygen debt is accrued. This is mainly a transitional phase where Wetmore's runners get used to going fast again.

Period C: Aerobic Long Specificity

This phase lasts six weeks and includes longer intervals than in Period B, while still avoiding anaerobic workouts. This phase is characterized by longer fartlek workouts, mile repeats, and long, hard aerobic efforts such as the ten-mile Dam Run. The rest between intervals will shorten towards the end of Period C as the runners advance their fitness. Because the intervals are much longer than in

Period B, his athletes start Period C running intervals at paces that are slightly slower than they will be running November 23rd. The paces drop over time. It is important to emphasize that through Period C the Sunday long run is emphasized, using the rule of thumb that it should be twenty percent of an athlete's weekly volume. As a rule, the steady runs on Wednesday afternoons through this phase are fifteen percent of an athlete's weekly volume.

Period D: Anaerobic Specificity

Now Wetmore introduces a heavy dose of traditional interval running: short, fast repeats with precious little recovery. The anaerobic work enables the runners to capitalize on the increase in their aerobic capacity while giving them what Lydiard calls "the vital edge" to race anaerobically. The Wednesday medium-distance run and the Sunday run are continued as aerobic maintenance, the difference being that with only six weeks until Nationals, the distance of the runs will decrease by 10 to 25 percent. The pace of the medium distance and long runs remains steady.

Period E: Anaerobic Speed

The season's last phase is marked by training sessions designed to induce deep anaerobic stimulus. In layman's terms, this is when his runners puke and come back for more. The hard training sessions will include sprinting and intervals at paces substantially faster than race pace. The end result of these sessions is a feeling of sharpness—a power and fluidity of stride that causes a reversal of traditional mind-body communication. Up to now the mind is employed to overrule the unresponsiveness of the legs that is a result of the cumulative fatigue from an ungodly number of training sessions. Now it is the legs that start telling the mind: *hey, you have the tools to raise some hell when it counts.*

The Wolfe Influence

Wetmore's training program demands a full investment from his athletes. He has expected nothing less from his athletes since he began his coaching career in 1972 as the coach and founder of the Edge City Track Club in Bernardsville, New Jersey. The Edge City Track Club begat the Mine Mountain Road Department, which led to an assistant coaching position at Bernardsville High School.

The Edge City Track Club would never have existed had Wetmore's father not given him a copy of Tom Wolfe's *The Electric Kool-Aid Acid Test* in 1972. This book, says Wetmore, "blew my mind." His father gave it to him as he was boarding a train to Massachusetts for a stint at Graham Junior College.

He read it cover to cover, finishing the text as he walked down Commonwealth Avenue towards his dormitory. Then, he sat down on the steps of his dormitory, and read it again.

Reading this book was the beginning of his interest in ideas, in life, and in plans. From that day forward, there has never been a day when he has not been reading one or two books, ever.

Until this moment, his life lacked focus and direction. In fact, he was going to Graham after a short stint at TCU so he could study to be a TV journalist. Now, he set himself a new goal: "to read everything in the world!" with the aspiration of becoming an intellectual. "I was voracious after that," he says. "I read 500 books in the next three years."

Wolfe's tale about Ken Kesey and the Merry Pranksters captivated him well after he finished the text. The hippies demonstrated to him the allure of living "on the periphery of existence." Wetmore took the lessons from their experiences and applied them to his coaching. He set about creating "an Edge City of physical wellness, always with a purpose" where he and his athletes would "suffer as much as we can to see how good we can be, safety be damned." This ethic infuses his coaching to this day.

Monster Island

Mark Wetmore moved to Boulder from Bernardsville, New Jersey, on August 17, 1991. Within "24 hours of moving to Boulder" he had discovered Magnolia Road. He was running it "probably the first Sunday I was living in Boulder." This was not by accident. He says, "Knowing where I am going to run is pretty important to me. I take the trouble to get a map, usually a topographical map, and I look for a squiggly wavy road. That usually means it is a little out of the way dirt road."

Not many runners had discovered Magnolia Road then, and Wetmore says, "the only person I saw up there in the first couple of months was Arturo." Arturo is Arturo Barrios, the former 10,000-meter world record holder from Mexico who was then in the prime of his career. Later that year he would take Bill Nann and Andy Biglow, two of his former protégés at Bernards High that were then running for CU, to run at Magnolia Road. Not once had they ever ventured there in three years at CU. A few days before interviewing for the position of volunteer assistant, Wetmore again went up to Magnolia Road and ran eight miles with Biglow and JD. "If I coach here," he said to them, "you'll be here every Sunday."

Then CU Head Coach Jerry Quiller had been searching for a volunteer assistant coach to help with the distance runners. He was allowing his athletes to select their mentor from among several applicants for the position. Biglow had been campaigning for Wetmore to his teammates, but it was this run on Magnolia Road that convinced JD that Wetmore should be their coach. JD was on the selection committee that voted for Wetmore, and in 1992 Coach Quiller brought Wetmore on board.

His initial charges were the collectively disgruntled and underachieving middle-distance runners on Quiller's squad. JD epitomized the group. A 1989 graduate of Campbell County High School in Gillette, Wyoming, he was the first schoolboy in Wyoming state history to run the mile under 4:20. He ran 4:13. An 800 meter in 1:51.67 was fast enough to garner him runner-up status at the prestigious Golden West Track and Field Invitational in Sacramento, California. Others in the group included Andy Samuelson, a miler from Colorado who ran 4:11 for 1600 meters *at elevation* to win his division at the Colorado state championships, and Mike Sobolik, a miler from Pueblo, Colorado. Alan Culpepper, a 3:50 high school 1500-meter runner from Texas, also fell under Wetmore's charge.

Despite their top shelf credentials, neither Andy Samuelson nor JD had qualified for a single conference final in four years. Each also had a full scholarship, along with Culpepper. None of the runners had ever made a Varsity cross-country team. They were dispirited and ready to try anything. Clearly, there was a lot of work to be done.

The first change Wetmore made was to add a long run to their program. Says JD, "Every Sunday morning we would do Mags." They started by running twelve miles, and by the end of the fall, they were all running fourteen miles every Sunday at Magnolia Road. They accordingly upped their volume so that they were all running seventy to eighty miles per week. Their legs were tired and they were hurting.

With the exception of current US marathon star Scott Larson, who would run with the group at Mags on Sunday and do intervals with the Varsity cross country guys on Monday, the distance runners remained skeptical. After all, they were interval-trained athletes experiencing moderate success under Coach Quiller's program. Any skepticism about Wetmore's system vanished at the end of the cross country season when the cross country team left to run the NCAA regionals. The middle distance runners ran a 3000-meter time trial at Potts Field. JD recalls their performances: "I ran 8:35, a PR. Sobolik PR'ed. Samuelson PR'ed. Al [Culpepper] didn't PR, but he ran 8:20 something. The distance guys were blown away. They gave in then [to Wetmore's methods], although they were pretty desperate then [to do well]." Culpepper's performances particularly impressed the distance runners. Says current US Army runner and 1994 CU graduate Shawn Found, "He [Wetmore] brought Culpepper back from the dead. By that winter he was running 13:53 for 5k in addition to his mile performances."

The group's success continued indoors. After having been the bane of the squad for their entire tenures, Wetmore's runners finally contributed some points at the conference meet. All four men made the conference finals, and all four scored. Running the 1000 meters, the mile, and the 3000 meters, they scored more points than any other group on the team. JD PR'ed in the 1000 (2:26). Now the rest of the squad was really taking notice.

Found recalls witnessing the startling transformation of the middle-distance runners:

> The reputation of the middle-distance guys was down the tubes. They were big guys scoring no points. They were running 4:10 in high school and 4:20 in college. In six months, he got them back running 4:05 again. He got Culpepper running 3:43 (for 1500 meters). We won Big Eight Cross without Wetmore, but by that spring the distance guys were getting spanked again. The middle-distance guys were scoring points and we were like "Shit, these guys are for real!"

Wetmore's runners validated their indoor performance by again making finals and scoring points at the outdoor Big Eight Conference meet. When all was said and done, all had PR's. JD ran 3:51. Culpepper ran 3:43. Sobolik PR'ed, and Andy Samuelson ran a 3:48 1500 meter—at elevation. In turn, their performances validated Wetmore. Found says, "It didn't take long to know he knew his shit."

Discouraged with his subpar performances, Found quit the team in the spring of 1993. Yet, the following summer saw Found also training under Wetmore. He recalls Wetmore telling him what he tells all his athletes: "It's all or nothing. Give me two years, then you'll start to see what's going on." Found was hesitant at first. He says, "That's hard to commit to." But he did.

At the time Found was a self-described "semi-alcoholic complete zero." He was fat, disillusioned, and working at 7-Eleven to make ends meet. Found laughs as he recalls how Wetmore dropped by to see him at work one afternoon. He was on his hands and knees in the parking lot sweeping up broken glass when "all of a sudden I see some feet. 'Can you tell me where the cliffs of Dover are?'" It was Wetmore. "Then he says, 'Here's the document. This station is temporary. See you in practice next week.'"

With that gesture, Wetmore won over Found. He sought out Found, and showed him in his typically understated manner that he cared about him. So Found went to work—hard. With Wetmore, there is no other way. Found says, "At the heart of it, and he'll say it himself, he's a martinet, a hard-ass. When you show up, you come to run. His methods are definitely Lydiardesque, and his temperament is like some hard-ass coach from the fifties. That's the enigma of Mark, but that's the appeal, too."

Like the others, Found ran long and hard on Magnolia Road. Eight months later, a new runner emerged. "I won a conference title, set school records and got second in the 5k at NCAA's indoors. Before that year, 14:17 was my best [5k]. I ran 13:51 at Indoor NCAA's all because of Mark, all because he had me see long term."

Furthermore, Found witnessed walk-ons enjoying as much success under Wetmore as those with sterling résumés. In the spring of 1994, Found was running a twenty miler on Magnolia Road while in 13:49 5k shape with Jay Cleckler and Jon Cooper, two Junior Varsity walk-ons. He was running a little over six minutes a mile, "and they blasted me. It was a preview of what they did that fall. Here were two guys from backwoods areas that no one wanted that became All-Americans. When they left they still couldn't break 4:20 in the mile."

The success of Cooper and Cleckler sent a message to all of Wetmore's guys: It does not matter how little talent you have, if you follow his instructions and work hard, you will succeed. According to Found, "ever since then, every Sunday run was a rumblefest." Wetmore would tell his guys, "When you live on monster island, someone's breathing fire every day." Now everyone has their eye out for the next Cooper or Cleckler, looking to see who is going to step up.

Last year it was current senior Matt Napier. A middle linebacker in high school with fair 4:30ish track credentials, he was so large when he came to CU that Wetmore thought he still had more of a football physique than one suitable for running cross country. Napier was also married and had a child. With these commitments, Wetmore questioned his decision to run on the squad, but Napier would not be deterred. "Trust me," Napier told him, "it will be worth it."

In his first season Napier ran only two races, finishing 31st in the Rocky Mountain Shootout and thirteenth at the Fort Hays State Invitational. His sophomore year he made greater strides, finishing 22nd at Big 12's and 99th at NCAA's. Last year the former linebacker finished eleventh at Big 12's before earning his first All-American honors by finishing 39th at the NCAA's. Napier is running Magnolia Road with the team this morning, and while he plans on redshirting the season, he stands as evidence to all the walk-ons that they, too, have a shot.

Wetmore did not speak to the younger guys yesterday, and the upperclassmen will not pull them aside and lecture them before today's first run up Mags either. Says Goucher, "When it's time to work, it's time to work. They'll find out on their own."

But why make the effort to travel and run at 8000 feet when there are plenty of runs in Boulder? While there are "debatable physiological benefits" of going up to 8000 feet for the long run (Wetmore claims "the best thing would be to live there and train down here"), Wetmore's primary motivation for running there is more pragmatic. They go there because "it's a relatively quiet dirt road, the air is clear and it's beautiful." Physiologically, he believes running on Magnolia Road offers his athletes the benefit of a "cardiopulmonary workout without hammering our legs because we're going slower. They can run at the same heart rate up there as they would down here, and we're not killing their legs."

The guys would find the latter part of his statement quite debatable. The run starts at the five-mile marker on the side of the road at about 8000 feet. After descending a slight hill for a quarter mile, the road starts to climb. And legs start to burn. Only fools summit this hill too quickly, for the road proceeds to ascend through rolling hills for three miles before a full-mile climb to the four-mile mark.

At last, there is a break from the climbing, but it is short-lived. The climb resumes for most of the fifth and sixth miles before rolling through the seventh mile. Those running fourteen miles turn around there. Those continuing to do 17.4 miles cross the Peak to Peak Highway and run out and back on the flattest stretch of the run. Such is the severity of the climbing on the way out that runners routinely average 45 seconds to a minute per mile faster on the return. Rest assured, the elevation and the climbing tax the lungs and the legs like no other run in the CU program . . .

On this Sunday the runners are meeting at the bronze buffalo that sits outside Balch at 8 a.m. Some, like Slattery, rise at a quarter to eight and bike from their dorm room to the buffalo. Others, like Goucher, rise considerably earlier.

Some birds are chirping at 7:50 a.m., and Slattery arrives first with a couple freshmen girls. He is clad in his standard Mt. Olive T-shirt and some long, baggy shorts. Johnson arrives five minutes later, followed by Friedberg and Schafer. The rest file in quickly after that.

There are roughly thirty people assembled by the buffalo as Wetmore emerges from Balch. He wears a white cap with a black Nike swoosh, a gray Nike sweatshirt and thick gray sweatpants. He is definitely kicking it old school.

He walks slowly and deliberately towards the group, document in hand. Conversations continue, but all eyes focus on Wetmore as he approaches. The eyes do not phase him. His businesslike demeanor does not change. Tessman and Schafer laugh as they ponder what he is thinking.

As is his custom, Wetmore passes the document to one of the athletes. Everyone is to come check to see his assignment for the day. The guys are relieved to see he is taking it easy on them today after yesterday's gaffe. Scrawled in thick firm cursive writing is the following:

Many of you have taken a big step in volume or intensity recently. I have under-assigned many of you because of that. We have ten more LD's (long days) coming, each of which will be harder.

Underneath his message he writes their assignments. Women's assignments are on the left, men on the right. Johnson, still just starting his training, is assigned eight miles. (He runs eleven.) Slattery is assigned ten miles, there is a group doing twelve miles, and Berkshire, Napier, Ponce, Friedberg, Severy, Batliner, and Goucher are assigned two hours, easy.

Batliner sees the document and says, "That is the second time in four years I've seen 'easy' next to a Sunday run." Knowing they *still* have to run Mags, Wes says, "Yeah, but that's like saying 'easy Flagstaff.'"

It is extremely hot on Magnolia Road. None of the runners wear a T-shirt. As they head out, Goucher and Severy establish a quick lead ahead of everyone. They talk casually to one another and Goucher asks

Severy how he likes living in his cabin. Severy has rented a cabin atop Flagstaff Mountain for the semester from a CU professor. He says he is loving it, except he found some black widows there

Severy's cabin

yesterday and he had to exterminate the place. Severy laughs when telling the story, as though their presence is really no big deal.

As they approach four miles, Friedberg catches Goucher and Severy. Goucher looks back and shoots Friedberg a condescending glance mixed with surprise. "Friedberg!" he says. "What are you doing here?" "Just running," he says. "Yeah, but you're supposed to be running easy," Goucher replies, "and your easy is not the same as my easy." Friedberg's face is flushed, and the exertion is clearly affecting him. He does not respond, or slow down.

Batliner is right behind Friedberg, and by four miles they are running together as a pack. The four run as one until there are only two miles to go, when Goucher finally pulls ahead. He runs the 17.4 mile course in 1:48 before tacking on twelve minutes to make it a nineteen- to nineteen-and-a-half-mile run. The run gives him 100 miles this week, with only one five-mile morning run in addition to his afternoon runs. "I'm gonna try to hold this (mileage) all fall," he says, "then I should be where I need to be." In his log he writes, *Felt pretty good, Mark told us to go easy, but you can never really go easy on Mags.*

Severy and Friedberg finish the 17.4 a few minutes later before adding on ten minutes to make it an eighteen-mile day. Friedberg struggles with the extra ten minutes, but it is nevertheless a huge day for him. It brings his weekly total to 98 miles. He is training as hard as anyone. After sticking with Severy on Mags, he has to be thinking of joining the club that Cleckler and Cooper founded and Napier continued.

Batliner runs the 17 in 1:57. He is tired, but not overly so. The same cannot be said for Ponce and Berkshire, who are nowhere to be seen as Batliner finishes. Wetmore heads out in one of the vans to check on the remaining athletes. "My dream," he says, "is to have ten men and ten women running the full Mags together at six- to seven-minute mile pace. But it'll never happen. Mags always claims its victims." As if on cue, Wetmore passes a struggling Oscar Ponce. "Look at Scar," Wetmore says, "he's hurting." Ponce squints from the sun, his shoulders are drawn high, and his strides are minuscule. It is the gait of a blown-out runner.

Behind Ponce, Berkshire is in even worse straits. When he finishes, he can do nothing more than wordlessly walk in slow circles before sitting in the shade next to the van. He just wants to get home. If he is anxious or worried he is not fit, his teammates will pick him up. Says Goucher, "If someone has a bad day, we all pull together. A lot of people get distressed after one bad day, but we're there to stabilize each other. We'll say, 'Don't be dumb, you're fit. There's no way you can't be fit.'"

Only O'Mara has cause for concern. He suffers through his twelve-mile assignment. Next to his name on the document Wetmore writes: "*dying.*"

Rest . . . Finally

Since organized practice began on August 18th, five out of the six days have been hard. The men earned a well-deserved easy day today. According to NCAA regulations, teams are only allowed to have organized practice six days a week. All season long, Mondays will be "OYO"—on your own.

Today they are assigned an easy 40 to 70 minutes with six to eight 100-meter strides. On the high end of the spectrum, Goucher runs the maximum 70 minutes. But he notes in his log, "need more sleep at night and rest, not getting enough rest for the amount of mileage I'm doing." Friedberg "rests" with a 78-minute run of his own in the a.m., and an additional two miles and strides in the afternoon.

On the lower end of the spectrum are the banged-up and lower-mileage guys. Reese was so beat up from Friday's run that he took Sunday off. Today, he runs easily for 30 minutes around a grass field by his house. If they are going to win in November, they will need a healthy Reese at the front of the pack . . .

Short Specificity

The sun is still rising, casting a dim glow through the clouds onto the Flatirons to the west. The cross country course, referred to by Wetmore as "The Buffalo Ranch," is located on the University of Colorado's southern Flatirons property. At this hour, it is deserted. The team will be practicing here for the first of many times later this afternoon. In anticipation of this, it was rolled yesterday as part of Wetmore and Drake's continuing effort to turn this rock-filled patch of land into a legitimate cross country course.

The course itself is a flat dirt trail about ten feet across in most parts. It is mostly hard dirt, but some resilient tufts of grass poke through. Light blue and purple wildflowers appear in patches. Every creature seems to be awaking; the high pitched staccato of crickets and a symphony of birds compete with the workday commuters for aural attention.

Goucher, whose apartment complex adjoins the course, approaches the starting line after a twenty-minute warm-up, ready to get to work. He is working out alone this morning because he is going to a MatchBox 20 concert this evening with his fiancée at the Red Rocks Amphitheatre. Classes started yesterday and today he has classes all day starting at 9 a.m., so he must practice now.

This afternoon a bridge that covers a shallow creek that leads to the course's one steep 75-meter hill will be in place. It is not there now, so Goucher has to modify the day's endeavor. He is going to run thirteen times 90 seconds hard with a full recovery between each interval. For Goucher, that only takes about 60 seconds.

Goucher sighs wearily and says, "Man, I'm not getting enough sleep." A restless sleeper to begin with, he will fight all season to get the rest he needs. He wears black Adidas shorts and a new white Adidas top. As he switches into his Nike Zoom cross spikes the power of his quads is evident. It is a lean power. The striation in his quadriceps is visible as the muscles dance beneath the skin when he rises from his crouch. Like the Kenyans, his calves are small and undistinguished in comparison. His quads are the engines that power him across the course.

Despite his contrasting outfit, the trees and thick undergrowth in the middle of the one-mile loop he runs camouflage him. He disappears and reappears from behind the foliage in no time at all. He carries some toilet paper in a little plastic bag in his right hand that he uses as a marker on his repeats. As he hits 90 seconds on his first interval, he emphatically throws it on the ground and starts jogging around. He bends down and picks it up before clicking his watch to start the next interval where the previous one left off. The efficient workout is over in no time at all. By 8 a.m. he has switched back into his trainers and jogged off into the distance . . .

By 4 p.m. the sun is blazing. The Buffalo Ranch has been deserted for the past eight hours. There is no shade on the course, no respite from the heat. The men are doing the same workout as Goucher, except that they are not running a fixed number of intervals. Rather, they are running 90 second segments until they cover four miles. Wetmore's only instructions regarding the rest are to take a full recovery before beginning the next interval. They are not timing the rest, but they are keeping a cumulative time to see how long it takes them to traverse four miles.

Severy (nicknamed "the Bus") and Batliner run out in front of the pack. They have quickly distanced themselves from their teammates by taking only twenty to forty seconds recovery between intervals. They are symbiotic training partners, feeding off each other's strengths. Batliner pushes the intervals while Severy pushes the rest, taking off before Batliner has a chance to fully recover.

Severy has a large wrap covering a gash on his calf. He bought a motorcycle in mid-August to get up and down from his cabin atop Flagstaff Mountain. His bike ran out of gas this morning and he slipped on some sand while he was slowing down, skidding on his lower leg in the process. The injury looks bad, but it does not affect his running. Wetmore sees him coming around the course and smiles while shaking his head. "Every year Sev manages to screw it up," he says. But Wetmore knows he is a diligent worker. "He's doing alright. If we can just melt the fat off of him we'll be okay."

Bat and Sev finish the day's endeavor first. They have run 19:37 and 19:38 for the four miles. The three milers, Slattery, Schafer, and Elmuccio also run 19:37, but they arrive several minutes after Bat and Sev because they needed more rest between intervals. Slattery is still thinking about his first Mags. "It sucked. My ankle is so sore from running those hills." But he is excited about how comfortable he felt out here today. "I took a little more rest, but I was feeling good. I think I'm adjusting well."

Reese pulls the surprise of the day. He ran an hour in the pool at Sev's sister Robin's apartment complex on Sunday to recover from Saturday's debacle, and today he does the entire workout. He runs 20:11 and finishes with Ronald Roybal. "My IT has been hurting since last week, but it wasn't bad when I warmed up today." He grabs his leg where he had knee surgery as he switches into his trainers and says, "My leg's just weak. But sometimes you just have to say 'what the fuck.'" He has an appointment next Thursday to see a "miracle healer" in Colorado Springs. He is hoping that will put his pain behind him. Nevertheless, Batliner is enthused to see Reese run so well today. He approaches him and tells him, "If you stay healthy, I think we're good for Nationals." It is something Reese knows all too well.

Jay Johnson finishes as the others lace up their trainers and prepare to cooldown. Today "J-Bird," as Wetmore call him, takes his time on the intervals and the rest; he pushes only as much as his body will allow. He covers the four miles in 22:30, over two minutes slower than any of his teammates. A week from today they will be doing this same workout, but with two-minute pushes instead of 90-second segments. That will be the first of many opportunities to start bridging the gap.

You *Need* the Melon

Ronald Roybal excuses himself to his Spanish literature professor as he arrives with two *huéspedes*, or guests, in tow, ten minutes late. The class appears to engage Roybal, a Spanish major, and only Roybal. No other student answers the professor's queries. Actually, most appear only semi-conscious. Despite his tardiness, in the professor's eyes Roybal is batting a thousand.

After class, Roybal and his buddy Pedro set off across campus on a beautiful 70-degree morning. "I think it's time," says Roybal. He pulls a knife and a beautiful ripe cantaloupe out of his knapsack. He proceeds to offer melon to any and all strangers passing by whom, in his estimation, "need the melon." "Oh, you see her," he says pointing to an attractive, petite blond, "she needs the melon. That guy, he needs the melon." Rejected once, Roybal will always ask, "Are you sure?"

Some will reconsider and take the melon. Others will try to rationalize it, but to no avail. There is no explanation for Roybal's actions other than his desire to see people smile. No doubt, it is odd. "But one time," he says, voice rising with excitement, "me and Pedro were on Pearl Street and this one guy came around like three times, and his eyes widened, and he was so excited 'cause we kept giving him the melon. It was awesome!"

Today maybe every third person takes the melon, a less successful rate than his trip down Pearl Street. Roybal appears unconcerned and is grinning from ear to ear. "We had honeydew then," he says. Of course.

Res Severa Verum Gaudia

A coach's duties never end. Wetmore has spent the morning schmoozing with a benefactor who is donating $200,000 to the university to resurface the indoor track. The university is matching his donation.

Goucher stopped by later in the morning and the two discussed drug use in the sport. It concerns them both. Wetmore asks rhetorically, "How long is it going to be before someone goes over there (to Europe) and comes back with the juice? There's no blood testing in the NCAA. It won't be long before collegians are taking EPO." He and Goucher discuss passively protesting drug use in the sport by having Goucher sport a "Test me" T-shirt when he goes pro. Wetmore stops abruptly. "Enough speechifying," he says.

Wetmore's computer sits on a stand perpendicular to his desk. A screen saver scrolls across the screen in bold white letters: "*Res Severa Verum Gaudia*." The quote comes from Gustav Mahler, for a decade a conductor at the Vienna State Opera House. He had it scrawled on a piece of paper on his podium. It means, "To be serious is the greatest joy." It is appropriately Wetmore.

"What joy is there," he says, "in being cavalier about your life or your endeavors? You should take your life, your joy, your endeavors, seriously." He leans forward in his chair. "Look," he continues, "I have the disadvantage of not believing in an afterlife floating on a cloud, playing a harp; so I'm not looking at this as something I just have to get through." JD appears in the doorway. Full into it now, Wetmore continues, "When my alarm goes off, and I've already been up a half hour, I'm fired up!" JD smiles as Wetmore jokes, "I got the reporter in here, I gotta show off."

The Right Stuff

Steve Slattery's roommate is Matt Ruhl. Ruhl is a 9:29 3200-meter runner from Triton High School in South Jersey, and he is running the time trial in hopes of making the squad. He has been running 70 miles a week and feels fit, but he has his doubts. "You never know what's going to happen on any given day." His nerves are tempered a bit by what Wetmore has told him, "Mark said me and this other kid got the best chance of making the roster this year. That helps me to see I'll do well at the time trial."

Wetmore is enthusiastic about Ruhl and the other aspirant's chances. "Almost all the guys who try to make it will make it. Those who don't get scared and run away." Those who do not make it are lacking what Wetmore refers to as "the right stuff."

"'The right stuff' on this level," he says, "is some combination of these four qualities: talent, durability, determination, and courage. Not everyone needs to have a monster four, but everyone has to have some combination of the four of these. You need some level of all four, and not having one will kill you."

He offers himself by way of example. "If I came out for my own team, I'd cut me. I have no talent." But a lack of talent can be made up for by an overabundance of courage. "You're not gonna die," he says. "This isn't jousting, but some people are just petrified. They can't do it."

One guy not lacking in courage is Goucher. "Yeah," Wetmore says, "he's a big talent, and he'll hold his hand in the fire. He's got above average courage. He'll go up against anybody. If there's a weakness, it's his durability. He's got allergies, chronically sprained ankles. But the allergies—Christ they kill him!" He sums up his star pupil, with an eye to the future: "He's got three out of four. If he's got durability and can do ten years of one-hundred-plus-mile weeks, he'll have four out of four, and he'll be hard to beat . . ."

Time to Work

The men are doing a "steady" medium-distance run this afternoon. It is not an easy run. In Wetmorespeak, "steady" means hard but controlled. The men will have four hard days a week—Tuesday, Wednesday, Friday, Sunday—all season long. It is the density of this training that separates Wetmore's men from most other teams.

The longest group will run the Marshall loop, 15.7 miles. Wetmore knows the exact distance, and it is one of the reasons he assigns this run. He says, "It's a quantifiable run. I like to know what we do." He reconsiders his choice of words before saying, "I need to know what we do."

The men head out *en masse*, and Goucher immediately takes the point with Berkshire and Batliner just a few steps behind him. Batliner and Berkshire are chatting with one another when Goucher pulls away from them just a mile into the run. Once he has distanced himself he pointedly remarks, "One thing I hope these guys learn is that when you're here, you're here to train, not to socialize. I'll socialize later. If I sit there and talk like Wes back there on a run, I feel like I am cheating, cheating myself. I know I can beat anybody in the country, but when I train hard, it gives me that extra confidence." He passes three miles in 18:12.

Is Goucher going faster than steady? He pointedly remarks, "No. If you're talking, you're not going steady. If I'm running and people are talking around me, I feel I should be running harder."

He burps, and his indigestion only adds to his irritation. "See," he says, "that's because I ate lunch. I ate a peanut butter and jelly sandwich at two o'clock." He burps again. "Shit! I like to feel hungry."

Goucher *never* eats lunch. If he is hungry, he will have a granola bar or another light snack. The guys, especially Reese, kid him that he does not eat enough. He used to eat more. Standing 5'9" to 5'10", he weighs in at just under 140 pounds. At the Olympic Trials in Atlanta in 1996, he weighed 145. After the 5000-meter final, where he finished a disappointing fourteenth, Wetmore told him he was fat. Goucher was livid. When he calmed down he realized Wetmore was right, and he has made a conscious effort to lose any excess weight since then. He feels the difference. "My chest was bigger, my arms were bigger. Losing the five pounds has helped me thin out, and it's cut me more. It's made a big difference."

Still cut, he does not lift weights. "I love to lift," he says, but it bulks him up too much, so Wetmore will not allow it. Now the only upper-body work he does are push-ups and situps. Still, much like Steve Prefontaine, the great American 5000-meter runner, he is blessed with tremendous upper-body strength. Pound for pound, there is arguably no stronger distance runner in the United States, and maybe even the world.

At about 3.5 miles, Batliner and Friedberg catch Goucher. Goucher turns to them and says in a slightly condescending tone, "So, you guys decided to start training?" Batliner, visibly pissed, replies, "Yeah, that's it." Soon after Bat stops for a pit stop, and Friedberg and Goucher decide to take one as well. Batliner takes his time. Goucher waits for a minute before departing without Batliner or Friedberg.

Goucher runs solo the rest of the way. As he runs a tune from country singer Tim McGraw plays in his mind. The song is one of many things that he will think about during the course of a run. Many times he thinks of the mundane, such as what he will have for dinner, or his homework. But right now the exertion is rising. "I'm thinking that I'm tired," he says, "but I just have to maintain."

He presses on wordlessly until about two miles from the finish at Balch, when he is forced to stop at a stoplight. "Shit!" he says. "I hate this." There are lines of salt streaking down his cheeks. He has hardly had anything to drink today, and he pulls his waistband down off of his hip to reveal a line of red irritated skin from the salt. "I'm not taking good enough care of myself," he says. "I'm dehydrated." The opposite light turns yellow and he darts across the intersection. He is easily running under six-minute-mile pace. He finishes shortly thereafter in one hour and thirty minutes. He has averaged 5:44 a mile.

Four minutes later, Batliner and Friedberg roll in as Wetmore waits for them outside the gym. They are followed by Ponce and Severy. The injury-prone Ponce has cautiously run a mile shorter than the others. "I gotta stay healthy," he says, "I don't need to get hurt."

Severy would do well to follow Ponce's example. Goucher takes one glance at his bandaged shin as he enters the gym and says, "Sev man, be careful, please!" Sev rolls his shoulder and laughs.

Reese is long gone. Yesterday's simulated fartlek on the course wiped him out, so today he ran easy for 45 minutes around Kitt field. He, for one, is unable to handle the density of training . . . for now.

So Many Gouchers

The document brings joy to the guys' eyes: *Easy aerobic run to Potts*. The two groups are either going 50 or 60 minutes before running eight 150-meter strides at "mile pace" on the track at Potts Field. Jason Robbie is one who needs the rest. "I'm exhausted," he says. "It's four days into classes, and I feel like I've just been through finals!"

Slattery does not join his mates. His ankle is still sore, so he is listening to the trainers and taking a day in the pool. Wetmore, however, feels no remorse about working his guys so hard. He looks at the other contenders for the national crown—Arkansas and Stanford—and he sees a large disparity in talent between them and CU. "Arkansas," he explains, "has a lot of Gouchers. Stanford—with Riley, Jennings, the Hausers—they have five or six Gouchers. Our only hope is to take our Friedbergs, hang it out, and see what happens."

"Us," he continues, "we got a Goucher, a Bat, a Reese, a Sev, and then the talent drops precipitously." There is an alternative to the density of training—mediocrity. "Some guys out there, who don't get it, they think they can be a Division I distance runner on 55 miles a week."

He pauses before thinking of how a tremendous work ethic has positioned one of his walk-ons to make the Varsity squad. "Wes," he says, "he's doing great. The only guy who's got less talent than him is me. But he really wants to make this team. He's waiting for September fifth." On September fifth Wes will get to show off his fitness at the time trial. But certainly Goucher, with all his talent, could afford to work less. "Sure," Wetmore says, "Goucher can be a Division I runner on 55 miles a week. But he'd be running 15:48, not 13:48." Berkshire and the others will take their next step tomorrow morning. Wetmore will be there to greet them at Kitt Field as the sun rises. They will be spiked up and ready to run at 6:30 a.m.

St. Crispin's Day

We few, we happy few, we band of brothers;
For he today that sheds his blood with me
Shall be my brother; be he ne'er so vile
This day shall gentle his condition.
And gentlemen in England, now abed,
Shall think themselves accursed they were not here;
And hold their manhoods cheap whiles any speaks
That fought with us upon Saint Crispin's day.

Henry V, Act IV, Scene iii
by William Shakespeare

Wetmore walks quietly between the men and women who sit on the grass, stretching and switching into spikes. It is a cool fifty-degree morning and the sun is rising in the east, casting a faint glow on the Flatirons looming straight ahead. "Six minutes," he says matter-of-factly. Three minutes later he speaks directly to those sitting on the ground who have not begun their strides. "Let's get going on the strides. We don't want to coddle tardiness, now do we?"

Why are they here at 6:30? For one, Thursday is always the easiest day of the week, so they should have had enough recovery to fare well this early. Second, practicing this early gives them more recovery before the week's key workout on Sunday. Finally, it makes their lives a little more difficult, and that serves to callus them a little more and develop a shared sense of sacrifice.

Everyone is here, except for Sev. He runs onto the field with two minutes to spare. There is now 100 percent attendance. Once Sev reaches the others, Wetmore explains the workout. They will be doing 300-meter repeats back and forth on the perimeter of Kitt Field before jogging around a backstop and back (a distance of approximately 200 meters) as a recovery. Then they will start again back down the stretch in the opposite direction. "This is a neuromuscular workout," he says, "so I'm not concerned about your rest. Take as much as you need." Although the primary purpose of the workout is to get a neuromuscular stimulus, they will still get an aerobic benefit from today's effort. Wetmore explains, "All we're really doing is training their legs today, so I don't care how slowly they run their 200's, although given 300 of every 500 is quick, they'll probably end up running sub-six minutes a mile."

Reese is scheduled to do eight repeats while everyone else is doing twelve to sixteen. Wetmore points to the slowest group, which includes Roybal and Robbie. "Reese, start with those guys," he says. The briefest look of indecision crosses Wetmore's face before he turns to JD, "I'm just worried we're being stupid." Reese had recently returned to running following his surgery, and Wetmore questions whether Reese should be doing any workouts yet. But this is Reese's last collegiate cross country season, and he is adamant about pushing the envelope to give himself a chance to do well at NCAA's. They are both prepared to live with the consequences.

Reese looks better. He still looks like he is favoring his good leg, but he has always run with a roll to his stride. He runs for the first time this morning without the knee strap he has used to stabilize his knee since the surgery. Scheduled originally to do eight repeats, he does twelve. He says afterwards, "I think we'll be fucking good this year."

If there is a flaw to the workout, it is that as it progresses and the men and women spread out, it becomes controlled chaos with runners going in all directions, narrowly avoiding one another. To limit potential mishaps, Wetmore is meeting the freshman here this afternoon. Through it all, Wetmore keeps a watchful eye on both teams, noting who is suffering and who is handling the work. He will not hesitate to pull someone early if they have fallen off the back of the pack.

Goucher hammers in front, running the 300's in about 50 seconds, two seconds ahead of the pack. Chris Valenti leads the chase pack. "Valenti's looking heroic today," Wetmore observes. By way of explanation, JD says, "He's been running 65 to 70 miles for the last month." "Oh," Wetmore replies, "that's why he looks so fresh out there."

It is hard to make any judgments from this workout because everyone is coming into it with varying levels of fatigue. While Valenti looks great, Berkshire falls off the back after the tenth repetition. However, Berkshire is running one hundred and ten miles a week. When he is rested and they race, he may get the best of Valenti, even though Valenti murders him today.

Berkshire is not the only one suffering. Chris Schafer is quickly off the back of the pack. He runs the 300's as fast as the others, but he needs more recovery time between intervals. Noting this, JD reasons that, "He might have done his 150's a little fast yesterday." "Yeah," concurs Wetmore, "that was his day to show off (in front of the freshman girls who were out on the track)." O'Mara looks flat-out beat. Wetmore has bookmarked the website showing results from the indoor meet last year when he ran 8:24 to remind himself that O'Mara possesses the right stuff. O'Mara has not shown a glimpse of those abilities yet. JD and Wetmore eye him as he labors past. "Well," says Wetmore candidly, "I think we're looking at our mistake."

As the men and women get deeper into the workout, Wetmore takes off to the opposite corner of the field, leaving JD and Lorie to take this side of the field. He turns his head and says, "I'm going here so I can offer ridicule and sarcasm to them." The men pass him as he walks; Friedberg is hanging onto the lead pack. "Okay," he says, "who's feeling bad today? Friedberg? Friedberg's feeling bad today."

Sev, Ponce, Batliner, Blondeau, Friedberg, and Napier run together towards the end. Roybal also mixes it up with them for the first time. Wetmore pulls him aside afterwards and says quietly, "It's about time." "Yeah," Roybal replies, "I know."

Goucher and Batliner are the last ones on the course. Goucher finishes their sixteenth and final interval with Batliner on his heels. As the men change into their trainers for their cooldown, Wetmore indirectly compliments their efforts. "It's like St. Crispin's Day," he says loud enough for all to hear. "Everyone here wants to be the real deal. Everyone in this town wants to be you, and everyone who wants to be you is in bed. I'm going to do my run so I can say I fought on St. Crispin's Day."

This last line would be a good slogan for a T-shirt: *CU Cross Country— Where were you on St. Crispin's Day?* Wetmore will have none of it. "No slogans," he emphatically states. "I hate slogans. I tell Goucher, you run fast and one day you can go on the Jay Leno show and just sit there."

The day's work done, most of the guys head to The Village Coffee Shop a half mile from Kitt Field on the corner of Folsom and Arapahoe. It is a blue-collar place, with the best hash browns and french toast in town. The team favorite is the #5: two eggs, hash browns, and wheat toast for $3.00. Catch Sev eating one of these, though, and you will have a tough time making out what exactly lies beneath a blanket of ketchup.

Laminated articles of the team from daily papers are posted on a wall by the front entrance of the village. If there is a place in town where the team gets star treatment, it is fittingly here. The waitresses love the runners, especially the steeplechasers. As Shana, one of the waitresses, sees Reese enter she says, "There's my favorite man in the whole wide world!" Batliner and 1997 graduate Clint Wells also get extra love for their hurdling exploits.

Bluebirds

Wetmore heads down to Kitt from his office in his university-provided Eddie Bauer edition Ford Explorer. He was ebullient this morning, and this was not by accident. "The team absolutely responds to me," he says. "If I show up at practice in a bad mood, no matter how good they're feeling, they'll feel worse because of me. I've got to remind myself every day that I've also got to be at my best in November. Jonathan Riley saved Stanford last year," he continues. "I want to make sure we win this year."

Slattery is the only guy down here, and he is joined by a large pack of freshman girls. There are five freshman girls, who make up the best freshman class Wetmore has ever had, along with a large group of walk-ons. Some of them are feeling exhausted already, so Wetmore reassures them this is how they *should* be feeling. "Every year from Pre-Nationals to Nationals we improve more than any other team because we are orchestrating our energy. Okay?" Even if they do not all buy what he is selling, no one argues.

Wetmore watches them go through their paces. Slattery is feeling better after a day of rest and some ibuprofen. He shows some of his speed as he runs ten intervals in 48 seconds. The pack of walk-ons moves way behind the recruits. Their pace does not discourage Wetmore. Out of this pack of walk-ons, or bluebirds, as Wetmore calls them, one may emerge as a Varsity runner, or even become an All-American. After all, the women have a walk-on to All-American legacy of their own.

Perhaps the most illustrious of the walk-ons is Shayne Wille Culpepper. She transferred to CU from Vermont in the fall of 1995 and did not make the roster to NCAA's. But by the end of the indoor season she was an NCAA All-American in the 3000 meters. She continued to improve throughout her career, and at the end of her senior year she placed third in the outdoor 3000 meters at the NCAA's in a school record 9:06.

The reality, though, is that these "bluebirds" are currently the worst athletes on a team that, combined, has over fifty athletes. Wetmore wishes he could give them more of his attention. "I'll say it again," he says. "If I had that last bluebird group ten years ago (when he was the distance coach) at Seton Hall, I'd have been psyched. I'd have taken those girls and finished in the top half of the Big East. Now I just have better athletes."

Oh, Goucher!

On a quickly warming morning at the Boulder Reservoir, referred to as the "Res" by local runners, the team heads out for a long run along the aqueduct canal. The rising heat is an unwelcome sight for the assembled harriers. While flat, the run snakes out along an irrigation canal that heads north out of town towards Gunbarrel, Colorado. There is no shade for the entirety of the out-and-back run. Six of the harriers, including Goucher, are slated to run out 60 minutes and back. Without water and without shade, the blue sky is unsettling.

A large group has assembled today, and the entire men's and women's teams toe a starting line drawn in the dirt by Chris Schafer. Some local runners looking for company have also arrived. Among the more distinguished of the "mercenaries," as Wetmore refers to them, are US Army runners Brad Hudson and Sam Wilbur.

While the CU veterans are heading out for two hours, the youngsters are embarking on runs of anywhere from twelve to fifteen miles. Wetmore gives the word, and the runners are off. A mile in, Goucher already has a substantial lead on the pack. He covers the first mile in only 6:30, yet he runs alone. It is a wise move on the other runners part to let him go, because he proceeds to slowly squeeze down on the trigger, almost imperceptibly, until he is running at an astonishingly fast clip.

He passes five miles in 29:21. Chris Valenti is the nearest CU pursuer, and he is already 200 meters back. Goucher runs purposefully along the canal, his effort controlled, yet constant. Eyes squinting behind a pair of Nike shades, breath audible, he pushes steadily forward. Before long an hour is reached, but Goucher elects to press on until he reaches the eleven-mile mark. He figures he will still run approximately two hours because "it's a bit downhill on the way back anyway, so it'll be faster."

Sixteen miles in, a jagged line of salt becomes visible on his shorts. Absent this visual cue, there is no way to measure his exertion because he has not changed his form or his visage since the start. But since he hit mile five, he has dropped the pace substantially. He clicks off miles sixteen through twenty in: 5:31, 5:29, 5:27, and 5:34. He has covered the first twenty miles in 1:52, a torrid pace of 5:36 per mile. As Goucher reaches the twenty-mile mark, the sun rises higher in the distance, and a slight breeze off the canal offers the only respite from the heat. The dawdling water that flows just a few feet away provides a tantalizingly cruel reminder of what reward awaits at run's end. A watersnake slithers upstream as Goucher heads for home, searching for prey of its own.

Entering the 21st mile, Berkshire and Ponce become visible in the distance. They are the first runners Goucher has seen since the run began. Spotting them, he again imperceptibly ups the tempo; his breathing is still constant, his turnover not visibly faster. He starts reeling them in, and he passes them right before reaching the twenty-first mile. He clicks his watch to check his mile split and sees he ran the twenty-first mile in 5:13. "I don't know what happened," he would say later when queried by Wetmore as to why he ran that mile so fast. "I guess I just saw those guys and slipped into competition mode. I didn't mean to run that fast." He eases up in the last mile, running a controlled 5:47. All said, he runs 22 miles in 2:03.

He immediately heads for the van, and downs some water from an old two-liter Gatorade bottle. A bedraggled Berkshire straggles in, with Ponce on his heels. Ponce is exhausted, and he immediately heads for a dip in the Reservoir. Ponce is pleased with his day's toil. He ran twenty miles in 2:06. That is the farthest he has ever run, and he did it running at a 6:18-mile clip. Berkshire is also wasted, yet satisfied with the effort.

All told, six Buffaloes run two plus hours today on the Canal: Batliner, Berkshire, Goucher, Nordberg, Napier, and Ponce. Out of town for his cousin's wedding, Severy runs nineteen miles in Steamboat Springs. For the last three miles of his run, Severy runs up the mountain for a mile and a half on some cat trails before turning back down. Counting Severy, seven men have run two hours or more this morning.

Those who run under two hours are no less impressive. Valenti, out to show Wetmore that he is for real, runs a solid fourteen plus miles in 1:23. In six days he will have his chance as he runs the time trial to guarantee his spot on the roster. Meanwhile, Slattery runs a little over twelve miles in 1:20—his farthest run yet. He may yet challenge for a spot at season's end. And then there is Roybal, who runs 16 in 1:48. It looks as if he, too, may round into form.

But the story of the day is undoubtedly Goucher. In his log he writes of the day's effort, *Felt really good. Just rolling them off, not out of control. Felt easy, got a little tired the last seven miles or so, started to feel it somewhat, but still not too bad; 21st mile 5:13.* For weeks to come Wetmore will field calls as word spreads around town about Goucher's effort. While pleased with Goucher's effort, he worries about the cumulative toll the hard work is taking on him. He has run over 100 miles this week, at elevation, in only eight runs. He will not run as far again this season—of that Wetmore is certain. But, the question lingers, is Goucher doing too much?

Tuesday, September 1, 1998
The Buffalo Ranch
4 p.m.

Seasonal Affective Disorder

The men have now been training together for three weeks. They will be doing another fartlek around the course today. A week ago, they did ninety-second segments; today, they will be doing two-minute segments. Everything is going smoothly, yet Wetmore is concerned. "There are a lot of neuroses today," he says.

Jen Gruia asks him what that means. "Seasonal affective disorder," he says. "It comes with the changing of the leaves, and it's worse later." Also referred to by Wetmore as "three-week syndrome," it is his term for the collective neuroses that suddenly crop up at this time of year. The initial feeling-out period is now over and the density of training is starting to catch up to his athletes. It occurs to them that all the hard work that has been completed is but a prelude for the more strenuous workouts that have yet to commence. For those who are already overextending themselves, it is a painful realization.

The neuroses are enhanced this week because it is the week of the time trial. Robbie, Valenti, and Ruhl still have to make the squad, and who knows who else is going to come out of the woodwork? But Wetmore need not have worried; everyone rolls today.

The course looks great. Another plywood bridge is in place. It goes over a little creek on the lower mile loop, eliminating the need to scamper across the dried-out creek that ran beneath it as they did during the last fartlek. One person who was looking to run the course in a CU jersey this season is now reconsidering. Slattery is leaning towards saving his eligibility. "I'd like to race because this is the best team we've ever had, but I'd also like to redshirt so I can have another season. If Mark calls on me, I'll be ready." He shows it today; he runs four miles in 19:44.

The men take off in packs, and finish in packs, with the exception of Goucher. He covers the course in 23:56, and finishes a minute and a half in front of the others. He is ambivalent about the day's work. "It wasn't hard," he says, "but I don't feel like I have the neuromuscular speed right now. I just don't feel like I'm really fast right now." Considering the volume he is putting in, his lack of zip is not surprising.

The chase pack is much more excited than Goucher about today's run. Berkshire leads in a pack of ten, including Batliner, Sev, Roybal, and Reese. Coach Roch saw them running a few minutes earlier, and she says, "Wes was way out in front of the guys he was with, but he might have just been working really hard." Others intentionally held back to keep the guys together. Despite continued tightness in his IT band on his good leg that he attributes to compensation, Reese is pleased. "It's good," he says. "We were all together. Some guys like me and Roybal were pushing it to stay with them, and Bat and Sev were slowing down to stay with the group."

As they come down the finishing stretch together, the excitement is visible in Wetmore's eyes, if not in his voice. In an even monotone he says, "No kicking," before repeating it a couple of seconds later. Out the back as the guys start kicking anyway, Sev recovers quickly to erase the gap and they finish as one.

Wetmore is relieved about the workout: "From the third week we get going to the end of September, it's always crazy, but they were rocking. Twenty guys just rolling along, talking . . ." But his day is not done.

The recruiting wars are starting to heat up, and JD and Wetmore have narrowed their search for the next generation of CU runners to a trio of promising harriers. The first two are twins Jorge and Eduardo Torres from Wheeling, Illinois. Two of the most sought-after recruits in the land, they have committed to visiting CU the weekend of September 19th. But getting them to sign letters of intent is a long shot. Both tremendous talents, Jorge has a shot this fall of becoming the only schoolboy ever to make the Foot Locker National Cross Country Championships four times. If Ed makes it, it will be his third trip to the national finals. Stanford and Oregon are also in the hunt for their talents, so it will be a recruiting dogfight.

If they do not land the Torres twins, there is a guy closer to home without the reputation or the results of the Torres twins who fits the profile of the typical CU runner. His name is Seth Hejny, and he is a two-miler from Grand Junction, Colorado. He ran a 9:33 two-mile at Air Force last spring to win the Colorado state meet. That is worth about a 9:16 at sea level, but it still may be slow enough to dissuade most schools from bidding for his services. What is even more intriguing about Hejny is that he has what JD calls the "Wyoming Factor" on his side. He is from a nowhere place and he has yet to really run consistently against top-flight competition. JD is going to go watch him run the Arapahoe Invitational not far from here on Friday, and while he cannot approach Hejny and talk to him, he can speak to Hejny if Hejny approaches him. Stanford has landed most of the best kids in recent years, and this will be a chance for JD to see if Stanford is eyeing Hejny as well.

The Tank

The team is running today at the East Arapahoe Trailhead. CU runners refer to it as "The Tank" because from the start a large water tank that serves as the six-mile marker is visible to the north. The trail goes slightly downhill for two and a half miles and then flattens out for a half mile before rolling hills bring one to the tank. The run does not appear especially difficult when compared to Flagstaff Mountain or Magnolia Road, but it is hard enough to keep one's heart rate humming.

The guys are running their second AT of the year on Friday, so no one hammers too hard today, including Goucher. He runs steadily with Friedberg, Severy, Batliner, and Ponce. They are the only ones going past the tank, and they run approximately fifteen miles in ninety-three minutes.

Reese does not go with them. As part of the requirements for his business degree, he is doing an internship with the athletic company Saucony. The company is based in Boston, but they have a sports-marketing department in Boulder. Not one to hit with books with vigor, he is investing a lot of time and effort into the job because it could lead to a position with the firm when he graduates. It also may lead to a coveted shoe sponsorship. His current responsibilities include making decisions on which athletes to sponsor, running expositions and promotions, and making sure the athletes Saucony sponsors receive their equipment.

Unfortunately, his work schedule conflicts with practice on Wednesdays, so he will run most of his medium-distance runs in the morning. Missing the Wednesday practices will not be much of a nuisance for him, though, because he lives with three post-collegiate runners—Brad Hudson, Kelly Lambert, and Clint Wells—who are often game for putting in a run with him. This morning, for instance, he ran for sixty-eight minutes on the Mesa Trail with Clint Wells.

Each Wednesday, the show will go on without him.

The Miracle Doctor

The men are going easy today. The assignments range from fifty minutes for the younger guys to eighty minutes for mileage hogs like Friedberg. It is blazing hot, and Goucher, for one, is feeling the heat. His training is catching up to him. Of today's run he writes in his log, *Very hot, feeling pretty tired, still not too bad of a run. Legs kind of sore all over, and not too responsive. Strides felt terrible.* Despite being sore and tired and having an AT with the others at 6:30 tomorrow morning, he still runs seventy-five minutes.

For the second day in a row, Reese runs in the morning. He is skipping practice so he can see a "miracle doctor" in Colorado Springs to help him with the IT band on his left leg. His left quad is still visibly smaller and weaker than his right quad as a result of the knee surgery performed last spring. To compensate, he has been putting more pressure on his right leg and now the IT band in his right leg is also becoming sore. Nevertheless, he is going to Colorado Springs to find relief from the pain in his left IT band.

The "miracle doctor" will attempt to alleviate his discomfort. His name is Doctor Michael Leahy, and he is an ART or "active release therapy" practitioner. He works by manually breaking up adhesions or scar tissue that can entrap muscles, ligaments, tendons, and nerves and cause pain or disability. Reese is hoping that such manipulation on his IT band will cure him of the chronic pain in his left thigh.

He is not the first athlete to try this therapy. Donovan Bailey, the former world record holder and Olympic gold medalist in the 100 meters, is a client of Dr. Leahy. In fact, it is he who helped make Dr. Leahy famous. Rumor has it that Bailey tore his hamstring one week prior to the Olympic Games in Atlanta. Without Leahy's aid, Bailey claims he would not have won the gold medal. Professional hockey players Al McGinnis of the St. Louis Blues and Gary Roberts of the Carolina Hurricanes are two other athletes who claim ART saved their careers when all else failed.

Reese learned about Dr. Leahy from his sister Angie. A reporter for the *Colorado Springs Gazette*, she recently wrote an article on Dr. Leahy and his company Champion Health. She told Reese about him, and with her recommendation and these testimonials, he is ready to give it a shot. It is not cheap. The initial fifteen-minute session costs one hundred and fifty dollars.

Reese arrives at the Champion Health building in Colorado Springs at 3:00 p.m. for his 3:15 appointment. The lower level has all the accoutrements of an athletic rehabilitation facility. There are medicine balls and rows of exercise equipment next to the waiting area and reception desk. Reese sits down on a white leather sofa as he completes the necessary paperwork. It is a pleasant atmosphere; stuffed cactuses are placed around the room, the walls are papered in light pastel colors, and easy-listening music plays softly over the speakers.

After finishing his paperwork, Reese goes upstairs and waits to see Dr. Leahy in his office. While waiting, he thinks of tomorrow's AT. Despite having only started running on August 9th, he is feeling somewhat fit. He has already lost eight pounds, and as a result he feels less "like a sloth" and more like a runner. If only he could alleviate the pain in his IT band.

Dr. Leahy enters the room wearing two-tone black and brown shoes, slacks, and a Goodwill Games polo shirt. He is tanned and fit. He informs Reese that he completed a full ironman triathlon in Canada over the weekend—his seventeenth one. The fact that Dr. Leahy is an endurance athlete himself reassures Reese that he understands the rigors and demands of distance running at an elite level.

Dr. Leahy asks Reese questions both about his knee surgery and what currently ails him. He feels Reese's quadriceps with his hands when Reese finishes explaining his aches and pains. Dr. Leahy then explains to him that the IT band is stuck to his quadriceps so they are moving together instead of properly sliding parallel to one another. He says that this is partially why Reese's knee continues to ache as well. He tells Reese that he will not be able to help the aching in the middle of the joint that is a result of the surgery, but that he can alleviate the other pain. His words are encouraging.

In the next instant Dr. Leahy is manipulating Reese's quadriceps with his thumb and hand. "Tell me if I go too hard," he says with a grin, "I'm pretty mean on Thursdays." He pushes down hard on Reese's leg and he has Reese raise and lower his leg as he applies the pressure. Reese appears unfazed, but Dr. Leahy grimaces with the effort.

The treatment lasts only a few minutes, and then the session is over. Reese has spent—at most—ten minutes with Dr. Leahy. Before exiting the office, Dr. Leahy tells Reese to schedule several additional appointments because he will need two or three treatments to get rid of the pain. Reese does not bother to schedule any more appointments. Instead, he heads straight downstairs towards the exit. On the ride back to Boulder he says, "I kinda get the feeling he was rushing me out of there." There will be no miracle cure.

AT

The sun is still rising in the east as the guys gradually file onto the track after finishing their warm-up jogs. One of the freshman girls looks none too pleased to be here so Wetmore offers her some encouragement. "Good morning," he says. "Just think, in an hour you'll be done for the day." Her smile does not reveal whether or not this offers her any solace at all.

Roybal enters the track and Wetmore throws a heart rate monitor at him. "Here, figure it out. Put it on." He looks ready to go; his right fingernails are painted purple. Wetmore throws heart rate monitors out to most of the top guys, including Goucher, Tessman, and Friedberg. Friedberg puts his on and turns to Tessman, "My heart rate's 22, just the way I like it." Tessman smiles and says, "You're fit as a whistle!" The humor is needed to help forget about the task ahead.

As they finish their strides, Wetmore addresses the team:

> I gotta give you a speech before you go. We're going with times today. In most cases I've slowed them down a little bit … I'm doing the best I can to make the best decision to get the best data for today. Occasionally, I want to know your heart rate. There's no good number. I'm going by how fast you're going, how I perceive your exertion to be, and how you perceive your exertion to be.

The intent of the workout is to run at a pace that Wetmore estimates is 85 percent of current fitness. Still, Wetmore later admits he intentionally under-assigned them. He says afterwards, "I'd rather they go five seconds slower and see 'em all together, vibing each other." The only exception to this is Jay Johnson. He is not ready to hang with the guys, so Wetmore instructs him to stay within a heart rate range of 168–172. That should be slow enough so that he does not go out over his head.

There are two main assignments for the others. The top eight guys, and Matt Napier, are scheduled to run 79 seconds a lap. In that group Reese, Roybal, Blondeau, Ponce, and Tessman are running 8k (in 26:20) while Napier, Severy, Friedberg, and Batliner are running 10k (in 32:55). As usual, Goucher gets to train alone. His assignment: 10K at 76 seconds per lap, or 10k in 31:40.

Fearing that they will go out too hard, Wetmore tells them, if anything, "start out too slow." Everyone takes off at once, and Goucher immediately sets off on his own. Everyone follows Wetmore's instructions, and the guys in the pack take turns leading, switching up after each mile. After they hit three miles, the pace starts inching ahead.

Everyone continues to look smooth into the fourth mile. Goucher increases his lead after every lap, and 76's appear to be no problem for him. But four and a half miles in, with only two laps to go, the pack loses a couple of guys. Roybal and Blondeau fall off the back. Everyone else in the 8k group stays on it, and they finish in 26:05. Roybal runs 26:40 while Blondeau, feeling sick, runs 26:45. Everyone's heart rate in the lead pack is between 175 and 180, including Roybal and Blondeau. Tessman, for one, is pleased with his effort: "It felt easy. It's going great. A couple of days a week I still can't run with the team because I'm still in my adjustment period, and it helps me recover when I don't run with them." Belying his track background, he excitedly adds, "26 minutes. That's still a good five mile time for me no matter where it is [never mind at elevation]. I don't know how fast it will go later in the season."

Reese is also pleased. "I felt fine up here," he says, pointing to his chest, "but neuromuscularly I felt really tired after 800 meters. But my heart rate stayed the same [180] the whole time, so that's okay."

And even though he fell off the back, Roybal is psyched, not at how he fared compared to the others, but compared to his form at this time a year ago. He says, "That's the closest thing I've done to a race since Nationals last November. I ran slower than them by 30 seconds but I wasn't out of reach of them until the last two laps. That's not that big of a deal. For sure, it's an encouragement to know I'm ahead of where I was last year." Wetmore agrees with Roybal's assessment of his progress. "He's coming around," he says. With Wetmore, that is as positive an endorsement as you are going to get.

While the 8k group recovers, Goucher and the others are still running. Goucher has dropped his pace and he now runs 73- and 74-second quarters. He looks relaxed and comfortable. He finishes in 30:59, an average of 74.4 per quarter. His average heart rate is 173, lower than everyone else on the team. In his log he writes, *Felt pretty damn good!!!*

While it is tough to feel great about your workout when you finish so far behind your teammate, Sev, Napier, Friedberg, and Bat are thrilled to run 32:20—an average of 77.6 a lap, well below their target of 79 a lap. Bat alone looks a little whipped. Like Goucher, he has upped both his mileage and intensity this season. But according to JD, Bat's fatigue is not unusual, "It's always like this a few weeks into the season when the guys have been training together every day rather than every other day like in the summer."

By 7:30 a.m. the men have finished their day's training. They head en masse to the Village Coffee Shop for some # 5's. JD does not accompany them. Instead, he departs to his other job with a geological consulting firm. Later he'll head to the Arapahoe Invitational to recruit for next year's team.

The Arapahoe Invitational

JD gets stuck in traffic on the way to the meet. After the AT this morning and a full day at work, he can think of other things he would rather be doing. He says, "It's hard to get excited after seeing our guys run 5:12 a mile for five miles this morning, then come to this meet where there's *maybe* one or two kids you would want out of everyone . . . They don't look as good as they do on the track anyway; with grass it's so damn slow. This guy I'm looking at, he looks pretty good anyway."

That someone is the aforementioned Seth Hejny of Grand Junction, Colorado. He has roughly the same credentials as Aaron Blondeau at this stage. But whereas Blondeau went on to finish 12th at Foot Locker Nationals, JD and Wetmore are secretly hoping that Hejny not qualify for the Nationals. Their reasoning is sound. "Look," says JD, "if he ran his times at sea level he'd have run 4:15 and 9:10 and he'd get recruited like crazy. [If] he qualifies for Foot Locker Nationals, he'll get recruited like crazy."

The reality is that most of the kids he recruits will not end up coming to CU. But it takes looking at hundreds, even thousands of kids before JD finds the runners he wants. It is an unrewarding task, one that in most cases belongs to assistant coaches at programs across the country. JD explains: "That's the thing about coaching. Most of our kids have no concept of what I do, that I'm on the phone at night, out here. There's no immediate satisfaction. Down the line they'll tell you. But it's an ego thing. You have to enjoy making people good. If you win NCAA's, you can see it."

Hejny could help make that happen down the road. What makes him an even more appealing prospect is that he is an in-state kid. Money is an issue both for the kids and the program. The CU track program is underfunded, and most of their dollars are tied up for the next few years. With an in-state kid, JD believes "we can make it affordable if we give him a fifty or sixty percent scholarship. Even if they get a half scholarship from an out of state school, it'll be more affordable here."

Another factor that weighs on JD and Wetmore's minds is the success they have had with Colorado kids. One need look no farther than this year's squad for evidence of this. Most of the contenders for the Varsity spots are from Colorado. The list includes Batliner, Berkshire, Blondeau, Goucher, Ponce, Reese, Severy, and Valenti. This list does not include Johnson, who has struggled thus far, but he has run at the NCAA cross country meet twice, in addition to running 3:49 and 14:20. The three CU cross country All-Americans who graduated a year ago, Ricky Cron, Zeke Tiernan, and Clint Wells, are from Colorado as well.

Wetmore's record demonstrates that he can field a top-five team at the NCAA's with a team comprised exclusively of Coloradans. That said, Wetmore and Drake are doing their best to encourage Colorado's best to stay in-state, and attend CU.

Hejny runs unchallenged today. He leads at the mile and his lead grows throughout. He is a tall and strong runner, but JD is right when he says that the athletes, Hejny included, look slow in this setting. JD gives greater credence to Hejny's time. He runs thirty seconds faster than a year ago. He is looking more and more like a national recruit.

Hejny's coach approaches JD after the race and Hejny joins them. JD was hoping to get him in for a visit before the Foot Locker Nationals, but Hejny does not want to take any visits before the state meet at the end of October. The news disappoints JD, but what follows is tougher to swallow. Vin Lananna of Stanford is after Hejny as well. His reputation as a phenomenal recruiter, coupled with the vast resources of Stanford University, make Lananna a colossal opponent to match up against in the recruiting game.

Traffic is no better on the way home. Hejny's news exacerbates JD's fatigue.

Stanford is on JD's mind the whole way home. He cannot believe they keep getting so many top athletes. But now his thoughts are not on the future, but this year's race, where Stanford looks formidable. "I know we'll run smarter than any team at NC's; we always do. But the only way we can beat Stanford is if they fuck up."

What Stanford does not have is the record of success that Wetmore has with walk-ons. Maybe tomorrow they will get another guy out of the woodwork. Who knows?

Vengeance Is a Very Useful Tool

Jason Robbie has to earn his spot on the squad today. But his chance took a turn for the worse late last night at Severy's cabin. Most of the men and women on the team showed up there for a BBQ. For some, it was their first trip to his cabin.

The cabin is not the only attraction. Sev's motorcycle is there, and Robbie, debating purchasing a motorcycle, decided to take it out for a quick spin. When a half hour went by and he had not returned, a couple of cars set out to find him. His teammates' fear that he had crashed was confirmed when they spotted Sev's abandoned motorcycle parked alongside the road. Robbie was at the cabin when the search party returned. He hitched a ride there from a passing motorist after wiping hard. Similar to Severy's crash earlier this season on August 25th, he was hardly moving when he fell. He was simply trying to turn the bike to head back up the road to Sev's cabin when the bike slid out from under him on a patch of gravel. He was banged up pretty good. Blood streamed from his right hand, elbow, and knee.

He fought hard to maintain his composure while Johnson and Sev scrubbed out his wounds with anti-bacterial Softsoap. They could not remove all the pebbles from his skin, so he went to the hospital to get disinfected. His ordeal didn't end until he arrived home at 2:00 a.m.

This morning his body is sore and stiff from the fall. Schafer spots him as he finishes his warm-up and says, "If you don't run well today, at least you got an excuse." Robbie will have

A bloodied Jason Robbie leads Sean Smith.

none of it. "Dude," he says firmly, "that ain't an option. If I don't run well it's 'cause my legs are falling off and I'm going back to the hospital." He glares up at Schafer, as he finishes tying his spikes. "You got that?"

Being Boulder, even this rinky-dink race is not without star quality. The mercenary du jour is none other than U.S. international marathoner Keith Dowling. A former resident of Albuquerque, New Mexico, he has been living in Boulder for several years now. He has just started training again and he is using this race to check his fitness.

Dowling's presence does nothing to help Slattery's nerves in his collegiate debut. Slattery is competing unattached and running in his New Jersey singlet from high school nationals, but he is nervous. "This sucks," he says. "I don't want to run." Wetmore is unfazed that Slattery is so nervous. "He's a good one," he says, "he's got courage. Not many of them have that."

That has been the knock on Valenti—that when push comes to shove, he turns into the Tin Man in search of a heart. If you knew nothing of the guys and were to watch one practice, he is the man you would pick for your squad—not Goucher, not Batliner, not Roybal. He will get his first chance today to show his practices are not a fluke. He, too, is not wearing a CU uniform. He is running in a T-shirt and shorts. And due to the hardness of the course, he runs in flats. He will earn his jersey today.

It is brutally hot. The heat contributes to a conservative early pace. A mile and a half in, Dowling, Berkshire, and Valenti have gapped the field. Berkshire is dropped in short order, and Robbie moves on him. His

elbow and hand are bandaged from the fall. Fearing a loss of mobility, he has not bandaged his knee. The motion has reopened the wound. Blood streams down his shin.

Chasing them are Darren De Reuck—husband of South African marathoner Colleen De Reuck—and an unknown in a sleeveless T-shirt and red USA shorts. A pack of guys including Slattery, his roommate Matt Ruhl, and El-muccio chase after De Reuck.

But all eyes are on the race up front. Valenti and Dowling run

Valenti, Berkshire, and Dowling out front.

side by side until they hit the downhill a half mile from the finish. Surprisingly, it is not Dowling who makes the move, but Valenti. "I figured I had nothing to worry about after that," he said afterwards, "so I just went." And no one catches him. He puts eleven seconds on Dowling in the last half mile. Wetmore grins as he eyes Valenti's finish and says, "Vengeance is a very useful tool." For his part, Valenti appears unmoved by his victory. Reticent and reserved, he offers nothing else. And nothing needs to be said. He ran 1:15 faster than a year ago. He did his talking with his feet.

Berkshire finishes third, 90 seconds faster than a year ago. "Those guys ran tough," he says. "I thought I might be able to go that last mile and get them, but I was rigging." He is pleased, and so is Wetmore. In most programs, it is the star who sets the example. At CU, the walk-ons have established a legacy of their own. Wetmore says of Berkshire, "He's 90 seconds ahead of a year ago. Great. Perfect. You can't underestimate 1000 miles in ten weeks. It's unfashionable now and it's unpopular, but he said I'm gonna risk everything, and he made it."

Despite his wounds, Robbie also makes the team. He finishes sixth, behind De Reuck in fourth and a freshman from Goucher's alma mater, Doherty High, in fifth (Cameron Harrison). While troublesome, Robbie's knee did not bother him nearly as much as his bruised ribs. He cramped up in the race, and he valiantly struggled to finish.

Schafer finishes seventh. Adam Loomis, a transfer from Portland, is eighth, and the Jersey duo of Elmuccio and Slattery finish ninth and tenth. Wetmore is not concerned with the Jersey boys' mediocre showing, since they have only recently been up at elevation. "For sea level guys, on the hills, in the heat, fine." The guy with the USA shorts who was up with the leaders early finishes eleventh. His name is Sean Smith, and he re-

Valenti drops
Dowling.

ceived the shorts for participating in the World junior triathlon championships last November. Last spring, he "decided to try the running scene a bit," and he trained 40 to 45 miles a week this summer to prepare for the race. Smith has earned a spot on the squad.

A non-CU student finishes twelfth before freshmen Zach Crandall from Fort Collins and Matt Ruhl from Jersey finish thirteenth and fourteenth. Both of them will also learn later today that they have earned spots on the squad. The last man to claim his spot today is someone who was already on the squad, transfer O'Mara. Despite his poor showing, he remains upbeat: "It was pretty tough, but I didn't back off on any miles this week so that made it tougher. It's my first season at altitude and racing, it just takes some time. If I run 29 or 24 minutes this season, it doesn't matter to me."

VARSITY/OPEN/ALUMNI
TIME TRIAL RESULTS

PLACE	NAME	TIME	PACE
1.	Christopher Valenti	26:55	5:21
2.	Keith Dowling	27:06	5:24
3.	Wes Berkshire	27:15	5:25
4.	Darren De Reuck	27:24	5:27
5.	Cameron Harrison	27:36	5:29
6.	Jason Robbie	27:42	5:31
7.	Chris Schafer	27:52	5:32
8.	Adam Loomis	27:55	5:33
9.	Steve Slattery	27:59	5:34
10.	Matt Elmuccio	28:08	5:36
11.	Sean Smith	28:14	5:37
12.	Geoff Streit	28:26	5:39
13.	Zach Crandall	28:28	5:40
14.	Matt Ruhl	28:31	5:40
15.	John O'Mara	28:52	5:45

Casualties

The density of the training is affecting the men. Although any weakness you have is exacerbated and exposed by Old Man Mags, today's casualties are unusually high—starting right at the top.

Even though he wore his trainers for the AT on Friday, Goucher's effort beat up his calves. For the first—and only—time all season, he will not be in front at the end of a Sunday run. Eric Mack, his old high school teammate and currently a post-graduate pupil of Wetmore's, impressively storms away from all assembled. Goucher and Severy, the aerobic monster, finish a minute behind "the Macker." As if Mags were not difficult enough, Severy's discomfort is magnified by a strange sensation in his chest. It forces him to stop along the side of the road four miles from the finish, where he vainly tries to empty his gut. The pain persists even after the run ends. Milling around and appearing more uncomfortable than his usual self, he explains, "It feels like there's a bubble in my chest pushing everything up." His only relief is that he is done, and even in less than ideal conditions, he and Goucher have run 1:46 for the full Mags—17.4 miles at over 8000 feet—a great time for the arduous course.

A minute later, Friedberg and Ponce cross the five-mile marker that signifies the run's end. Both athletes have run huge PR's for Mags. Friedberg has slashed two minutes off of his previous best, while Ponce runs an astonishing ten minutes faster than he ever has. The 100-mile weeks have strengthened him.

A minute and a half behind that duo, Big Papa Napier chugs across the line. After running with Ponce and Friedberg for the first 15 miles, they surged, pulling ahead in the last two miles. However, while this "racing" is discouraged on other campuses, it is accepted and understood as a matter of course on Sundays at CU. Jason Robbie explains: "There's only one thing you're out there to do on Sunday, and that's to better yourself by running as fast as you can. That's it. Dude, you don't wait for anyone."

Wetmore's enthusiasm for their runs is tempered by the knowledge of those who did not finish. Batliner, Roybal, and Tessman were all forced to quit mid-run. Roybal's hamstring, the same one that caused him unending grief a year ago, is acting up again. Six miles in, he calls it a day. Sore since Wednesday, Batliner ends his run after feeling no progress in his aching calf. Four miles from the finish, Tessman joins the pair at the makeshift water station that JD has set up for the runners. An aching knee forces him to throw in the towel.

While discouraged, none of the three are down because of their effort. Roybal knows he must listen to his body, and push only when he is ready. For him, this is part of the process. Batliner, meanwhile, has been injured so often that he would rather be cautious and miss a day than have another lengthy absence ruin a season. And for Tessman, this is a whole new world of fatigue; a former half-miler, he understands that there are going to be days like this. He has almost two full days to recuperate before practice resumes Tuesday with the first long specificity workout of the season: repeat miles (referred to as "milers") at the Buffalo Ranch.

Sophomore Blondeau is more down than the others. He was sick with flu-like symptoms for Friday's AT and today he pukes after running the fourteen miles in 92 minutes. Last year at this time, he ran this course a full five minutes faster. To compound matters, his shins are sore from the AT and the downhills on Mags. His only positive thought is that, hopefully, his immune system will be strengthened after these trials, so "at least [he] won't get something the day before Nationals."

Tessman and Roybal's injuries will disappear as quickly as they appeared. But for Batliner and Blondeau, today's troubles are but a prelude.

GOUCHER AND MACK

Goucher and Mack finish today as they did when Goucher first started running cross country as a sophomore at Doherty High School in Colorado Springs, with Mack setting the pace. Two years older than Goucher, Mack entered his senior year in high school as the favorite to win the state championship. Having only started running as a junior, Mack had rapidly progressed to that point. Goucher, meanwhile, almost never ran high school cross country despite winning the City Championship 1600 meters in 4:42 as a ninth grader.

Goucher had his eye on football. Meanwhile, Judy Fellhauer (known as Flower), the Doherty High School cross country coach and an Olympic Trials competitor in the marathon in 1988, had hopes of coaching Goucher since she watched him win the 8th grade City Championship in the 1600 meters in 5:03. She spoke to Goucher for the first time after he won the mile title again as a freshman, telling him she would love to coach him. More important, she spoke to Goucher's mother. Adam's mother explained to Flower that no one in her family had gone to college, and that her only goal for Adam was that he do well enough in a sport to gain a scholarship to college. Goucher only weighed 125 pounds then, and Flower explained that in order for him to get a football scholarship, he would probably have to gain 50 to 60 pounds and perform really, really well. If Goucher ran, well, she would not promise anything, but she speculated that he may get a scholarship out of it in the end.

Flower watched in disappointment at the beginning of Goucher's sophomore year when she saw him in line to sign up for football. But while in line, Goucher realized he was going to be late for work, so he left for his job in a feed store, figuring he would sign up for football the following day.

That evening, Goucher's mother and sisters persuaded him that Doherty's football team was not that good, and that he was too small to really excel at football, anyway. They encouraged him to try something new and run cross country. Flower stayed out of it, not wanting to influence Goucher's decision. Goucher called Flower later that evening. "Flower," he said, "this is Adam Goucher. I don't know if you remember me, but is it too late to sign up for cross country?" "Of course, I remembered him," Flower says. "He had no idea everyone [on the cross country team] was talking about him."

Goucher showed up for practice the next day in a pair of Reebok Pump cross-trainers, ready to run. Flower sent him on a five-mile run, and when he came back, she says, "He was muddy, moaning and groaning." Goucher recalls thinking, "Holy shit! This is crazy!" Nevertheless, he asked two fellow sophomores on the team who Doherty's best runner was. They pointed to Mack. "Alright," he told them, "I'll beat him by the end of the year." His friends laughed.

A week and a half later, Goucher ran his first ever cross country race. He asked Flower beforehand who the best guys in the race were, and she pointed out three or four of the top guys before warning him to pace himself out there. Mack won the race, and Goucher finished fifth, in 16:50.

"Oh my God," Flower thought to herself, "what have I got here?" As the season progressed, Goucher improved dramatically, inching closer and closer to Mack in every race. At the regional qualifier for the state meet, Goucher finished only five seconds behind Mack. Seeing Goucher's progress, Flower gave both Mack and Goucher the same counsel before the state meet. "You're the guy," she told each of them. "You can work together or you can run your own race. Go for it, and don't hold back."

Until the eve of the state meet, Flower says, "Mack appreciated Goucher's talent, but he never gave him too much thought. He was worried about the other seniors in the state." Now Goucher was a threat.

At the state meet, Goucher caught Mack a mile and half into the race. They ran neck and neck until Goucher broke him with a half mile left and went on to win the state championship in 15:27. It was the first cross country race he had ever won.

Flower had planned on going to the Kinney (now Foot Locker) regional cross country championships with only the seniors. The top eight finishers from the regional meet advance to the national championship race. But now that Goucher had won, she extended the invitation to him as well. Goucher and his family raised funds for him to make the trip, and he finished fourth in the regionals in Kenosha, Wisconsin, to qualify for the national meet. Only one other sophomore in America, Brian Young from Oklahoma, qualified for Kinney Nationals. Mack would finish a disappointing tenth in Kenosha, missing Nationals by an agonizing two spots.

Flower recalls that Goucher "didn't realize what an accomplishment it was to make it." Rather than rest on his laurels when Goucher returned to Colorado Springs, he trained with the intention of winning the national championship. Two weeks prior to the Nationals though, Flower's mother had a stroke. She would be unable to accompany Goucher to the national championship.

By himself in San Diego for the Kinney championship, Goucher says, "I was blown away. I was treated like a king." Racing in the seventh cross country race of his life, he finished an admirable thirteenth. But Goucher was less than elated when he called Flower to tell her his result. "When he called," Flower says, "he was like, 'I'm the biggest loser in the world. I got thirteenth.' He was completely mad at himself. But we talked him into it. We explained that it was really a pretty good deal."

That race, says Goucher, "was the turning point. It told me I have the potential to be good." Forced to miss the basketball season because he had "skipped" the tryouts to run Kinney Nationals, Goucher focused his energy on running. That spring, Goucher finished third in the 800 at the state meet in 1:57, in his second 800 ever, and he also finished third in the 1600 meters. Mack, meanwhile, capped his high school career with a state title in the 3200-meter run.

Each year, Flower had her athletes write down their goals, both for the season and long term. In the summer following Goucher's sophomore campaign, Flower says, "We had long talks about his goals. He was now the man to beat. It was such a difference from his sophomore year." During these meetings, Flower helped Goucher set his short-term and long-term goals. Goucher wrote down his goals prior to his junior year. They were as follows: "Achieve leadership skills, be a good role model, State Champion for a second year, State Champions as a team, work hard and do the best I can, go to Regionals and make it to Nationals, be top three, or better yet, first in the nation, and 1996, Atlanta."

Goucher dominated his junior year. He won every race throughout the cross country season, set course records, and repeated as state champion. At the state championships, he set a state record for 5k, running 15:03. His team had won the championship his sophomore year, and this time they finished sixth, but otherwise, he had thus far met his each of his short-term objectives.

But at the Kinney regionals, disaster struck. He finished ninth, seemingly missing the Nationals by one spot. Seeing that, Flower says, "I just died. When I saw him, I just said, 'I'm sorry.'" But Goucher had a surprise for her. "I made it," he said. One of the runners ahead of him was Canadian, so he qualified again for Kinney Nationals.

He was lucky to qualify. But Goucher was not about to waste the second chance he had been given. Flower says, "We went there to win." But again, things did not go as planned at Nationals, and Goucher finished a disappointing fifteenth. Flower says, "He felt so good, and quickly ended up in front of the pack. Eventually, the whole pack passed him. He forgot all of our strategies because he was feeling good. I think he learned a lot from that race. He learned more from that than any race he has ever won. He learned about using your head as much as your body."

Goucher skipped indoor track, because Flower feared burning him out. "I think we could have cleaned up," she says, "but I wanted him to stay really hungry for it. I thought, 'If he's going to be in it for the Olympics, I can't burn him out now.'" Goucher's precocity mandated that Flower consider such grand ambitions. She says, "We talked about the Olympics right away. Talentwise, I thought he had it, and I think one of his biggest assets is his pain tolerance and focus. Then there is his competitiveness. He will pay the price. He will train." Her intuition about his physical skills was proven when he was subjected to a battery of tests at the Olympic Training Center in Colorado Springs following his senior year. Flower says, "He excelled in every level. His muscle strength was exceptional. His VO$_2$ Max was exceptional, and his muscle biopsy was exceptional."

In the spring of his junior year, Goucher continued to improve, winning the 1600- and 3200-meter runs at the state championships in 4:18 and 9:35. By this time, none of Goucher's teammates could keep up with him, forcing him to train alone. This did not deter him. "Most of the time," says Flower, "he was alone. But he never complained about it. Never."

Entering his senior year, it was time for Goucher to make new goals.

They were as follows:

1. Win State championship for third time, and break his state record of 15:03.
2. Win Footlocker Midwest Regional Championship, Kenosha, Wisconsin.
3. Win Footlocker National Championship, San Diego, California.

4. Be first Colorado runner to break 15:00 for 5k—Goal: 14:53.
5. Long Term–Collegiate National Champion, Make Olympic Team in 1996, 2000 and beyond.

Goucher wrote his goals on poster board and blue construction paper. He decorated the poster with black spray paint, "to make it mysterious," and printed the goals in large black letters. He hung the poster high on the wall of his bedroom, he says, "so when I woke up, I could see it. When I went to bed, I could see it. I was constantly thinking about what I wanted to do."

Flower also wanted to "hold him publicly accountable" for his goals, so during his senior year, the team brought a banner to meets that read 14:53. Flower devised a training plan "with everything focused on Foot Locker [formerly Kinney Nationals]," and more than ever, Goucher dedicated himself to accomplishing his goals. In midseason, he accomplished his fourth goal, running a spectacular 14:41 for 5k on the state meet course. And at the state meet, he again covered the course in under fifteen minutes despite the fact that it was covered with three inches of snow.

Unfortunately, Goucher was unable to savor his state meet victory for long. Only three hours after the race, Goucher was on a plane to Florida to visit his ailing grandmother. She passed away while he was there. She was originally from Worcester, Massachusetts, so Goucher and his family then went to Massachusetts for the funeral. There was a blizzard in Massachusetts, yet every day, Goucher ran in preparation for the regional meet. "I have to turn this negative energy into positive energy," he told himself. "I have to focus on what I want to do, for the family."

Goucher won the Midwest Regional in 15:13, tying the course record held by former U.S. 10,000-meter champion Todd Williams. It was on to the Foot Locker (Kinney) National Championships for the third, and final time.

This time, his family accompanied Goucher to San Diego. Throughout the season, Flower had studied the competition by reading results in *X-C Express*. "I felt it motivated him to see how he compared to the rest of the guys throughout the year," she says. "We knew that when we got to Foot Locker, we knew everything about everyone."

Once there, they were surprised that Goucher was overlooked as one of the favorites. Instead, all of the pre-race talk was centered around local favorite Mebrahton Keflizighi of San Diego, Matt Davis of Oregon, and Bob Keino of New Jersey. "Adam," says Flower, "was a little miffed at the lack of respect." "This is great," she told him, "because they [the favorites] were not left alone. They couldn't even get lunch. I said, 'Okay, wait till tomorrow.'"

On race day, Flower says, "Adam could hardly wait. He had no fear, just a sheer joy about being there and competing. He had fire in him." There was one major hill on the course, and this is where he envisioned breaking away. Keflizighi had broken from the pack with a mile and a half to go, and Goucher plowed up the hill, catching Keflizighi.

On the descent, Goucher rolled away from the field to win the Foot Locker national cross country title in 14:41. His widowed grandfather was there to enjoy Goucher's win along with the rest of Goucher's family. "It was," Goucher recalls, "a great moment for the family." His grandfather passed away a week and a half later.

For Flower, Goucher's accomplishment was all the more impressive because of everything he had had to overcome. She says:

> I love Adam like a son, and he has not had it easy. His dad left when he was in the fifth grade, and his mom struggled to raise him and his two sisters. It was a financial struggle; she was trying to make it a good life for them, and he was the man of the house forever. He worked throughout high school, sometimes closing restaurants at midnight, to pay for his own expenses and fees ... He struggled with his dad leaving, and his mom made up for it ... [but] he had it a little hard ...

Goucher's tough upbringing did not deter him in the least. In fact, Flower says that Goucher was the most coachable athlete she has ever had. "He listened. He was loyal to me as a coach, and he listened to what I said, no questions asked. He never doubted what we were doing. He believed in it. And he always expressed his gratitude."

Goucher did not have to have blind faith in his coach. She was a proven competitor herself, and she studied the sport, because she "wanted to know why you did what." She took exercise physiology and sports psychology classes at CU Colorado Springs, she earned her USA Track and Field Level One coaching certification, and she sought out advice from anyone who could help, including Ed Burke, the US Olympic cycling physician, who explained to her athletes the physiology of heart rate training. She also studied because she "felt a real responsibility to be careful with what I did with Adam, with someone with such big goals."

Goucher appreciated the enormous effort she put into her coaching. She laughs when she recalls an incident that occurred during the recruiting process: "A prominent coach said to Goucher, 'Hey, I hear you have a girl coach.' Adam told him, 'Yeah. And if you got a problem with that, you can go to hell!'"

After Foot Locker, Goucher says, "I was just fried. For so long I had visualized it, and when it happened, I was ready to be done." He still ran the U.S. Junior Cross Country championships in Memphis, Tennessee, and the race was a disaster. Wearing a soft orthodic in his racing shoe for the first time, he developed tremendous blisters, and finished a disappointing eleventh, missing the U.S. team by four spots.

His health worsened on a trip to Chiba, Japan, for an international 8k race. He finished a respectable fifteenth in a field of 600 runners, but on his cooldown, he severely sprained his ankle, and the injury effectively ended his high school career. All that was left for him to do was decide where to attend college.

ON TO THE UNIVERSITY OF COLORADO

Flower was "bombarded by college coaches. I got at least a call a night." Goucher listened to Flower's counsel, "but the whole decision was Adam's. I was there to help him." Both were impressed with then Wisconsin coach Martin Smith, but Goucher clicked with Wetmore immediately. "Adam convinced me," Flower says, "more than Mark convinced me, that Mark was a good guy." In spite of being taken aback by Wetmore's ponytail and relaxed appearance, "Mark," Goucher says, "would fire me up." In the end, Goucher decided on Colorado. "I could sense Mark had what it takes to make me the best I can be."

Flower will be in Kansas to cheer on Goucher in his last collegiate race. She will be looking for the fire she saw when Goucher won the high school national cross country title as a senior, and she will be praying for another victory.

It's My Last One, Bitch!

In years past milers have commenced at the end of September. This year Wetmore is starting them earlier—over the hilliest part of their course—so that they will be ready for the sweeping hills in Lawrence at the end of the year. The men will do these today at "elevation date pace"—what they could do right now for a race at altitude. They run milers three more times this season, and each time, their cumulative times should be faster than the last. They will run their last session of repeat miles on the track. That last one is always on the schedule, so they will get to see where they stand next to teams of years gone by before the Big Dance.

Wetmore gathers his men together before they start the workout. It is brutally hot. They listen attentively as he addresses them all:

> *Today is either three or four or five miles. They're slow. I'm giving you a deliberately slow set this year. This time of year is high-level aerobic long specificity. I want you doing about what you're supposed to be doing up here, this time of year. I wanted to give you four sets [of milers workouts] this year instead of three like last year. When in doubt slow down. Men, the PFB's [peach fuzz babies] are doing four, the rest of you are doing five, but controlled.*

The runners are doing the mile repeats on an eight-minute cycle, so Wetmore splits them into groups so they all get the right amount of rest. (For example, if Goucher runs a mile in five minutes, he will have three minutes rest before the next mile repeat.) Tammy, their trainer, has set up a van at the finish line of their mile repeats so they can hydrate after every interval. He instructs them to stay cool. He says, "Tammy's got Gatorade, water, and Miller High Life in three separate coolers. I want you taking water after each one. Actually, it's better on you than in you."

Goucher is assigned five miles at 4:50, while Friedberg, Napier, Ponce, Reese, Severy, Tessman, and Valenti are assigned five at 5:10. Another group is doing five at 5:20, while the freshmen (peach fuzz babies) are doing four miles at 5:30. Batliner, Roybal, and Blondeau still are not up to going, so they run four to eight miles on the course at 6:30 pace. Bat's calf is a bit better, but still sore. "It's a little looser," Bat says, "but it's still there, whatever my fucking problem is." Bat and Wetmore are getting nervous.

As they line up to begin the workout, one change is readily apparent. Slattery wears running shorts for the first time. "I was sick of all the shit," he says. Wetmore is one of the first to notice. As they are stretching he tells him, "You're a minute faster already. Just because of those shorts."

From Wetmore and JD's vantage point at the start of the interval they can see the men head out and up the big hill. They disappear then for the majority of the interval before Wetmore and JD catch them for the last 100 meters.

As Goucher comes down the stretch at the end of the first mile, Wetmore checks his watch and is satisfied that he is running under control. "Good, good," he says. "He listened." "[4]:52" Wetmore says. Goucher checks his watch and yells over his shoulder "51!" Severy and Friedberg lead the charge across the line for the rest of the men in 5:12. It is the slowest mile they will run. Friedberg is on Sev's heels the whole workout and they average 5:07 a mile. In Batliner's absence, they are establishing themselves as the early two and three runners.

Wetmore moves around onto the hill before the start of the second mile. It is here that he will offer some of his best pointers. As the freshmen start the climb he instructs them to "release, relax, and flow down that hill, don't fight it. A lot of energy is wasted fighting it. I don't expect you to master it, today you practice it." To the group he says, "Okay, easy up the hill but then you gotta gain it back down the other side."

The strategy of going slowly up the hill and then charging is advice that is counter to what most coaches teach. It is a survival tactic at this elevation since it is next to impossible to recover once in oxygen debt. In order to race well here, the best bet is to conserve energy going up the hills by slowing down the pace, or at most maintaining it. In races, while their opponents are recovering from charging up the hill, the CU guys start to roll. The strategy is particularly effective late in races when a rapid rise in effort sends guys into oxygen debt more quickly. Since the CU runners have maintained an even effort throughout, in the last mile or even the last kilometer they are still feeling good. It is then that they kill you.

Goucher struggles on the next two miles, running 4:53 and 4:55. He is working harder than he has yet this season, and his exertion is apparent in his final preparation before each interval. With five seconds to go he high steps to the line while taking several audible deep breaths where he forces the air out, "WHOO, WHOO, WHOO!"

Robbie struggles just to run. His right knee is swollen, tight, and full of fluid. He is still able to run 5:21's today while getting all the lift in his right leg from his hip flexor. Like the others, he suffers under the intense sun. They all dump water over their heads for some relief from the heat before taking off onto the fourth interval. As they climb the hill, someone is right on Goucher's shoulder. "Who's running with Gouch?" Wetmore asks incredulously. Closer attention to the long powerful stride reveals the answer: Slattery.

Goucher is none too happy to have the frosh sitting on his shoulder. He turns to Slattery and says, "Run your own workout!" Slattery responds as any self-respecting Jersey boy would: "I am. It's my last one, BITCH!"

Goucher does not respond. "Okay," he thinks to himself, "if you're gonna run with me, you're gonna pay." What happens next is no surprise. "He took off," says Slattery, "and I died." Goucher runs 4:54 and he is followed by Severy and Friedberg in 5:07. An exhausted Slattery crosses the line in 5:14. He stumbles off to the side and vomits. "I shouldn't have eaten those freaking corn chips at lunch," he says.

Goucher still has one more mile. He nails it, running 4:50. Sev and Friedberg finish a great workout with a 4:58, leading a charge of guys under 5:10. When Goucher finishes, he pulls Slattery aside for a little talk. "It's a process," he tells him. "My body took two and a half, three years to adapt to Wetmore's workouts. Don't feel bad about getting your butt kicked; it's part of being a freshman in college." He later tells Wetmore of his little talk with Slattery. All Wetmore can do is shake his head. "Yeah, he's a strange bird, isn't he? He's hard to communicate with, but that's OK, the best ones are."

Goucher is also salty about the workout itself: "It sucked so hard. I know I ran too hard. I wasn't feeling good. I don't know if it was the heat or whatever. He said to be controlled. It wasn't controlled."

Wetmore has several possible explanations for Goucher's inability to hit his splits. He tells the guys, "I'm pretty sure the miles are 20 to 30 meters longer than last year. But, that's OK, what matters is what happens the next time, the next time, and the time after that. The last time, nothing can go wrong, right?" That is right, because the last one is on the track. Wetmore's other explanation for Goucher's difficulty is just as valid: "Twenty-two [miles at the Aqueduct] two Sundays ago."

Flagstaff Again

Most of the men are doing another thirteen up Flagstaff today. O'Mara and Batliner are among the missing. After another disappointing workout yesterday, O'Mara has gone AWOL. (He is spotted later running alone on the Creek Path.) Wetmore addresses the team while they stretch. He instructs them of some eligibility matters that must be resolved, and then he exits the gym to catch a plane to Dallas for some Big 12 meetings. He would rather be with the team, as most coaches would, but this is part of the bureaucratic tedium he must reckon with daily.

The lanes are being painted on the new indoor track today. The mondo surface looks fantastic. It is being completed just in time, for the Torres brothers are coming into town next weekend for their recruiting trip. Anticipating this, JD asks the runners returning from Flagstaff if they could have a social function that weekend to allow the twins a chance to meet some of the runners. It is important they have a good time and really like the team, because Wetmore and CU will not be able to offer the twins full scholarships for their first year while practically every other school in the country will be offering them the moon.

Batliner does not join his teammates up Flagstaff. Instead, he goes for an easy ten miles down Fourth Street to Wonderland Lake and back. He skipped all his classes today to tend to his sore calf, spending the entire day alternately massaging it, icing it, and stretching it. The therapy has paid off because his calf feels better today than at any time since he first injured it. He runs without a hitch.

He could have run up Flagstaff with the others, but he elected not to. Batliner's restraint is admirable. In a sport that demands compulsion, sometimes the hardest task is having the confidence to rest. As he runs easily along Fourth Street, he tries to deduce why his calf is injured. He is running more volume than a year ago (85 a week), and, like Goucher, he has upped the intensity. Whereas last year he ran twelve miles easy on his recovery days, this year these runs have been at 6:30 a mile at the slowest. "Even my easy days are intense," he says.

He is not second-guessing himself for upping his intensity, because it is, as Wetmore would say, the next logical step. But he is questioning not doing calf exercises that he started doing last winter after an up-and-down weekend in Boston. That weekend he ran a huge PR in the 3k—7:58—to automatically qualify for the NCAA's. The next morning he hit the bank of the Charles River for a twenty-mile run. His calf cramped on him, and as a result he did not run again until indoor NCAA's. Once up and running, he performed calf raises diligently before every run to get good blood flow going. The routine served him well. He trained uninterrupted through the start of the outdoor season—until a stress fracture in his fibula threatened to sideline him yet again. Despite another bout of intermittent training, he finished a stellar third in the steeplechase at outdoor NCAA's.

A new year upon him, he began to "feel invincible," and ceased doing his exercises. He is starting them again now, and on Friday morning he will attempt his first workout in over a week. He knows no one counted on the rise of Ponce and Friedberg (Bat says, "They're definitely All-American material now"), but even with their emergence, if Batliner goes down, CU's title hopes might go down with him.

More Trouble

The guys are OYO (On Your Own) today for some easy jogging and strides. Ponce stops by the gym to stretch before heading out. He has a slight lump under his eye. Trouble often seems to find Ponce, and as he went back to his place last night after practice, it found him again.

He went to the Varsity weight room in Dal Ward to lift after practice yesterday. By the time he rode his bike back to his abode it was already after eight o'clock, and he had yet to eat dinner. When he got there, he found someone had parked in a "No Parking" spot right in front of his door, making it impossible for him to get inside.

He waited a minute to see if someone was going to come move the car, and when no one did, he slammed his bike against the car in frustration. A guy was walking by as he did this—the owner of the car. An argument ensued and, underestimating Ponce because of his small stature, the man started swinging at him. Ponce is small, but he is wiry and remarkably quick. Ponce did his best De La Hoya impression on him, and before the guy could react, he was down. He did not wait around to see if Ponce could dish out any more. He scrambled for his keys, climbed into his car, and left.

Ponce is distraught about the rumble. His freshman year he was involved in a similar incident that went one step farther. A party he was attending got busted by the cops for underage drinking. There were close to a hundred people at the party. Only one person got put in cuffs and taken away: Ponce. "Why," he thinks, "am I the one always getting into these altercations? Is it because I am Mexican?"

He had a conversation with Wetmore then, and Wetmore offered him some advice that he thinks about now. "Look, Oscar," he said then, "four years from now, it won't matter. It's not about white, black, or brown. What everyone gives a damn about is green, and you'll be telling the punk who told you to go back to the hood, 'Here are the keys to my Lexus, don't scratch it.'"

Strength Kills

The seniors who are not racing tomorrow at the CSU meet are on the course ready to get started. Goucher, Reese, Robbie, Napier, Severy, and Johnson are here for some neuromuscular work: 6x600 meter repeats up and over the Ranch's primary climb. It is the first hill workout Goucher has seen Wetmore assign him during his tenure. "Yeah, you know why we're doing that?" Wetmore says. "Because Kansas has some big swooping hills and I want to get ready for that."

Wetmore is in a surly mood as the runners are finishing their preparations. JD does not put much stock into it. "He gets moody in September." Apparently Wetmore is also susceptible to seasonal affective disorder. JD says, "You've got to learn not to take it personally. He's just moody. It's just the way he gets. He's still listening to you." JD thinks for another moment before adding, "He had to go to the coaches' meeting, and he hates to be pulled away from here."

There is another reason for Wetmore's grim disposition: Batliner. After a comfortable run on Wednesday, Batliner has regressed. His calf tightened again on him yesterday, and today it feels worse than Sunday. He saw a masseuse yesterday afternoon who offered a possible diagnosis for his ailment: compartment syndrome. Compartment syndrome is a condition where the muscle in the shin grows too large for the muscle sheath. The sheath then pinches the muscle, causing enormous pain because the muscle has no room to expand and contract. Corrective surgery would require four slits in the muscle sheath to release the muscle. Wetmore has seen people running again—not 100 miles a week—but running nonetheless, in three weeks. But that is a best-case scenario.

Wetmore offers the guys some final instructions: "This is a 600-meter neuromuscular workout. Go up the hill slightly faster than race pace, AT pace up top, then release down the hill. Jog as easy as you want back to the start. I want to simulate Kansas. The watch is useless; there's no sense using a watch. I'll be somewhere on the hill using ridicule and sarcasm."

The guys are relieved to see the workout. They feared another session of milers this morning. Wetmore laughs at the thought of more hard aerobic work right now. "You've certainly had enough of that," he tells them.

It comes as no surprise that Severy leads the charge up the hill next to Goucher with Reese, Robbie, and Napier right behind them. Johnson falls back early. This is the only strength workout that the men are assigned. The women have mandatory lifting sessions to supplement their strength workouts, but the men do not. "The men are doing 85 to 95 miles a week," Wetmore explains. "Trying to do circuits would be borrowing from Peter to pay Paul. That'd be taking away energy from their running. Plus, they have a better strength to weight ratio than the women. I leave it up to them if they want to pursue it."

JD and Wetmore stand towards the top of the hill. On the fourth repeat, Goucher pulls away from the others. JD estimates that Goucher is going about 5:40 a mile including the 1000-meter jog back to the start. Both Wetmore and JD offer encouragement to the guys as they come past. Robbie grimaces as he climbs. He has a robotic-like motion that amazes with its consistency. Whether he is climbing, going downhill, or on the track, it *never* changes. Sensing he has little chance of making the Varsity this season, he has just elected to redshirt. Now there is one less man on the depth chart.

While Robbie would not be contending for All-American honors, his decision to redshirt leaves CU with one less man that they may need. Reese is hurting, and he is quickly off the back. "I think all the work is catching up with him," Wetmore says. With the exception of Goucher, everyone looks beat. Severy and Napier drive past Wetmore. "Relax the head and shoulders," Wetmore advises, "calm mind." As the runners wearily trudge past them, JD asks Wetmore, "Think that Sunday run [at the Reservoir] is catching up with them?" Wetmore does not hesitate. "Definitely."

Calm mind. With Reese, Bat, Blondeau, and Roybal hurting, Wetmore is questioning the workload. He glowers in silence, and it appears he is beating himself up for their ills. Calm mind.

Ponce Has His Day

For most of the squad, the season's first meet has arrived. The day begins inauspiciously. The team (traveling on an old school bus to Fort Collins) departs from Potts Field on schedule at 7:00 a.m. without Ronald Roybal. He is running late, but they do not wait even a minute for him. While Wetmore makes no mention of his absence, Friedberg cannot believe Roybal has missed the bus. Roybal is notoriously absent-minded, and the thought occurs to Friedberg that he should have given Roybal a wake-up call. Then he thinks better of it. "He's 21. Don't make me responsible for waking him up." Batliner bails out Roybal by giving him a ride to the race.

Ponce sits alone on the bus, nodding his head to the beat from his headphones. His team-issue Nike sweats are so large they threaten to swallow him whole, and he wears his pants with his right pant leg rolled up to his knee.

Ponce went to a University-sponsored Mexican-American dinner last night, and then he went over to Batliner's house to have some of the two trays of lasagna Batliner cooked for his teammates. All the food made him drowsy, but sleep eluded him. He has not raced since last October, almost a full year ago, and he lay awake thinking of today's race.

Wetmore is holding his top two guns out of today's contest. Goucher and Batliner will make their debuts at the Rocky Mountain Shootout on October 3rd. As planned, Reese is also a spectator today. Wetmore will only run Reese when Reese informs him that he is ready to go.

The CSU meet offers Wetmore's remaining harriers a chance to shine before Goucher begins his season and grabs the limelight. It also presents Wetmore a much needed chance to see how some of the Junior Varsity guys have progressed. He has two goals for today's race: to average 25:45 and to win the team competition. While Fort Collins is at the same elevation as Boulder, the race will be faster than the Shootout in Boulder because the meet is being held on a pancake-flat golf course. Past history tells Wetmore that his guys will run approximately a minute faster here than at the home course. Since Chris Valenti ran 26:55 at the time trial, he is expected to run 25:55 today. But Wetmore does not expect Valenti to be his first man. That distinction goes to Friedberg. Friedberg has looked great thus far, and Wetmore is looking for him to run about 25:25 for the 8k course.

As is his practice before every race, Wetmore writes down his predictions of how fast his men will run. He does not share these predictions with his guys, but he is rarely off by more than ten seconds. He does, however, post a document on the board with goal times for each of the harriers. If they go out faster than the pace the document calls for, Wetmore will let them hear it. None of the runners disagree with Wetmore's expectations for them today.

Wetmore likes this course. Two years ago, the district race was here. Overnight, on the eve of the race, 24 inches of snow fell. From his hotel window, Wetmore would get up every hour all through the night. JD, who shared a room with him, recalls, "Every hour, he'd get up and I'd hear him say, 'Shit! Still snowing!'" Says Wetmore, "I just had to tell myself, 'This will help us. This will help us.'" It did. CU swept the top five spots, and Batliner emerged late in the race to defeat the field. Wetmore grins unabashedly while recounting the memory: "Batliner comes out of nowhere and wins it. A complete unknown! It was beautiful."

When CU arrives at the course, many of the teams are already milling around. Wetmore waits for everyone to disembark the bus before gathering the men together for some brief instructions:

> I want you all to run a controlled first mile. Wes, that means 5:10 to 5:12. If you run 5:15's, that's 26:15. That's pretty good here. When in doubt go out slower. If you go out in 5:20, you go four seconds faster the last four miles; it's no tragedy. JD and Lorie will wheel out the first 400 meters and 800 meters, so if you go out too fast, we'll fix it early. I'll be at the mile mark. After that, you're on your own.

Wetmore makes no mention of the other teams or the other runners. None. He wants his harriers focused solely on executing their plan and running the times they should hit. Still, there are three formidable competing athletes headlining the field. Jeff Simonich, a senior from the University of Utah, earned All-American honors last spring in the 5000 meters. Brian Berryhill, a former high school quarterback representing the host school, Colorado State, finished second in the mile last year at indoor NCAA's. Finally, there is Jason Hubbard, the defending Division II 5000-meter champion from NCAA Division II powerhouse Adams State.

At 9:25 a.m., five minutes to race time, the men amble slowly to the starting line. It is nice and cool, and the sky is replete with large cumulus clouds. As the Buffaloes do their strides, the men from Adams State gather in a huddle and loudly cheer, "ASC! ASC!" This is in stark contrast to the CU runners, who laugh and joke between their strides. Chris Schafer alone seems anxious. A half-miler/miler by trade, Schafer readies himself to suffer anonymously in the pack. He occupies himself by taping his wrists, a ritual he began in high school to keep his wrists rigid when he races. Wetmore reminds his troops one last time, "Be smart, be patient." He makes eye contact with Roybal. "You be careful, Ronald, alright?" Roybal nods his consent.

A mile in, the runners are right on pace, except for Friedberg. He passes the mile in 5:00, five seconds fast. Meanwhile, Simonich has already jumped out to an early lead. The runners race around the course, and thirteen minutes in, Simonich has 50 meters on the pack. Adams State has two runners in second and third, and Friedberg is in fourth. Ponce has quietly gained on Friedberg and he slips behind him into fifth place.

Four minutes later, Ponce passes Friedberg and moves into third place. Friedberg falls to fifth, and right behind him, Tessman, Blondeau, Valenti, and Berkshire run beautifully together in a pack from seventh to twelfth place along with a couple of other runners from Western State. JD waits anxiously as they pass the four-mile mark. "Alright," he says, "this is where it happens."

The last mile. This alone is CU's province. Historically they have always gone out controlled, taking over a race in the last mile. Rarely will one see CU's men running backwards in the last mile. Today is no exception.

Simonich dominates through to the end, winning easily in 24:48. Ponce, however, is outkicked by three runners in the final stretch. He does not die, but he simply does not have the ability to switch gears so early in the season while he is running 100-plus miles a week. Despite being outkicked, his sixth place finish leads the team. Blondeau, Friedberg, and Tessman finish right in a row behind him. Valenti finishes eleventh to round out the scoring.

CU wins handily, outdistancing Adams State, 41-57. CU's top five averages 25:32. They have accomplished both of Wetmore's objectives. Still, Wetmore is unfazed. "On one hand," he says, "we're happy with how they did. On the other hand, Jay Johnson ran 25:29 here last year, and he was our tenth man. They'd better get better." A brief smile creases his lips as he walks by Ponce while he stretches. "Scar's our number-one man now!"

Ponce smiles. He is pleased with his effort: "I haven't raced since last October, so it felt good to get it out of the way. I felt good 'til that last half mile, then I just locked up. Three guys passed me in that last 50, but I'll get them at the [Colorado] Shootout [at the Buffalo Ranch]. It's all good. They never have that kick at the end of our course, because of the hills. And it's a 25-second PR, man. I'll take that."

Also turning in a notable performance is CU's sixth man, Wes Berkshire. The junior walk-on far exceeds Wetmore's goal of 26:25, running a solid 25:50. Two years ago, he ran 27:20 at this meet. He credits his improvement to Wetmore: "I'm happy with my time, although I'd like to have a race like that more towards the end of the year . . . Putting in the miles, that's all it is. That's Wetmore's system. Running as many miles as you can for as long as you can. Put in all the miles you can possibly handle." The guys pass around the official results on the bus ride home, and Berkshire beams when he sees he has beaten CSU's Sven Severin. "That guy used to kill me. He used to run laps around me and give me the business for sure. I love that [beating him]. That is the coolest thing ever." The interminable hundred-mile weeks now seem worthwhile.

The only CU harrier to miss his goal time is Friedberg. He is also the only one who did not follow the plan and went out too fast. He went out fast because he was "worried they wouldn't come back to me," and he paid the price. Though he would have liked a better result, he is not concerned. After tomorrow's run, he will have over 90 miles for the week.

Unquestionably, though, Ponce is the story of the day. And on his warmdown, with Wetmore's comment ringing in his ears, he silently pondered just how far he has run to become CU's number one man . . .

A LONG ROAD FROM JUAREZ, MEXICO

In 1996, the track team went on their annual spring break trip to Tucson, Arizona. While there, Ponce and some of his teammates went on a day trip across the border to Nogales, Mexico. Once in Mexico, the guys were instantly besieged by seemingly ubiquitous Mexican children selling gum. Other children washed the windshields of passing cars for spare change. The children were willing to do anything, it seemed, for the smallest bit of change.

Seeing these children had a visceral affect on Ponce. In an instant he was transported back to his childhood in Juarez, Mexico, when he, too, was washing windshields and walking the streets, famished, having not eaten for several days. He would search out tourists to whom he could sell something, anything, for money. Money to buy food for himself, and for his family. For survival, for one more day.

Some days were more successful than others. Some days Ponce would eat. On others, he would go hungry. If the opportunity presented itself, he would steal, not only to feed himself, but also to feed his sisters. What else, he reasons now, is a seven-year-old boy burdened with the responsibility of caring for his sisters supposed to do? Then, there was no reason to reason. He had to survive.

Every day Ponce would awaken on a little bed he shared with a sister and two cousins. He would stand on the dirt floor of their homemade wood and aluminum shack, and then he would leave. More often than not, it was not to school, but to the streets, where he would sell gum and such, fight, or steal.

He quickly learned to fend for himself. When he was six, his mother gave him a belt for his birthday. Brandishing his new belt, he went to play soccer with some friends. Seeing his new belt, they beat him up, took the belt, and ran away. A sobbing Ponce went home to tell his mother what happened. His mother did not offer him her condolences. Rather, she gave him a licking of her own before warning him that he had better go and come back home with that belt, or he would *really* get a beating. Ponce found the boy who had his belt, beat him with a stick, and returned home with his belt.

His uncle helped Ponce hone his fighting skills. He was a boxer, and he was five years older than Ponce senior. His uncle owned a pair of boxing gloves and would parade Ponce around the neighborhood, looking for someone to fight him. When he found a suitable opponent, he would give one glove to him, and Ponce would get the other. Towels were wrapped around the other hands to cushion the blows, and then the boys would go at it. Ponce recalls, "I wasn't necessarily the toughest, but I wouldn't give up. Bloody nose, crying, I would still stand and take more."

Growing up in such abject poverty, Ponce often dreamt of a better life. He could see across the Mexican/American border into El Paso, and he thought "that if we just went a little further, there would be trees with money, and we could just take money out of the trees."

The irony is that Ponce was an American citizen, so he was free to go. But his mother was not an American. She sneaked into America when she was pregnant, and gave birth to Oscar in East L.A. Soon thereafter, they were deported to Mexico.

Then one day, when he was almost fourteen, in late July 1991, Ponce had his chance to flee Mexico for a better life in the promised land. Leaving her two daughters with his grandparents in Juarez, Ponce's mother set off for the United States with him. They piled into the back of a "hot, smelly immigrant truck for what seemed like forever." After a long harrowing journey, they made it to Amarillo, Texas.

Their stay in Texas was brief, and full of hardship. They spent their first week in Amarillo with his grandmother's sister. She then abruptly kicked them out of the house. At the time, neither Ponce nor his mother spoke any English, and they were forced to spend the next two nights sleeping in a park. His mother's cousins learned of their predicament and found Ponce and his mother a place to live. More important, they found her a job cleaning houses and nannying.

Ponce spent the rest of the summer in school trying to learn English. Then, in early fall 1991, Ponce's mother met her future husband. He asked her to move to Denver with him. In Denver, he promised, was the opportunity for a better life. She agreed, and they were off.

Ponce and his mother settled into his aunt's apartment in the projects of North Denver. They were there for four months. It is difficult to conceive of this as the good life, and there certainly was not money falling from trees, but as far as Ponce was concerned, it was the American Dream. "It was tough," he says, "but then, it wasn't. It was better than Amarillo and it was better than Juarez because it wasn't survival anymore. First, I was going to school, and second, I was staying out of trouble. In Juarez, trouble was everywhere. I mean, in Juarez, I saw someone get his brains blown out in front of me . . . I went a week without eating anything . . . So, it was easier [in the projects] in the sense of the progression we made. Compared to now, though, it was tough."

At Denver North High School, Ponce flourished. The tenacity that enabled him to survive the streets of Juarez, coupled with his mother's love, now enabled him to prosper in a more stable setting. His largest obstacle was learning English. He feared not speaking properly, so he applied himself. "My mother taught me not to quit at anything," he says, "and she taught me to be tough. She's the foundation, all the passion, all the strength." He learned to count watching *Sesame Street*. He would stay home and read the dictionary for hours on end. Soon he was speaking fluently, with only traces of a Spanish accent.

Before his English caught up with his Spanish, his legs started speaking volumes on the track. Mark Mounsey, a CU runner in the early seventies, was Ponce's first high school track coach. More important, he was the first white person to treat Ponce with dignity and respect. Says Ponce, "Before him, I didn't like white people. But he's just a caring person. He was the first one to see me not just as a brown kid. He treated me like a human being." As Ponce's career progressed, Mounsey called Jerry Quiller, CU's track coach at the time, to tell him about Ponce. "Because of him," says Ponce, "I came to CU."

Ponce's track and personal development in high school was assisted by the aide of Dr. Jeffrey Young, a Boulder veterinarian and runner. He provided more structure to his training, "and he gave me the biggest opportunity with financial support. He would take the whole team out to eat. No one had ever done that for us. He would take us to the movies, and pay for everything. He even co-signed to help my mom get a house."

Dr. Young still plays a prominent role in Ponce's life. Says Ponce, "I consider him my father. He's just there for me. Whatever I need, emotional, financial, whatever." Ponce now lives in a file room he converted into a loft next door to Dr. Young's clinic in Boulder. There is no plumbing, and it is certainly not a luxury accommodation. But Dr. Young is letting Ponce live there rent-free in exchange for the work he did to transform the place. Living here, a year away from graduating with a degree in

Spanish literature, Ponce feels blessed. "Sometimes I feel like I'm dreaming," he says. "I'm gonna wake up washing windows, or selling gum. I'm so thankful. In the ghetto they say, 'It's all good.' But it's not true. But here, right now, that's true for me. It's all good. I'm here, I'm alive, and I've got my family, my treasure."

Two years ago when he entered CU, Wetmore told Ponce, "We have a pack of lions. And every day a different lion roars. If you want to be part of this team, be patient, and work hard. I'm looking for an investment from you. You won't see changes for two years. You'll be sore for two years."

After two years, he told Ponce, he would start to reap the benefits.

Ponce made it out of Juarez. He made it out of the ghetto. He made it out of Denver North, a rough inner-city high school. When he graduated from Denver North, he tied for first in the Colorado state championship 1600-meter run. His PR was a modest 4:28. But he made it through the soreness as a Junior Varsity understudy for his first two years at CU. He is on track to graduate, and he has his eyes set on becoming the first ever All-American athlete to graduate from Denver North. And today, he made everyone take notice as the University of Colorado Cross Country team's number one man. On this day, Ponce was a lion, and he roared.

CSU INVITE

PLACE	NAME	UNIVERSITY	TIME
1.	Jeff Simonich	Utah	24:48
2.	Jason Hubbard	Adams State	25:14
3.	Bryan Berryhill	Colorado State	25:20
4.	Rees Buck	Western State	25:22
5.	Shawn Nixon	Adams State	25:25
6.	Oscar Ponce	Colorado	25:27
7.	Aaron Blondeau	Colorado	25:31
8.	Mike Friedberg	Colorado	25:32
9.	Brock Tessman	Colorado	25:33
10.	Chris Cole	Colorado State	25:35
11.	Chris Valenti	Colorado	25:41
15.	Wes Berkshire	Colorado	25:50
18.	Ron Roybal	Colorado	26:04
22.	Adam Loomis	Colorado	26:14
36.	Matt Elmuccio	Colorado	26:35
37.	Cameron Harrison	Colorado	26:36
55.	Zach Crandall	Colorado	27:15
58.	Chris Schafer	Colorado	27:24

Money in the Bank

Local runners mingle among the Varsity CU runners at the Buffalo facing Balch gym as 8 a.m. approaches. The forty to fifty runners waiting for Wetmore's arrival are the only people on the CU campus at this time on Sunday morning. No doubt many CU revelers have only recently drawn the curtains on their Saturday night.

Wetmore approaches the Buffalo from his office, carrying a document that contains the day's assignments. He walks purposefully, and the glint in his eye indicates the delight he takes in the controlled chaos that he has presided over in one way or another each fall for the past twenty years. But as much as he enjoys the sight of all his charges, it is not without its downside. Because of the number of athletes waiting to run, Wetmore has but a minute to chat with Batliner about his leg before Wetmore sends him to Kitt Field for some easy jogging. For Bat it is a good day: thirty minutes of jogging and he "feels great."

The runners pile into cars and head north of town for a run known simply as "the Grange." It is a relatively flat run primarily on dirt roads through farmland speckled with horses and cottages. There are six loops, ranging between twelve and eighteen miles, that extend from the run's nexus off of Nelson Road, along with a two-mile segment that can easily be added on. The gentle descent that extends for the first five miles makes for a quick early pace—and a long finish for those who go out over their heads, perhaps forgetting that all the runs finish with a three-mile ascent back to the start.

The usually desolate dirt lot that adjoins the road at the starting line is packed with cyclists of all shapes and sizes. A bike tour is in progress, and the cyclists have stopped at the refreshment and aid station that has been set here. The thought of people paying money to go for a ride amuses Wetmore. He compares them to the thousands of recreational runners who jog the Bolder Boulder road race every year. "There'll be 40,000 people running the Bolder Boulder," he says, "but only maybe 500 people will be racing. The rest will talk about it for six months, train for one to three weeks, then pay twenty bucks so they can run six miles. Amazing."

The leaves are changing, and for the first time this fall the morning sun does not seem oppressive. But a quarter mile into the run, Goucher starts to heat things up. He quickly creates a fifty-meter lead. "What's he doing?" Friedberg condescendingly asks. Berkshire comes to Goucher's defense, "Ah, he just wants to run alone." Severy then takes off and quickly catches Goucher. They remain about fifty meters in front of the others until they reach five miles. JD has parked his van at the five-mile mark, opened the back doors, and placed cups of water and Gatorade there for the runners.

Despite early indications to the contrary, the men are running controlled. Goucher and Severy reach JD in a shade under thirty minutes. Perhaps due to their cumulative fatigue, Goucher and Severy do not extend their lead, and the main pack also maintains the same steady pace throughout. Tessman runs fifteen miles in 1:31—just a shade over six minutes a mile. Even better, Roybal also runs 12.4 miles at a six-minute mile clip, and he "feels great."

The mileage monsters also have a good day. Ponce, Berkshire, and Friedberg run nineteen in two hours, while Severy runs twenty miles in 1:59, finishing a minute behind Goucher. More money in the bank.

Elmuccio is the day's only casualty. His hamstring is sore from yesterday's race, so he stops eight miles in and gets a lift back from JD. His injury frustrates him, but he does not dwell on it because he is preoccupied with the afternoon's activity. The team is going to his house—fleas and all—for brunch. He let it slip that he thinks his french toast may be better than the Village's supreme french toast. "The secret's in the spices," he says. "I gotta run to the store and get some vanilla."

By the time Ponce and Berkshire have finished their runs most of the runners have already hitched a ride back to campus. The cyclists are long gone, but four cases of bananas remain in their stead. Sev runs over from his car and grabs a bunch. As he does this, Wetmore barks at him from his truck, "Sev! That's it for you. That's all you eat—for a week!" Sev laughs at Wetmore and flashes his goofy grin. Wetmore says, "Look at him. Does he look like an athlete? He doesn't, but he's an amazing athlete." No one is going to confuse Sev with a gazelle when he runs, but on skis he is grace personified. Ever the outdoorsman, Sev's day is just beginning. He is driving to Crested Butte to go kayaking with a man who may be the next cross country All-American in the family, his little brother Jonathan. The Bus just has endless endurance.

Brunch is a smashing success. Although the verdict is still out as to whether Mooch's french toast takes the blue ribbon, everyone is well fed and no one gets attacked by the fleas that call Mooch, Berkshire, and Loomis's place home.

There are ten weeks until Nationals.

The Dam

Says Batliner, "In my opinion, this is the toughest workout we do." Ten miles, all out. Tougher than Mags, tougher than Flagstaff. In years past Wetmore has run the ten miles down the creek path to a dam that serves as the five-mile mark and back. Hence, the dam. Goucher has run 53 minutes for the dam (as they refer to *any* practice where they run ten miles hard, regardless of the locale where it is run) when he is fit. Reese's roommate Kelly Lambert, preparing for the Chicago marathon, recently ran it in 52 high. Today, though, the guys will do the ten miles on the cross country course. What used to be the toughest session just got tougher. And to add to their misery, it is 80 degrees, and there is nowhere to hide. The sound of crickets fills the air. It is as if they, too, are commenting on the heat.

Batliner is not "damming" it today. He does not have compartment syndrome, but he may have a stress fracture. He is seeing a doctor in the training room at 6:00 p.m. Until then, he has a meeting with "the devil, the inferno of hell." The pool. Wetmore and JD are extremely concerned. JD cannot stop thinking about Bat and the ramifications of his absence. He says: "We're *screwed* if Bat's out. I think we're already hurting a little bit. With Bat in tenth and Gouch one or two, we're in pretty good shape. But with Bat twentieth, then what do we do? Can Sev be seventeenth again? He had a summer of a lot of mileage that year (1996), but he missed all of last year racing. Sev is so obsessive though that a summer in the 80's might get him there." Exasperated, JD shakes his head. "And Reese, what can he get back?"

Severy is running the dam, although he, too, can be added to the list of the walking wounded. His hamstring is sore where it connects behind his knee. But his soreness might not be related to running, but rather, to his car ride back from Glenwood Canyon. Two and a half hours away from Boulder, a tire blew out on his car. Wetmore shakes his head as Sev recounts the story and says, "That's why I don't allow any fun in my life, Sev." Sev has to laugh. "There's no doubt about it," Sev says, "something will always come and get ya."

If Sev's nuisance is not bad enough, Goucher now has a sinus infection. "I woke up with it on Sunday morning and it just got worse." His eyes are a bit swollen, and he sniffles constantly through the warmup. Is *anyone* healthy?

Before departing, some of the guys start negotiating about switching up groups. Wetmore overhears this and quickly defuses any such thoughts. He claps his hands to get their attention. "Don't switch groups. Don't switch groups. You don't have my permission. I'm the big man who gets paid all the money. Don't go up groups [to faster group], please trust me. Okay, [Jodie] Hughes? Don't go out with Goucher."

Point made, Wetmore lines up with them at the start. He often runs while they do, and today he runs in the opposite direction so he can intercept them during their run. Wetmore lines up with them and says, "Set, go, goodbye!"

JD sets out water cups in the back of one of the vans the team has driven in to the course. He wonders aloud about the health of the guys after learning that Blondeau is not running today because of a sore back. "The one thing I remember about Wetmore's program is I was always dragging ass and beat up. But I was only in it a year, and I think it takes longer to come around. I was always worn to hell. I mean long runs, I'd never done that."

Tessman is currently feeling as worn out as JD once did, but today he looks better than ever. Halfway through the run he comes up a small incline, smiles, and shrugs, palms in the air, as if saying, "I don't know, man, but I feel great." He finishes the run tied for fourth with Ponce in 55:46. Afterwards, he is still amazed at how comfortable he felt out there. "It was weird, I don't know what happened." His heart rate at the finish is a placid 144. He adds, "I got this stuff down. Anaerobic stuff, milers, that's what kills me, but it's great, I'm doing that the next six weeks." "Brockford Files," as Reese calls him, appears to be getting fit when the team needs it.

Reese cannot relate to Tessman's experience. "I'm fit enough to race," he says, "just not enough to do the CU workouts. That's a long way. After one mile I was like, 'fuck!'" He still runs 56:01—a full three and a half minutes ahead of Roybal, who now also has an ailment of his own. "I rolled my ankle, and when I did it, it hurt like *hell*."

Despite his cold, Goucher rolls a 54:15, twenty seconds ahead of Severy. He credits his good workout in part to a rare and cherished three-hour nap this afternoon. Thoughts of how a sinus infection killed him at NCAA's last year have him determined not to let history repeat itself. He says, "I'm starting to get on top of it with shots and medicine."

To help his body recuperate from the hard training, Goucher has added massage work to his regimen. He saw local masseur and Fiji Olympian Binesh Prasad on Sunday and he is seeing him again tomorrow at 11:30. The look in his eye says he is fearing this more than any workout Wetmore throws at him. "I'm not too fired up about this appointment," Goucher says. "It will hurt. I mean, I've never heard anyone say 'I went to Binesh, it was awesome!' It's one area where I'm not very tough—people sticking fingers and elbows into my sore spots, but he told me last week I need a lot of work."

Perhaps too beat up to face the "dam," O'Mara is AWOL again. Says Wetmore, "There's a meaning to every behavior . . ."

Back on campus, Batliner waits to see a physician in the training room in the Dal Ward Athletic Center. He is not optimistic. "I tried jogging up the hill [to Dal Ward] and I couldn't even do that. But I don't know, maybe I'm looking at this wrong. Maybe pain is good."

Wetmore, not wanting to delay the inevitable, heads right there when he gets back to campus. He fidgets while awaiting Bat's results. "If Bat has a stress fracture," he says, "I'm gonna kill myself."

Again, the doctor has no conclusive information for him. Batliner tells Wetmore: "It's not acting like a stress fracture, but it could be. He doesn't think it's compartment, because I'm missing 90 percent of the symptoms. There is an inflamed muscle with a shinsplint on top of that. I'm getting a bone scan."

Wetmore, hiding his anxiety, tells Bat, "Don't panic. We'll still get 99 percent done."

Recovery

Goucher is leaving no detail to chance in his quest to win his first NCAA cross country title. He has upped both his volume and his intensity this season, and in order to aid his recovery from the daily pounding, he is electing to pay forty dollars per session out of pocket to receive periodic massages from one of Boulder's premiere masseurs, Binesh Prasad. Binesh's office is located in his house on the edge of the Reservoir in North Boulder, and Goucher arrives for an appointment around noon. This is his second appointment with Binesh, a two-time Olympian in the 10,000 meters for Fiji with a lifetime best of 28:30. Despite such illustrious credentials, Binesh is not the most revered runner in the household; Binesh is married to Nadia Prasad, a French native who is one of the world's premiere road runners.

It was while working with Nadia at a training camp in France in 1995 that Binesh first considered going into massage therapy professionally. As he tells it: "We were working on each other when Khalid Skah [the Moroccan 10,000-meter Olympic Gold Medalist] walks in and says, 'Hey, I want one too.' I was not a trained masseur then, but I worked on him, and after that I worked on the other French athletes. After that, Khalid told me, 'Hey, why are you wasting your time? You should charge us, do this professionally.'"

Binesh took Skah's advice, and his business is prospering. A sign on the door outside Binesh's office reads, *When you walk through these doors, you join the best athletes in the world.* This is not hyperbole. Thanks to Binesh's ability and Boulder's continuing status as one of the world's premiere training grounds for endurance athletes, Binesh's clientele includes top marathoners who have done training stints in Boulder. Belgian marathoner Vincent Rousseau, South African Olympic Medalist Elena Meyer, and several domestic distance studs, such as 1996 Olympian Mark Coogan and emerging 10,000-meter star Pete Julian are among the elite who have patronized Binesh. Photos and letters from his clients cover his office walls. Hiromi Suzuki writes: *As you know, I got the Gold Medal at the World Championship in Athens. I really think that I got this happiness result because of your massage. Thank you very much to you.* In fact, at every major track and field competition, from the Goodwill Games to the Asian Games to the European Championships, there are athletes who rely on

Binesh's hands to keep them going. Says Binesh, "At every big meet and every big marathon, there is someone that I have worked on."

Amid the autographed letters and photos is an autographed photo from Romanian middle-distance star Anuta Catuna. She writes a statement with which Goucher will shortly concur. *To Binesh*, she writes, *the* **hardest** *massage therapist I know.*

Goucher's first massage from Binesh last Sunday was a painful experience, and Binesh adjusted his hips for him when he found they were slightly out of alignment. Goucher is a relative newcomer to massage, so today, Binesh promises to go lightly. He tells Goucher, "Today, we're just going to get you into massage. We're going to go deep, but not the regular Binesh."

He starts in on Goucher, paying particular attention to his right hamstring, which has been giving him problems as of late. "If it's too hard," he says, "let me know." Kneading Goucher's hamstrings, Binesh tells him, "Today, with good pressure, we'll flush the muscles out, then the body makes the next step of changes." He admonishes Goucher to relax and communicate: "If you're tight because you are not relaxed, I'll think your muscles are tight and I'll work them harder—so you have to let me know if it's OK." It is a message some are not quick to grasp. Two weeks from today, Severy shows up to practice with a bruise the size of his fist on his thigh. "See this," he says to Wetmore, "I got a massage from Binesh."

Goucher is in obvious discomfort as Binesh works. Grinning, Binesh says, "The stronger the muscles, the more painful it is too. It takes a lot more to release them, so you have to break them more."

When Binesh gets to Goucher's upper gluts, the usually stoic Goucher moans, "That didn't feel good, *at all*!" When Binesh hits his calf, Goucher says, "Good Lord!" Binesh finishes by pulling and pushing on Gouch's back. "This," he explains, "will open up your chest." He has to remind Goucher to keep breathing, and Gouch's back reddens quickly when Binesh applies pressure, the result, Binesh says, of excess toxins in the area. To help Goucher clear his system of unwanted toxins, Binesh suggests he take an Epsom salt bath once a week. Goucher asks him why once a week, and Binesh tells him if he wanted to, he could do it every day, but no one would do that. As with massage, he advises establishing a routine, and doing it consistently. Binesh, almost condescendingly, tells Goucher that his "elite" Boulder-based clients, such as Coogan and Julian, regularly see him once a week. On the way home, Goucher, bristling, says, "What the hell did he mean by that? Does he know who I am?" Binesh meant no disrespect, but in a town full of Olympians and World Record setters, it is possible for someone of Goucher's caliber to be small-fry, even in the running community.

As Binesh wraps up the massage, he reiterates that he went easy on Goucher today. Later, he will beat him up. "The pain," he says, "will fix the injuries. You have to know if muscles are strong; you need to work them harder to eliminate the tight spots. The stronger the muscles, the deeper the massage, the more benefits you'll have from it."

Goucher does not think this was so easy. "My God," he says, "I'm gonna die. That fucking hurt so bad. Especially when he got to my back." Yet, despite the pain, and the forty dollar hit to his pocketbook, he will be back to see Binesh. After all, he could have signed a lucrative shoe and endorsement contract after winning NCAA's in the spring—but he elected to return for this one final season to "maximize my options and increase my marketability. By sticking around, most likely I will." He is not cutting any corners, and if all goes according to plan, the forty-dollar bi-weekly investment will help him sign a six-figure contract after winning NCAA's in November. By then, perhaps, Binesh will know who he is . . .

Roybal has just received his equipment today. Wetmore has withheld it until now because last year he caught Roybal trading one of his CU shirts for an ARMY T-shirt at a meet. Needless to say, Wetmore was not pleased.

Wetmore gives Roybal all extra-larges. Roybal puts the sweatshirt on and the sleeves extend half a foot past his hands. Roybal shakes his head in disbelief as he moves his arms up and down and the sleeves flap around. He is disappointed and exasperated. Wetmore is still in his office, so he turns to JD and says, "JD! What am I gonna do with this?" JD asks rhetorically, "Well, are you gonna complain to the boss?" Again, while flapping his arms, Roybal says, "No, but JD, what am I gonna do with this?" JD just laughs.

Wetmore, conversing with Goucher in his office, says, "What you gotta say to yourself is, 'The best thing I can do for my marketability is to have a monster cross season.' So that means not thinking about Nike, [agent] Brad Hunt, or anything else; just eliminate all distractions. Then you'll be able to go on David Letterman and just sit there and not say shit."

Goucher agrees. While most of his teammates come from relatively secure financial backgrounds, Goucher does not. Winning the NCAA title will have a tremendous impact on his financial future. He knows his priorities. "If it comes between getting an A in class or getting rest for Nationals, I'm gonna get my rest! The rest is what's gonna help my marketability." Given Goucher's situation, Wetmore voices his approval. "Well, I think I concur with that."

Goucher puts all distractions aside this afternoon and runs the 15.7-mile Marshall loop in 1:27. "I felt good. I was going sub-six's and it was easy, considering I thought I'd feel terrible." Tessman, yesterday's star, runs a solid 79 minutes for twelve and a half miles. "It was tough," Tessman says, "I was pretty tired."

The Buffaloes will need Tessman to go the extra mile. Batliner just called Wetmore to inform him that he has a stress fracture in his tibia.

They All Want to Be You

They all want to be eagles, but they don't want to act like eagles, so we're going to have to do it ourselves.

Ken Kesey in *The Electric Kool-Aid Acid Test*
by Tom Wolfe

Time to get those legs turning over. The men are doing anything from twelve 300's on the grass in 56 seconds with a slow 200-meter recovery to 24 times 300 in 50 seconds for Goucher. In case there is any confusion about today's task, Wetmore addresses everyone at 6:28. "OK folks, this is a neuromuscular workout. It's a leg workout, not a cardiovascular workout. I'm not trying to get a deep aerobic stimulus. These 300's will be faster than race pace, faster than you will run a race this season, barring a miracle. Get your groups together, let's get going." He cautions them before they head out, "Don't get greedy. Bad things happen when you get greedy."

Getting greedy, that may be why many of the men are getting hurt, but that is also why they are good. Bat's news has all the guys thinking about their training. Ponce says, "I think that the problem is we're all trying to chase Goucher, and we're not at his level. Look at Bat, that's why he's hurt. But it's also what makes us better."

Goucher certainly sets the standard. On his rest day yesterday, after having run over fifteen miles on Wednesday, he ran eighteen miles. He is no worse for the wear. The 300's are slightly uphill on the way out, downhill on the way back, and Goucher averages 51 out and 48 back. He runs powerfully with that slight roll of his shoulders, and he leans into every stride. He runs shirtless, and Wetmore notices his ripped appearance: "Goucher's looking lean enough, huh?"

In terms of leanness, Goucher also sets the standard. After practice yesterday, Wetmore reached out and pinched Slattery's stomach. "Pretty good," said Wetmore. Slattery has lost ten pounds since arriving in Boulder. Then Wetmore held his hand out, rubbing fingers. "Goucher" —he paused— "he's like paper."

Tessman has made the jump and is now in the second group with Friedberg, Sev, Napier, and Ponce. Tessman leads the charge. Wetmore likes what he sees. "Well, this is a good-looking group here, better be, needs to be" (especially Tessman)! Losing Batliner is a huge blow, and someone needs to pick up the void. Can Tessman help? "Brock is the un-known," Wetmore says, as he eyes his athletes. "After three or four years of being with a guy, you know what to expect of him. I spent most of last night fantasizing about him making a big jump."

Not that Wetmore is giving up on Bat. "We'll give him 30 days in the pool, put him on the conference team, and try to race him into shape." The runner whose spot he is going to take is going to be pissed, so Wet-more will address the men this afternoon regarding the situation.

Roybal, meanwhile, moves through the third pack, at times leading the group. Like Schafer, Elmuccio, Napier, and Slattery, Roybal is blessed with natural speed. Today gives him an opportunity to show off a bit. "Roybal's mostly well, at least he's weller than a year ago," exclaims Wet-more. "If I can get the same improvement curve as a year ago, I guess I'd be pretty satisfied."

Elmuccio and Slattery are going at each other with some vigor. The Jersey boys always seem to have a little something extra when they run against each other. Wetmore is pleased to see them battle like this. "Slat-tery's finally feeling his oats today. This is his style of workout. See Elmo, he'll run himself to death if I put him with Slat." Wetmore keeps his eye on the third pack, and he focuses his attention on Johnson, who runs comfortably with the Jersey boys. Wetmore watches him as he bounces from foot to foot, his long, curly blond hair flopping up and down with each stride. "Good J-Bird, good. Looking great!" he says.

Goucher is the last one out there. Some Marine ROTC cadets play a spirited game of flag football on Kitt, oblivious to Goucher as he flies by them on the perimeter of the field. Wetmore alone offers some en-couragement. "All right, Adam, good poise, practice feeling poised . . ."

The men and women sit in the stands above the indoor track while Wetmore directs the proceedings from the front aisle. He passes out a form for them to choose their training shoes. "You don't have to put your event down on these yellow things. I know your event. Your event is to follow instructions." Everyone laughs at Wetmore's characterization of himself as a disciplinarian. He gets them to do what he wants, but he never needs to assert his authority over them to accomplish his goals.

As the runners fill out the paperwork, Wetmore begins telling Friedberg, seated in the front row, his tale of the seven-dollar running shoes. A minute later, he has everyone's attention. "One day when I was a poor young coach running 130 miles a week, I said, 'This is ridiculous, I keep paying $75 for a pair of shoes!' I figured, it's brilliant, I'll go to K-Mart and pay seven dollars for a pair of shoes. I figured I could get at least 100 miles per pair of shoes. Great. That'd be seventy bucks for about 1000 miles. I get a pair and go for a fifteen-mile run in the rain. Six miles in, they fall apart. It turns out the glue is water soluble."

When the team finishes filling out their forms, Wetmore addresses them for the first time this season. It is a memorable speech:

> This is our first meeting and it's one month into the season. I wanted to wait until we finalized the roster. We're done. We're not taking anybody else. Some people were here a year ago, and they're not here today.
>
> Those of you who ran the time trial, I wanted to know if you had the stomach for the fight. Some people were annoyed that I made them run. Sixteen women and some guys didn't have the stomach for the fight. Sean Smith made it. He had the stomach for the fight. I want you to know you guys paid a stiff price to be here, you should be proud of yourselves.
>
> Everyone in Boulder wants to be you. The dilettantes, the posers, the dreamers, the schemers; they all want to be you.
>
> The Wally Rutherfords [walk-ons] of this team, you're the envy of them. Being the real deal is the price of this team.
>
> We're interested in doing it. We're here to run races. I run the time trial to scare off people who think this is the camera club. Races are scary. You could vomit.
>
> We're here to run races. This is leading up to the caveat emptor. Because we're not the jogging club, I have to pay attention to the first nine athletes first. There are 54 people on this team, 50 are here now. I need

fourteen. Seven men and seven women to go to conference, districts, and Nationals.

I have enough money in the budget for 36. But everyone who's in here had gumption. I'll find a way to give you a chance. But understand I have to pay attention to some people more than others.

Look at Friedberg. Last year we practically ran him off the team, now he's up to the point where I speak to him one on one twice a week. The majority of my attention has to be for the fourteen people on the team. I hope you understand that inequity, that you'll forgive that unfairness . . .

If we go four days without talking, understand: our number-one priority is to beat people. Wait your turn like Friedberg, you'll be on a higher echelon, you'll travel to meets, and get to race.

October 3rd . . . Rocky Mountain Shootout. I hope you're all running that day. I want everybody running. It's the first time we open the floodgates and we want to show off.

October 10th . . . I need nine men and nine women to run the Pre-National championships on the [championship] course. Competition for those spots will be pretty heated. My decision will be a subjective decision, not an objective decision. I'll say, I feel good about these nine people. It's based on what I've observed and what I feel. The best thing you can do is run well and train well for conference on October 30th.

October 17th . . . Our next nine, numbers ten through eighteen will travel to sea level to Ft. Hays, Kansas, for a good, fast meet. It's a fun meet. You want to be on that bus if you can.

October 30th . . . Conference Championships. This is when I really have some handpicking. If you're not in that nine, it'll be tough to make the districts two weeks later.

Remember, it takes 100 days to impress me. No one day impresses me.

November 7th . . . For those of you not running districts we have a small meet here to monitor your progress. The cool part of running is watching you get better and better and better. That's the fun part. This is the last chance for those folks.

Then [with the Varsity] we're going from nine to seven. It's a subjective decision. It's the seven I feel best about. It's not always the same seven as at districts.

Judging from the time trial and Fort Collins, we are not the best team we've ever been, but we do have the most potential we've ever had. We're not there. I thought we'd start there, but we're not. But by November, I think we'll have the two best teams we've ever had. The women are ranked fourth, the men are ranked third [nationally] right now. We're not deserving of that right now.

We have these rankings because Colorado has a record. We lose four of our top five women, and even though we're cleaned out, they're thinking, "That nasty son of a gun up there, he's gonna dream up something."

We have a good, good year coming. I don't like to give a lot of rah-rah talk . . . for ten years [as a high school assistant coach] I had to listen to Tuesday and Thursday speeches. I came to hate speeches.

I don't need to build you up. I don't want you to leave here smashing your head against the wall. Be businesslike, patient, and methodical. Do a little head smashing every day for one hundred days.

Not just everyone in Boulder wants to be like you. Everyone in this university wants to be like you. You're the top-ranked team in the school.

We live in a city on a hill. When your alarm goes off and you're tired, think, they all want to be you. No one knows that Heather [Burroughs] or [Jen] Gruia are one minute ahead of last year. No one knows I have six freshman women who one month from now will be among the top ten freshman women in the country. I like it that way.

Rules. I have only one rule: that you be a young man or young woman of character. You follow that rule, and I'll take care of the rest.

See you all, at 7:59, at the Buffalo.

No one moves. A moment later, Wetmore points to the other end of the bleachers, and pulls the men aside. He has already explained to them that choosing his teams is subjective. Now he must address Batliner's situation, and he does not beat around the bush.

As you all know by now, Bat's x-ray came out positive; he has a stress fracture. My fullest intention is to find a way for him to be on our team at NCAA's. He's not running the next month. Nonetheless, at conference and districts, it's gonna be our eight best, six best, and Bat. He's one of the best runners in the country.

I'm gonna gamble. I think I can get him in shape in a month. I want the contenders to know that someone in here is going to be pissed.

I told him, he has a responsibility to tell me if he's not ready. Matt, [he looks at Napier] you already know, you're the number-one man on the bench. [Napier laughs.] You're on hold. We won't use you unless we have to.

Bat, [Wetmore looks straight at him] I'm planning on taking you, whatever it takes.

OK, [he turns back to the others] I just wanted to let you all know the status of Bat. I want to be fair to you all. OK, that's it, you're out.

As the men get up to go, Wetmore singles out Chris Valenti in front of everybody. He was not at practice this morning. "Valenti, where were you?" he asks. "I was sick." Wetmore gives him a scornful glance, then turns to Goucher. "Gouch, where were you this morning? Have you finished your sinus medication yet? How did you manage to make it out here to practice?"

"I wouldn't miss it for the world, too much fun." Point taken.

Forty. Four Zero. Forty.

Magnolia Road. Again. Guaranteed, on this morning, not everybody wants to be them. With Bat out, someone has to pick up the slack. Tessman is willing to take it up a notch. He is running Mags to the Peak to Peak Highway, fourteen miles, for the first time. "Someone's gotta step it up now that Bat's out," he says. He is going hard again despite not being fully recovered from last week's training. "Last week was tough with a race Saturday, long Sunday, and hard Tuesday and Wednesday. I was feeling beat Thursday." Such is the life . . .

He is not the only one picking it up. Reese joins Tessman and his roommate Clint Wells on Mags today. Reese adds on a little at the end, giving him fifteen miles for the day. "Two weeks ago I could barely hang with the freshmen. Today I felt controlled. I was psyched. I felt good today, man."

The Torres twins are here on their recruiting trip, and they, too, are doing their twelve-mile Sunday run at Mags (they run by themselves because NCAA rules forbid training with the team). They are small and slight in stature—maybe five feet, seven inches, 125 pounds. But as they run out along Mags next to one another the efficiency of their stride is immediately evident. Coming from sea level, though, they hurt more than the other guys. After they finish, they discuss their first Mags and their impression of CU.

Of Mags, Jorge says, "It was hard on the way out, but on the way back it was a lot easier. Coming from Illinois, the elevation hit me right away. When I finished the run it took me two minutes to become undizzy." Despite the elevation, Ed is impressed with the surroundings: "There's no place like this with the scenery, the campus—I'm like, oh, wow! And the people here are so nice."

Jorge is not as easily impressed by the five-star treatment they are receiving. "But on recruiting trips I guess they're all nice to you." Virtually every major university has courted them, and only three schools remain in the running along with Colorado: Oregon, Montana, and Stanford.

An advantage Colorado has is that it is a training mecca. Jorge visited Boulder this past summer, and his eyes light up when he says, "Man, we saw world-class runners all over the place!" It just so happens that there are three Kenyans running Mags today.

Ponce and Berkshire spotted the Kenyans loping fairly casually, maybe 6:30 a mile, up ahead of them on the way back. Wanting to say that they had run with the Kenyans, Ponce and Berkshire put in a push to catch up to them. They catch the Kenyans and run in silence next to them for two miles before one of the Kenyans, seeing Ponce's cut-off Mexico shirt, asks him if he knows the Mexican marathoner German Silva. Ponce informs him that he does not personally know Silva, and then he discovers that all three Kenyans are marathoners, and that the one doing the talking is running the Chicago marathon, while the others are running the New York City marathon.

The Kenyan asks Ponce how far he is running, and Ponce tells him he is running twenty miles. Ponce asks the Kenyan how far he is running, and he tells him that he is running forty. "Fourteen," Ponce asks him, "or forty?" "Forty," the Kenyan replies. "Four zero. Forty."

Ponce shakes his head, recalling the scene. "I was hurting, and once I heard that, I was like, 'Fuck, I'm a little bitch.' I didn't even feel my pain anymore, I was like, 'Fuck, I'm feeling sorry for *him*!'"

Berkshire jumps into the conversation. "Fuck that," he says. "Those guys are assholes! My whole conquest today is ruined. I'm so pissed! I thought I was a badass when I passed them, then I found out they're doing forty. Fuck!"

The Kenyans glide past the assembled CU runners as Ponce re-counts the story. Seeing them puts all of Wetmore's needling about being thin in perspective. They are *skinny*.

Ponce need not have felt too sorry for the Kenyan doing forty. Ponce thought the Kenyan meant that he was doing forty *miles*. An article on the Kenyans in the *Boulder Daily Camera* later reveals that they were running forty kilometers, not forty miles. It is still a run of over 24 miles, but not quite forty miles.

The man who spoke with Ponce is Ondoro Osoro. He goes on to win the Chicago Marathon later in the fall in 2:06:54. In addition to being the fastest debut ever, Osoro's run is the third fastest marathon in history.

As Goucher and Severy come up the final hill to the finish they both look strong. It is Sev's first twenty miler on Mags in two years, and he runs it in 2:03—just what Wetmore wanted. Two years ago he ran twenty with Goucher in 2:04, and it destroyed him. Today, in a role reversal, he dishes out the punishment to Goucher.

Goucher was dragging ass at the beginning, and getting more riled every step because of the presence of a post-graduate, Dave Collum of the Palo Alto–based Farm Team, running with them. Collum's presence irks Goucher and gets his competitive juices flowing. He says afterwards, "I don't like these guys coming out to hang with us and race us so they can say, 'I ran with Adam Goucher.'"

At the turnaround they picked it up for a mile, and Sev continued cranking up a mile-long hill. "Gouch was pretty good," he says. "He didn't really complain." But Sev started pulling away from Goucher in the middle of the hill. As he started pulling away, Goucher looked up at him and said, "Goodnight!" Not even Goucher can hang with the Bus when he is rolling up here on the hills.

Goucher turned the tables on Sev later in the run, punishing him over the final four miles. They covered the last four miles in 5:35, 5:45, 6:00, and 5:20. After already having run sixteen miles on Mags, that is hauling ass!

Step It Up

Today is their last simulated fartlek on the course, and it is the longest one yet. They are running two-minute-and-thirty-second segments this time, with equal rest. Fortunately, it is a mercifully cool 65-degree day. Wetmore is exuberant as everyone heads off toward the starting line. They react to his moods, and today he is animated. Four of his freshman women run in a group. He proclaims, "Alright! There they go! The four horsewomen of the apocalypse."

From the gun, Goucher rolls. Wetmore yells encouragement to him as he reaches for the finish line. Eyes open wide, Goucher grimaces with the effort. He looks like he is running on rage. Wetmore did not expect to see him coming around to the finish so quickly. He excitedly yells to Goucher, "They'll see you run next week; you're gonna put on a show! Run tall, run tall!" It is the most animated he has been all year. Wetmore wanted Goucher to run 23:45—4:45 pace. Goucher covers the course in only 22:53. This is an astonishing 63 seconds faster than what he ran on September 1st, and today's workout is more difficult because the segments are 30 seconds longer.

Wetmore gets even more excited as the next pack rolls in. Nine guys come barreling to the finish line. Roybal, Napier, Ponce, Sev, Tessman, Berkshire, Valenti, Reese, and Friedberg. Everyone looks good, and no one is in danger of falling off the back.

They run 24:35, ten seconds faster than three weeks ago, with longer segments and less recovery between intervals. The guys cannot stop talking about how good they felt as they switch into their trainers. Each guy half listens to the others, waiting to get their two cents in in the excitement of the moment. Roybal, up in the pack again, cannot believe it. "It felt so easy! It felt so good. It was an amazing workout!" Reese, too, is excited to be in it after getting dropped on the dam workout a week ago. "Today was the first time I felt like a runner. We were keeping it relaxed, no one had to push it."

Only Severy struggles today. He says afterwards, "I didn't feel so good today. It was Sunday I think. But it was a good team workout. It was fun running with all the guys again. I'm extremely happy with our team. I was concerned when we lost Bat, but I'm not so worried now." "Hey," says Friedberg, "did you see how pumped Mark was?" As he says this, Wetmore makes his way to the guys. "Good work. Good day today, good day."

Adding to Wetmore's good mood is that Goucher's workout comes two days after having run twenty on Mags, with a lingering cold. Goucher has finished his antibiotics, but he still cannot seem to shake it. All things considered, it is a tremendous breakthrough for him today, but as Wetmore will say, it is still only a workout. "Gouch is running 4:35 a mile out there. If he runs 24:00 at the Shoot-out, and he's 30 seconds fitter than last year, then I'll be impressed." His pessimistic, or realistic, nature is trying to get the best of him here, but his excitement still bubbles through. He continues, "Gouch didn't even look tired or winded. I've said all along that he hasn't even touched what he's going to do yet." Again, Wetmore looks for a reason not to get overly excited. "This workout is deceptive, you can run great, and it won't necessarily translate into a race." But Wetmore cannot deny that the guys are, if nothing else, getting fitter. "They're a step ahead of where they were last time and that's what you look for. That means they've adapted to the workload." Ever the perfectionist, his thoughts turn to what has not gone according to plan. "Maybe we'll save Bat, I don't know . . ."

But Goucher is improving, and Wetmore attributes his gains to changes he has made in every aspect of his training. Wetmore told him he was fat, he objected, and then he lost the weight. Wetmore told him he had to run 100 a week, he grumbled, and now he is doing it.

The only one not overly excited about Goucher's practice is the man himself. Instead, he is thinking about how much better he could be doing if he could better manage his schoolwork. He can skate by all he wants, but he had better not fall through, because he needs to graduate. "I need to focus, but I can't focus right now. I only think about running. I wanted to work on this homework last night, this show; I did nothing. I've got twenty-one credits this semester, and I've got a lot of homework this week. I'm not happy about this."

He is more jacked at how well his teammates have done today. He tells them, "We need all you guys to step up big time. You can do it too, you just *need* to do it." In all the excitement, Friedberg reminds them of Batliner's absence. "We need Bat is what we need." Goucher's not worried. "Yeah, he'll be back."

JD is also thrilled about the guys' work, but he is also distracted. He does not like CU's chances of getting the services of the Torres twins. They had a great trip, but he thinks that they left disappointed. Why? One word: cash. "We told them before they came we couldn't give them two fulls, and when we told them again here with the closing speech, their faces just dropped."

They have one additional worry. Blondeau, the only freshman to make the Varsity squad last year, did not finish today. He is so quiet that he is easy to overlook. But they can ill afford to lose him as well.

Edge City Blues

The team is busing out to the East Arapahoe Trailhead to run "the Tank" today for their medium-distance run. Blondeau and Bat are not going with them. Blondeau is getting a bone scan today on his hip and lower back. He really started to notice the pain there two weeks back at the Grange, and, he says, "I haven't been able to run well since."

Already saddled with his positive reading on the bone scan, there is nothing for Bat to do but rehab: bike and pool. He still thinks about the bone scan he got at the Boulder Medical center. After injecting him with radioactive material, he lay still on a table while they took pictures of his leg. By looking off to his left, he could see the image of his bone forming. Having been through this process before, he knew what to look for. Two bright red spots instantly appeared, the outline of his shin forming around them. It is a moment in time he will never forget.

The reality is that he has to stay in the best shape he can so that Wetmore has something to work with when he tries to "save" him. But, a scheduling snafu causes him to lose a day today.

Bat got confused and arrived at Dal Ward today at five p.m. thinking that the weight room would be open until six. At 5:30 one of the trainers told him in no uncertain terms to get out. At 6:30, Batliner is still pissed. He says, "It's a bunch of crap. I wouldn't be in there if I didn't have to." If only he could just slip on his shoes and head out for a run . . .

Out at the Tank, Wetmore wastes no time getting Goucher's goat with some news he received today. "Hey Adam, Iowa State got two more Kenyans to go along with the two they have."

Goucher does not flinch. "Good," he says, "bring 'em on, 'cause I'm hungry, hungry for some Kenyans." He does not fear the Kenyans, and he does not give Wetmore's news a second thought as he runs 15.5 hilly miles in 1:28. Ponce, Friedberg, and Berkshire roll in a couple of minutes after him.

Again, though, someone falls by the wayside. Roybal's hamstring, the same one that bothered him all last year, is acting up again today. He stops at a trailhead two and a half miles from home, and JD goes and picks him up. Getting "Binesh-ed" has helped his hamstring, so he will drop some cash and go see him this weekend to get the problem ironed out. Roybal is just the latest in the long line of wounded men. When one considers that Wetmore is as preoccupied with the women as he is with the men, it is amazing that he gets any sleep at all. Living in Edge City, it seems, has its perils.

We Believe in Our Fitness

The sun lies low on the horizon. The sky is burnt orange. Most of the men are here, switching into their spikes and stretching after having warmed up. Wetmore launches into a story: "I saw an article in the paper this morning. Only ten percent of all non-human species are monogamous. Of those ten percent, only two percent are really monogamous. I guess the point of the article was to forgive our president. What I want to know is, of that ten percent, how many lie about it?" He looks at Mary Baretto, one of the freshman women. "You think many lie about it, Mary?" She shrugs her shoulders. She, like the others, is not nearly awake enough for this.

As usual, the men notice Wetmore's demeanor. Ponce looks at Robbie, and says, "Wetmore's vocal this morning, dude." "Yeah, he's fired up." Wetmore checks his watch before continuing his monologue. "We're going to be late this morning, I can tell, there are certain late people." The comment is aimed at Severy, who walks in through the gate to the track as Wetmore says this. Sev just grins sheepishly.

Wetmore turns to Friedberg: "Mike Friedberg! Today you're going for your 10k PR. Forget the heart rate monitor! Fuck the document! There's a 53-second NCAA [altitude] conversion today, boys! If you're within the qualifying time, fuck it and go!"

Reese does strides while Wetmore rants. Every twenty steps or so, like a frisky colt feeling his legs, he snaps a leg back towards his butt.

Two former Buff cross country All-Americans are going to do the workout with the boys. Wetmore announces their presence: "We have some guest leaders today. Zeke [Tiernen] and Clint [Wells] are our guest rabbits. They're going out in 6:40!" Everyone laughs at this one and Robbie joins in, "Zeke trains all week for Friday morning." "No," says Wetmore, "he doesn't train all week, then he comes."

Now that he has spoken up, Robbie has made himself a target for Wetmore's humor. "Robbie, are you ready? Have you done your strides?" He does not miss a beat. "Yes, Coach," he says, needling Wetmore, "I thought the workout started at 6:30." It says something about the importance of the workout that Wetmore does not rush the men.

"Alright," he says, "let's get cracking, a couple of strides." He is bouncing around. "Man," says Goucher, "he is fired up!"

Robbie is still needling Wetmore about the time. "Alright," he says to

Robbie, "here's what you do. Go over there and just stand on the starting line." The guys crack up as Robbie does it.

Wetmore and JD position themselves at the starting line as Goucher heads out on his own. He is scheduled to run 74's, or 4:55 a mile. If he is concerned about doing it, it does not show. Most of the guys are in spikes, but Goucher is wearing his trainers, hoping to minimize the damage to his calves.

Everyone else is running 77 or 5:10 a mile. Friedberg, Napier, and Severy are running a full 10k, while the others will stop at 9k. Sev is reliable, so he sets the pace. He is a bit more nervous than the others, because he ran his easy day yesterday with Goucher; in other words, it was not very easy. As he passes the first quarter right on pace, JD notices how fit he appears, "He's looking thin. I've never seen him that thin."

Wells and Tierman go through the mile in 5:07, and Sev comes through, on pace, in 5:10. He looks anxiously at Wetmore as he passes on every lap. "Calm down, Sev Dog, calm down." Then Wetmore adds, "Sev, you're looking good, I can see two of your ribs." "Great," Sev answers, "only six to go."

It is brisk—standing still, you can see your breath—but the chill is welcomed by the runners because it is perfect distance-running weather. Goucher comes by two miles in 9:45, looking effortless.

Eleven laps in Reese flashes a big grin as he passes. Wetmore sees this, and remarks, "Good guys, just training, just training. We race next week." Sev has gotten nervous and pulled away with Wells and Tiernan. Napier is all alone leading the pack past three miles in 15:30. "Am I alright?" Napier asks. "Little fast," Wetmore replies, "but OK."

Tiernan and Wells pull off at 8k, having run 25:25. Sev keeps going. "Nice and controlled, nice and controlled. Feel good." He is running all alone, in Goucher territory.

Goucher, meanwhile, is just flying and making it look easy. He passed 8k in 24:11. Every mile has gotten progressively faster. 4:53, 4:52, 4:52, 4:49, 4:45. Tiernan watches him and shouts encouragement, "Good job, Big Dog, looking hot!" "Look at Goucher," he exclaims, "he's an amazing runner. He's going to run 10k in 30 minutes! That's an automatic NCAA qualifier right there!"

He would come close. He runs the sixth mile in 4:42 before closing the last quarter in 70 for a 30:09. That converts to 29:16 at sea level. The mark would be an provisional qualifier for NCAA's, and he does this at 6:30 in the morning, in training shoes, at the end of a hundred-mile week, with 95 miles in singles. Wetmore gives his star the data: "30:09—that's a 29:16. That's what you ran at Furman [at the NCAA Cross Country

Championships] a year ago. Compare the efforts." It does not take him long. Says Goucher, "I'm fired up. I feel good."

Goucher is continuing an incredible run of training that even his teammates and former teammates, like Wells, find hard to fathom. Says Reese, "Last year I was running with him on Tuesday workouts, and now there's no way I can hang. He's stepped it up. He was training last year like the Dog [Sev] is now." Goucher's run is all the more impressive when one considers that he ran eighteen miles yesterday, and that this is his seventh consecutive 90-plus mile week, mostly in singles. "Man," Reese tells Goucher, "it hurts to get that much." "No," Goucher replies. "I'm used to it now. I felt good, really good, really under control. It got hard toward the end, but that's expected. I was close to my heart rate threshold today. I'm still stuffy though."

Leave it to Goucher to find something to complain about. Such a temperament is why he has been tagged with the nickname "Groucho" from the guys. In Goucher's defense, he has an uncanny ability of getting screwed. Sev recalls such an instance: "We were in Pasco, Washington, our sophomore year. We go to a Dairy Queen and I wanted a small cone. It was huge. Gouch got one too, and his was puny. Another time, we were in Washington at Dairy Queen, and we all got cones for 99 cents. He goes to a different window and pays a dollar seventy-nine." Incidents like these happen so often that the team refers to getting screwed as getting "Gouchered." There is a caveat though. "It's only on the small stuff," says Sev. "On the big stuff, I don't think he gets Gouchered."

Severy finishes ahead of schedule, running 31:39. Napier follows in 31:51 and Friedberg runs 31:54. Sev is more excited about Wetmore's comments than about his performance. "That was the first time I've ever heard that from him. I only hear, you're looking fat. I guess I'm getting in shape, huh?" There's no doubt about it.

But what about Friedberg? He runs a 30-second PR. Clearly, Goucher is not the only one making big leaps.

And the pack? Valenti and Robbie, the tenth and eleventh guys on the depth chart, run 25:40, right with everyone. For Robbie, it's an 8k PR that converts to 25 and change at sea level. It is amazing to think this is a guy they were going to cut from the team. Berkshire, Reese, Roybal, Ponce, and Tessman stay together, running a stellar 28:50 for 9k. The shocker here is Roybal. In the last anaerobic threshold run he was off the back and on Wednesday he had to get a ride back to the van. But today he looks great.

The improvement in the pack helps soften the latest blow to the team. Blondeau is out for the season with a stress fracture in his back. Wetmore called him last night to console him and convince him "that it's not a tragedy." But as the injuries mount, Wetmore is forced to look at the training to see what is causing the rash of injuries. In Blondeau's case, the challenge is discovering "why he's had two stress fractures in six months on 60 miles a week. Particularly because it's not in the same spot as last time, that's the confusion."

Still, Wetmore's mood is jocular and upbeat. His moods, like his practices, are to a certain degree orchestrated. They know that he is pleased. If he were mad, he would not have to tell them. Says Wetmore, "They know I'm pissed when I withdraw my affection."

Every guy ran better than expected this morning. Their depth right now is better than any previous CU team. Reese says, "Freaking Wes! How is he able to do that? He ran 28:40 through 9k. Any other year, that makes our top seven. I think he's got issues with leg turnover. That's the only thing stopping guys like him and Jason Robbie." Adds Wells, "That's what [All-Americans] Cleckler, Cooper, and [Tim] Catalano were all running when we got second at Arkansas [at NCAA's]." Reese credits Wetmore for the result. "With Mark, it's the power of suggestion. He says it and you just do it, even though you may not be fit enough to do that."

If Wetmore has a fault, in Reese's eyes, it is that he does not encourage them to take a leap of faith in their own ability come Nationals. Wetmore's faith is based in fact. Reese admits, "We believe in our fitness." Reese also knows Wetmore analyzes an athlete's practices and results to predict what they should be able to run in the next race. So, Reese understands that Wetmore is not going to give a rah-rah speech asking someone to run a superhuman performance to get the job done at race time. He just wants his athletes to do what the data tells them they can do. But, to win it all, Reese thinks they need a little more. "At Nationals, you have to believe in big things. You gotta believe in miracles. After Nationals last year I wrote in my log, 'Ran pretty well, but I gotta get out a little better.' We believe in our fitness, not in miracles. But somewhere I think we got to have faith that we can have a breakthrough performance." But for now, Reese's focus is not on NCAA's. He is looking no farther ahead than the Shootout, or "N-Day" as he referred to it on the first day of practice. "It's going to be weird remembering the pain of racing again. I haven't gone in a long time."

Before the Shootout, the men are running on Sunday on the Sante Fe Trail in Colorado Springs. Wetmore knows the training can get monotonous, so he spices things up by taking his runners to cool places to get in the miles. The Sante Fe trail promises to be one such run. Goucher asks Wetmore if it's cool if he meets them there so he can go home to Colorado Springs until Sunday morning. "I don't know if it's cool," Wetmore replies, "but it's OK. You'll have to check with MTV to see if it's cool."

Bluebirds

The Bluebirds now get their opportunity to match the morning's heroics. Johnson, the Mooch, and the freshmen fall five seconds short of their goal, running 27:12 for 8k—5:26 per mile. No one overexerts himself to hit the pace. "Good," Wetmore says to them with a mile remaining, "that's the way I like it, nice and controlled. When in doubt, slow down."

Wetmore addresses them when they switch into their trainers. "Good run, nice and controlled. I'm proud of you guys." He chit-chats with Slattery before speaking to the group. "You want a story?" No one responds. "Well, I'll give you one even though you don't want one. I had an essay once in high school: *Explain the meaning of life.* I wrote, 'Life is a sugary sweet cereal made by the Quaker Oats Company.' I got a D." Wetmore never was one for sitting in class. "I was too fidgety," he says. "I hated it." He laughs with the others, before addressing Adam Loomis, the Portland transfer who has been battling injury problems, and himself. "Stick to the plan," Wetmore says, "and you'll be surprised what you can do. There are no miracles in running. I don't know about other sports. Actually, I know about wrestling and there are no miracles in wrestling. There may be in other sports, but there are no miracles in running."

Death March

After the long two-hour ride to the Sante Fe Trail, Tessman is ready to roll. On the way out, he really pushes the pace, jumping way ahead of the pack. He has not been putting in the volume that some of the others have; he has "only" been averaging 70 miles a week, but he has been pushing the hard and long days. He cuts down his load by often running an easy six or seven miles around Kitt Field on recovery days.

Early Friday afternoon, Tessman stopped by Wetmore's office to see what time the buses were leaving on Sunday morning to the Springs just as JD and Wetmore were talking about how much he has improved since practice started in late August. "Tessman," Wetmore said to him, reclining in his black leather chair, "there's a consensus around here that you're going to be the X-Factor for us in November." Tessman's eyes lit up at the thought. "Oh definitely, I definitely think I can be."

Already in front, Tessman crushes everybody on the way back, finishing sixteen miles a full five minutes ahead of the pack in 1:37. That is just a shade over six minutes a mile, at an elevation over 7000 feet. "I wanted to make it a death march," he says afterwards while sitting under a tree, "I wanted to hurt."

He accomplished both objectives, and Roybal was a victim of the first. After cranking most of the way, Roybal, Mr. Inconsistency, walks and jogs the last two miles back to the bus because of hamstring pain.

The mileage hogs—Berkshire, Friedberg, Napier, and Ponce—finish in a pack. They run a solid 1:53 for eighteen miles. Only Goucher and Severy have yet to return from their run. Although they are doing twenty miles, Goucher arrives just a few minutes after the eighteeners. Sev hung tough with Goucher until they reached ten miles together in 57:25, but on the way back, Goucher was too much for the Bus. Goucher's time for twenty miles is a blazing 1:56:20. Severy finishes only a minute behind Goucher, completing a tremendous run of his own.

A year ago the team ran this same trail. Batliner remembers it well. "It was kind of a bummer. We drove all the way out there and there was this super-thick fog. It was kind of rainy, and it got worse as we went along. In spots it was so bad that you would be running along, and it wouldn't be until someone was 30 meters out that you would see them coming at you."

Today the sun is oppressively unrelenting, and everyone is grasping for water and searching for shade when they roll in. Goucher, though, seems remarkably unaffected by the endeavor. Perhaps it is because today's run is yet another demonstration of the improvement he has made since last year. In last year's fog, he ran 1:58 for eighteen miles, two minutes slower than he ran this year for twenty.

Milers

Sev has a bruise the size of a fist on his quad, courtesy of Binesh. He is not the only one battling sore legs now. Goucher is starting to break down under the weight of his training. As he does his strides, he occasionally breaks form, his right leg buckling beneath him. It is a disconcerting sight for everyone on the team. "I don't know what it is. My IT [illio-tibial band] is sore, but I can't put a finger on it. The pain builds, then I take a step and it gives." "Great," says Wetmore, "that's all I need to hear." Sev and Goucher do not let their aches affect their workout. No one does.

They are doing the same workout as the one on September 8th. Wetmore is looking for continued improvement to signify that, again, his runners are advancing their fitness. Here are the results:

NAME	9/8 PACE	9/29 GOAL	ACTUAL
Slattery	4 x 5:18	5 x 5:25	5:10
Ruhl	4 x 5:32	5 x 5:25	5:14
Crandall	4 x 5:30	5 x 5:25	5:20
Elmuccio	5 x 5:25	5 x 5:20	5:08
Johnson	NT	5 x 5:20	5:17
Harrison	4 x 5:24	5 x 5:20	5:17
Smith	NT	5 x 5:20	5:16
Loomis	4 x 5:22	5 x 5:15	5:12
Robbie	5 x 5:21	5 x 5:15	5:12
Valenti	4 x 5:19	6 x 5:10	5:06
Schafer	5 x 5:18	5 x 5:10	5:08
Roybal	NT	5 x 5:10	5:12
Napier	5 x 5:16	6 x 5:10	5:06
Tessman	5 x 5:14	6 x 5:10	5:06
Reese	5 x 5:14	6 x 5:10	5:10
Ponce	5 x 5:12	6 x 5:10	5:06
Berkshire	5 x 5:11	6 x 5:10	5:06
Friedberg	5 x 5:07	6 x 5:05	5:00
Severy	5 x 5:07	6 x 5:05	5:00
Goucher	5 x 4:53	6 x 4:45	4:45

Afterwards, Goucher has more aches and pains. "I'm past tired. I got no sleep last night, and I ate lunch today." The result is a cramp down his right side during the last interval. Wetmore's counsel to his star on the last part is simply, "Hey, don't eat lunch."

Sean Smith is particularly tired today. The quiet walk-on has not said two words since he has been on the team. Nonetheless, he made Wetmore livid yesterday afternoon. After practice, Wetmore walked into the gym from his office to see Smith doing plyometrics in the corner of the gym. (Plyometrics are ballistic jumping exercises that are used to develop leg strength and explosiveness.) Wetmore pursed his lips, and his eyes shrank. It was as if he was thinking, "Are my workouts not tough enough for you?"

As it turns out, Smith was not doing any "secret training," but just trying out some drills one of his buddies on the ski team had to do to pass a fitness test. Wetmore understood, but Smith is reminded of it after today's practice. Looking at Smith, Wetmore says, "He's not worn out from me, he's worn out from doing ski team plyometrics."

Without Limits

The team ran a nice and easy loop down the Boulder Creek Path that they call Old Tale. For once, no one got injured. Everyone is jacked, not for Saturday's Shootout, but for the preview showing this evening of the new Steve Prefontaine biopic *Without Limits*. A running movie alone is enough to get them excited, but a free one about Pre, with a cameo appearances by Reese's roommate, Brad Hudson, has them giddy.

The glitterati of American distance running are here for the show: Keith Dowling, Mark Davis, Shawn Found, Brad Hudson, Dan Browne, Sam Wilbur, and the list goes on. The entire men's team and most of the women are here as well. Guys on the team were at the University Memorial Center (UMC) this morning getting as many passes as they could for the event so that anyone who was in class would get to see the movie, and they got enough for everybody.

The movie is impressive. Some of the guys hoot when Hudson flashes on the screen, but otherwise, everyone is silent throughout, intently watching the film. Afterwards, the CU guys and some of the runners mill around in the lobby of the UMC. Davis argues that the last scene where they say that Pre still has the American Junior 5k record is incorrect. He claims that he now has the record.

Goucher is impressed with the film. And he feels some of the loss that so many American distance runners felt for the charismatic star felled in his prime. "It's so intense," he says. "It [Prefontaine's death] still brings tears to my eyes. It puts a knot in my throat, you know?" Sentimentality aside, does Goucher think he could compete with Pre, head-to-head? Goucher thinks for a second, then says, "I could take him."

Percolation

Today it is 55 and sunny—real cross country weather. Everybody is wearing sweats and winter caps. For the first time this season, they are really resting. In addition to yesterday's relaxed run, this afternoon and tomorrow they will jog easily in preparation for their first test of the season at the Shootout. Wetmore is resting them so that he can use the race as an accurate barometer of their current fitness.

Before the course is race ready, there is still some tending that needs to be done. The Buffalo Ranch is covered with rocks. Once the men and women arrive at the course, Wetmore assigns them a chore. "There's a lot of rocks on the course and especially up on the hill. JD says they percolate out of the soil, and he's a knowledgeable cross country course builder guy so listen to him. You all throw 50 rocks, that's 2500 rocks. That's pretty good."

The runners head out from the starting line like obedient soldiers. Robbie hurriedly grabs a rock from the edge of the road and obliviously throws it onto the course. Wetmore lets him have it, "ROBBIE, YOU NIMWIT! DON'T THROW IT ON THE COURSE!" JD, for one, is surprised at the vigor with which they are performing this exercise. "Jeez," he says to Wetmore, "they're really going to town." A satisfied Wetmore responds, "Good. They're recognizing it's their course and there are a lot of rocks on it."

There are two conscientious objectors to this exercise: Goucher and Sev. Sev believes the course is already too easy, so he refuses to participate. "This is my least favorite course," he says. "It's a pussy course, and they're making it easier." He much prefers the Kansas course, with all its ups and downs. The more irregular a course is, the better it is for Sev.

When the men clear the course, assistant Lorie Roch arrives with some spray paint to make a sign that will advertise tomorrow's race. Lorie, JD, and Wetmore set about making the sign to place off of the road tomorrow for the visiting teams and for spectators to the Buffalo Ranch. Everyone on the team has posted some fliers around campus and town advertising the race; the race could attract some attention since it will be Goucher's last race as a CU Buffalo at home.

Most programs in the country have already been racing since mid-September, but this will be the Buffs' debut. Wetmore prefers this late start to the season: "We've been able to do one month of uninterrupted training while other teams have been racing. But, if you notice, Arkansas and Stanford haven't run their heavy hitters yet, at least not all at once. That sucks. They're getting smarter. It makes my job more difficult."

He explains: "How many 10k's can a world-class runner run in one season? Three? They may run four 5's and three 10's in May, June, July, and August. That's four months. Geb [Haile Gebressalasie] is quoted in *Track and Field News* this month saying the Golden League is good, but not for distance runners. There are too many races in too short a time."

If only everyone's training was uninterrupted. Bat now has a nasty cold to complement his stress fracture. "I'm a disgusting mess. I've been hacking and wheezing around my apartment with the bone stimulator on. It was pretty cool," he jokes, "so I figure I'm healed now."

JD and Wetmore walk the course in the cold, periodically throwing rocks, long after the runners have departed. One gets the sense that the state of the course is not all that concerns them.

Shakeout

The runners trickle into Balch in groups of twos and threes. Everyone is doing a shakeout today (four to six miles easy), and everyone is wearing T-shirts and shorts. It seems that yesterday's chill was an aberration. Today the weather has climbed back into the seventies.

Wetmore has posted a document with some details for tomorrow's race, and the guys glance at it on their way to the stretching circle. It reads:

Can men average 40 seconds faster than at the Time Trial?
Men's Top 5 average 25:37?
Go out smart!
Watch your breathing!

Reese, Robbie, Schafer, Batliner, and Goucher are relaxing in JD's office, putting in some new razor-sharp spikes for tomorrow's race. The guys argue about how much Goucher should run today. He ran a total of 98 minutes yesterday. He is debating running eight miles this afternoon so that he remains on pace to hit a hundred for the week. A year ago, Goucher was averaging 84 miles a week. He does not want to slack now because he wants to maintain his higher volume for as long as he can.

The guys tell him to relax and just run an easy half hour. Reese laughs, thinking of the role reversal that is taking place. In years past, it was always Goucher who was telling Reese to chill out. Reese says, "Man, I don't know if I like the new Gouch," and they all bust up laughing.

A few minutes later, Wetmore gathers the team for a few words. They form a semicircle around him on the indoor track, and he receives their undivided attention:

Those of you in the open race, remember not to wear any CU gear, or it counts. Those in the open race will want to be there at 8:30 to 8:45. For the rest of you I'll have a van here at the Buffalo at 8:30.

Tomorrow will require a certain amount of autonomy and peer leadership because I'm gonna be the course builder, and I'm gonna be talking to parents for three minutes apiece for 162 minutes. So, I won't be there to tell you how to warm up, etc. You young guys turn to the elders for that.

There are nineteen teams entered. It's our best turnout ever. There are gonna be 160 runners in this year's race. Adams State's men have two good guys. One of them is the NCAA DII 5000-meter champ. We'll have the DII and the DI champ. There's a showdown already! [Everyone laughs.]

Men, we want to average 25:35. We can have four guys at 25:50 and Gouch at 22:30, or we can have some other guys at 25:30. We have to average 25:35 if we're gonna do what we want to do later in the year. Those of you who ran the time trial should run 40 seconds faster. That's a good projected goal.

On the course itself, the mile markers are wrong, but overall it's OK. Adam averaged 4:45's for the milers. None of them were in 4:45, but that's what he averaged. He's hoping to go 4:50's without any rest on Saturday . . .

When in doubt, pay attention to your respiration, and pay attention that first mile.

Today we're doing a race shakeout. Do whatever you're comfortable with, a couple snappy strides, and some stretching. I'm going out to the course. It's in the best shape it's ever been in. I'd wear spikes. With spikes, I could run maniacally down those hills, but with flats, I'm like "Oh, oh, oh!" But, if you wake up and it's raining, you better break out the monsters. OK, that's it. Take care of the shakeout. I'll see you tomorrow.

Everyone scatters to do their own shakeout loops. Goucher heads to the course in his Mazda pickup; it is one of the few Mazda pickups on the road today, even in truck-crazed Colorado. The guys have talked some sense into him, and he is heading out to the course to do a twenty-minute run and some strides with Reese. He expects to see significant improvement from a year ago. "24:10 would be pretty good," he says matter-of-factly. "I can definitely run twenty seconds faster than last year. The only reason not to is if I am too beat up from my training. I'm sore and I'm tired, but I'm not too beat up." Yesterday he felt some lingering soreness from Wednesday's fourteen-mile run in his left IT band. He is monitoring it, but he is not too concerned.

Goucher expects some soreness since he has made a jump in volume and a slight increase in the intensity of his training from a year ago. He has taken, as Wetmore says, the next logical step in his training. "I'm not doing anything so much faster. I'm just training," he says. The time is now to take the next logical step in his racing. He is ready. "This is what it's all about. This starting tomorrow. It's my eighth week over 90 miles. But this starting tomorrow, for the next seven weeks, is what's it's all about."

Time for dinner. Goucher goes to Reese's place for a steak dinner. They cook a couple of fat steaks on Reese's barbeque, and Reese teases

Goucher for not finishing his. Goucher tries to convince Reese that he has eaten most of it, but he has really shifted a lot of it around on his plate. They eat steak, Reese says, "because we want to be a couple of carnivores out there tomorrow."

Roybal hits the town with his parents and a slew of relatives who have road-tripped up from Pojoague for the race. It is a joyous occasion. During dinner, his cousin addresses Roybal in front of all assembled: "I have everyone back there praying for you. We love you back there. You're just a little Mexican from Pojoague, you have everyone back there rooting for you." Roybal is ready to race.

Unleash the Lions

The fickle cross country weather is back. It is cold, damp, and overcast. Men's and women's open races start off the day's events. South African Simon Morolong throws down the gauntlet, winning the men's open race in 25:16. But, ironically, it is the professionals that serve as a warmup for the collegians. Everyone here today knows Goucher is the star of the show, and most of the competitors from the open race hang around to get a view of this kid everyone in running circles has been talking about. A couple hundred fans join the open competitors, and all told, there appears to be over a thousand fans lining the course—quite a turnout for an early season cross country race—or a cross country race anywhere, anytime, period.

The men are all bundled up in their CU sweats. Severy is anxious to get things under way. "I'm nervous now," he says. "I haven't raced in a while. I just don't want to finish worse than second." He glances around and tugs on his jacket by his left shoulder. He laughs and adds, "I better find the guys, I don't remember how long to warm up. I seriously don't remember."

Goucher stands by the start in his sweats, chatting with his teammates. He oozes confidence. He fears no one in the field, and he appears completely at ease. In fact, he has appeared more tense before training

Severy crouches amid his teammates moments before the start.

sessions than he does now. But today he has his race-day necklace on, a necklace he has made from beads that Wetmore has given him. Though he says, "I can win with 'em or without 'em," they hold some significance for him. The shrunken head bones are something Wetmore used to give out to signify "the shrunken heads of our pulverized, beaten, destroyed, and weakened opponents." Wetmore stopped doling them out several years ago, but Goucher had already acquired enough to make a necklace. Goucher adds, "I like to wear 'em because these were one of the first things that were really cool that Mark gave us. I want to use 'em when I race and that's it. I just like it." He is particular, however, about having it just right before he toes the line. He adjusts it just so before every competition. It is part of his pre-race ritual:

> I always like to start the race with it in the right place. It's just the way I am, a little anal or something. Quickly thinking about friends and family, please be with me type thing. Alright everybody this is it, send me energy everybody. And I will get on one knee, and gather my final thoughts. It may look like it, but I am not praying or anything.

Goucher believes in his fitness. At 10 a.m., the gun goes off, and Goucher immediately grabs the lead. A couple of Adams State runners, including Jason Hubbard, try to stay with him, but Goucher drops them on the steep 50-meter hill past the half-mile mark. He hits the first mile

Two and a half miles in, no one is in sight.

in 4:46—an astonishingly fast clip considering the first mile is by far the toughest on the course. Even Goucher cannot hope to sustain such a murderous pace. After the race, Goucher would say, "that first mile killed me." A full twenty-some seconds after Goucher passes the mile mark, the two Adams runners come charging down the hill with Chris Severy right on their tails.

A crowd of spectators gather at the intersection that is roughly at the two-and-a-half-mile mark. Goucher passes the crowd first. He crests the small grade, and, remarkably, appears not to have slowed at all. He does not appear to be laboring excessively. The length of his lead serves as the only indication that he is moving exceedingly fast. Half a minute later, Chris Severy comes powering over the little climb. Face flushed, he stares intently ahead. Only later would he reveal the thoughts his face concealed.

On April 17, 1998, five and half months ago, Severy's father died after a long bout with cancer. It was, says Sev, "a worse hell than I've ever seen anyone go through." Today, Sev's uncle was standing at the two-mile mark. As Sev ran past, he shouted, "Go, Christopher!" For an instant, Sev imagined it was his father calling out to him. The thought brought about a torrent of emotions. He struggled mightily to keep from hyperventilating. It is only at the three-mile mark that he is able to regain his composure and focus on the task at hand.

Despite the ordeal, Sev does not relinquish his position, and he makes it home in second place overall in 25:11. His time is five seconds faster than that of Morolong, the victor of the open race. Wetmore is

An emotional Severy
gaps the field.

fired up. "[Two and a half years ago] in outdoors of '96 he ran his last race at the conference meet in May. I'm thrilled with him. I was hoping he would run 25:30 and he ran 25:11." In the open race, Sev might have taken home the $400 first prize. But Sev only finished second in the collegiate race. In this race, the victor was waiting for him at the finish line—as he does for all his teammates—cheering like mad. Goucher's new course record time of 24:12 substantiates his status as the best of the Shootout.

Wetmore, while impressed with Goucher's run, feels there is still room for improvement. He says, "I got him a little too worked up. He wanted to put on a show. He was way under five minutes at the mile, about ten seconds too fast. He hit two miles in 9:28. He was on the edge for five miles when he was supposed to be in control. But I'm pleased." He concludes, "He might have broken 24 if I hadn't worked him up."

Rebounding from a disappointing showing in his first race at CSU, Friedberg surprises everyone except himself with his third-place finish in 25:20. What makes his finish even more impressive is that his time is a minute faster than what he ran just a year ago at this same meet. The two weeks prior to the CSU Invite had both been 100-mile weeks. This time, Friedberg was coming off two 90 mile weeks. He feels the extra rest gave him the boost he needed. His phenomenal performance earns Wetmore's praise. Wetmore starts calling him the "Iceberg" for the coolness under pressure that he demonstrated today.

Reese finishes sixth in 25:35 behind a pair of runners from Western State. Ponce finishes seventh in 25:38 before his buddy Roybal crosses the line in 25:44, ninth overall. Roybal's result delights all his relatives who have come from New Mexico to see him race.

Reese has been gunning for this day since he proclaimed it "N-Day" on August 18th. His desire to beat "Nordberg" did not come to pass, but even he could not have predicted Friedberg's improvement six weeks ago. And, having only been running for seven weeks, he is not altogether disappointed with his result.

Roybal has also improved his performance from last year by over a minute. After the race, he and Ponce jump around jubilantly and give each other a bear hug. "*Damn,*" Roybal says in his New Mexican accent, "I felt fucking good. I've gone through this a million times in my mind: thinking about this race, what I'm going to do. Turns, tangents, I *knew* it, *perfectly*, without even *thinking* I was *doing* it. I was really patient, I *knew* exactly where I needed to be with the team. And to do it with my dad and all these guys here, the energy of having all these people that love you, well, when I *finished* I felt like I could go more."

Finishing in twelfth, in the most tenuous team position—seventh—is Brock Tessman. He has looked so great in practice that Wetmore has called him "the X factor" that could lead them to the title. Yet, he knows that if he does not improve his position relative to the team, Batliner could take his place at NCAA's. Wetmore made it perfectly clear that if Bat can run, he will run at NCAA's. "I don't think I ran that great today,"

Tessman says. "I don't feel that good about how I competed." Nevertheless, he sees the silver lining. Redemption is but a week away at the Pre-National meet in Lawrence, Kansas. "But I'm going to Kansas," he says with conviction, "and that's the preliminary goal."

There is disappointment in the camp. Wes Berkshire, who has been training so well, bombs today. He is never in it and he finishes 14th on the team, and 38th overall. Before the race he was all but assured of traveling to Kansas for Pre-Nationals. Now it is doubtful that he will be on the traveling squad. His face says it all. "It's just pretty fucking disappointing. I mean, what can I say?" He is inconsolable; it was the wrong time to be off.

The men get down to business and get moving on their cooldown. Their excitement is tangible as they bop around the course, jubilantly bantering and laughing with one another. Their exhilaration is well founded, for they far surpassed Wetmore's goals. Even Wetmore is overjoyed, "I'm thrilled with them all. We were third in America last year, and we had six guys finish faster than our second guy last year. Some of it's the weather but some of it's fitness. No matter what, this is a better team than a year ago, and we're still hoping to get Bat back."

Goucher and Severy run out in front on the cooldown. They are joined by a guest luminary—Jonathan Severy, Christopher's younger brother and a strong runner in his own right. Sev's been following his younger

brother's progress, and it appears that the high school junior has a shot at winning his division at states. Christopher and Jonathan run up the back hill by the mile mark in stride, with Goucher beside them. Shoulders slightly hunched, legs flexed like a mogul skier's as he comes down a mountain trail, Jonathan's form mimics his older brother's.

In their excitement, the rest of the squad catches the trio. Everyone is thinking of one thing: Nationals. Sev cap-

Ponce presses in mid-race.

tures it best when he turns to Goucher and says, "Well, Gouch, we may get our senior year present after all." "Yep," Gouch replies, "we just might . . ."

Later this afternoon, Sev hosts a barbecue at his cabin atop Flagstaff Mountain for his family, friends, and teammates. The cabin offers a spectacular view, and on a clear night, one can see Denver alight miles away. More important, the cabin offers ample time for reflection and study without distraction—assets Sev craves.

Sev is not a hermit, or a deranged technophobic recluse yearning to be off the grid and all alone. He is an eccentric, yes, but he is living here because he believes the experience of living here through the fall cannot but enrich him personally.

He wants to share the experience of living here with his family and friends, and the weather cooperates. While the sky in Boulder remains overcast and the temperature cool, there is nothing but blue skies up at the cabin. It is a joyous time.

UNIVERSITY OF COLORADO
ROCKY MOUNTAIN SHOOTOUT

PLACE	NAME	UNIVERSITY	TIME
1.	Adam Goucher	Colorado	24:12 CR*
2.	Chris Severy	Colorado	25:11
3.	Mike Friedberg	Colorado	25:20
4.	Michael Aish	Western State	25:25
5.	Rees Buck	Western State	25:33
6.	Tom Reese	Colorado	25:35
7.	Oscar Ponce	Colorado	25:38
8.	Jason Hubbard	Adams State	25:43
9.	Ronald Roybal	Colorado	25:44
10.	Humberto Sanchez	Western State	25:47
12.	Brock Tessman	Colorado	25:54
13.	Chris Valenti	Colorado	25:59
23.	Matt Elmuccio	Colorado	26:29
24.	Jay Johnson	Colorado	26:31
27.	Adam Loomis	Colorado	26:40
32.	Sean Smith	Colorado	26:50
35.	Zach Crandall	Colorado	26:55
38.	Wes Berkshire	Colorado	27:02
39.	Chris Schafer	Colorado	27:05
40.	Cameron Harrison	Colorado	27:08
45.	Matt Ruhl	Colorado	27:17

*Course Record

Mags

The celebration does not last long. This morning, they go back to work. Wetmore rewards his runners, if you can call it that, by easing the pace of today's run because of yesterday's effort. To make sure the men run controlled and do not start racing, Wetmore staggers the groups in one-minute intervals.

It is bitterly cold on Mags this morning. Everyone has hats and gloves and bounces in place to keep warm while they wait to go. But before they depart, Wetmore announces his studs of the week—runners who made the largest improvement yesterday from their previous PR—to all assembled. Matt Elmuccio takes the prize for the men. He improved 1:39 over a year ago, finishing ninth on the team. Nine men will travel to Pre-Nationals, and he is confident the performance is enough to get him there.

The bitterness of the cold is exacerbated by the knowledge that it is a beautiful sunny morning down in Boulder. Wetmore, however, is not about to change their plan to make life more comfortable. On the way out, a stiff wind makes Mags ridiculously difficult. Forty-five minutes after the men head out, the sky opens, and it starts snowing. Goucher was intending to do twenty miles with Friedberg and Sev this morning, but the cold prevents his sore muscles from loosening up, so he stops after 18. The pounding from the Shootout and Magnolia's hills leave him "just feeling trashed."

Wetmore looks over some results as he leans against his truck after the run. The guys come by crowding around, looking over one another's shoulders, anxious to evaluate the numbers over which Wetmore pores. Arkansas has won the Cowboy Jamboree, beating a good Dodge City Kansas Community College team that the Junior Varsity runners will meet later this season at Ft. Hays. Big 12 rival Oklahoma State also looks solid, running third there. The story of the day, though, is the performance of Julius Mwangi of Butler at the Notre Dame Invite in South Bend, Indiana. He crushed the field and stamped himself as a contender for the National title along with Goucher, Abdi Abdirahman of Arizona, and Bernard Lagat of Washington State.

No one stays to banter for long. It is too cold, and the guys hitch a ride back to campus as soon as they can. Elmuccio is the exception. He hangs around until the others have left so that he can ask Wetmore if he is going to Pre-Nationals. Wetmore informs him that Berkshire is going in his stead as a reward for all the hard work he has done. Elmuccio did beat Berkshire fair and square at the Shootout, so he is rightfully disappointed that he will not be making the trip to Lawrence. But Wetmore's decision to run Berkshire is also a sign from Wetmore that he still has confidence in him despite yesterday's sub-par performance. Will Wetmore's trust in him be enough to restore Berkshire's faith in himself?

Welcome, Captains Reese and Burroughs

As the men and women gather round the stretching circle, Wetmore passes around a few pencils and some scraps of paper so that the runners can vote for this year's captains. Wetmore says, "Traditionally the captains are upperclassman, but not always. You've been around here long enough, if you think someone younger is uniquely qualified, you can vote for them." Reese was captain a year ago, so it is logical that he will be reelected. He is an accomplished All-American, well liked by all, and he is the social ringleader as well. At CU, it is a captain's responsibility is to help foster a synergy within the team, and in this regard, he is as good a choice as anyone. There is a smattering of votes for the others, but Reese handily retains his captaincy.

Elsewhere, it may be logical that the swiftest, most talented athlete bears the honor, but Wetmore is happy with the election results. He is glad Goucher is not captain because "he has enough to worry about." Wetmore is also pleased that fifth-year senior Heather Burroughs has won the women's captainship. She is the workhorse of the team, and she sets a fine example with her tenacity. As demonstrated by his decision to bring Berkshire to Pre-Nationals, Wetmore likes to reward those who toil hard. Burroughs fits the bill, "although," Wetmore says, "she'll be the most reluctant captain in the world."

He announces the results of the vote in typical underhanded Wetmore fashion: "Lots of people got votes on the men's side. Everyone got one vote, Reese got two." "Come on," jokes J-Bird, "no one voted for Schafer." "That's not true," Wetmore replies, "I saw one with girl's handwriting. She crossed out Burroughs and wrote Schafer." Everyone laughs and Wetmore gets them back on track. "Let's go, let's go! Captain Reese, get these guys into shape! Captain Burroughs, let's go!"

The sign the coaching staff made for the Shootout will not win the blue ribbon at the county fair, but it was effective. Wetmore arrived at his office yesterday to find an elderly gentleman waiting outside Balch. "Are you the track coach?" he asked Wetmore. "Oh God," thought Wetmore, "whose house did we throw a rock at now?" But the gentleman was not there to admonish his team. The gentleman continued, "I saw that sign for the CU cross country race. Now, I don't follow running and I've never been to a track meet in my life, but I wanted to tell you that guy Goucher is really something. I've never seen anything like it in my life. He runs like an antelope."

Goucher does not feel like an antelope today. His left IT band is sore and the insertion to his hamstring on his right leg is acting up again. Thankfully, today's workout is just a neuromuscular exercise designed to generate some turnover and get his legs feeling responsive. The runners are doing 300's around the perimeter of Kitt, jogging a little over 500 meters for the recovery. "We're doing something faster than race pace," Wetmore says. "I want to do something fast, but you can't do too much or you'll be complaining of soreness in your legs. The recovery is steady, between steady and easy. This is a neuromuscular workout, if you want to make it a little aerobic you can, but the main thing is going hard on the repeats."

It is an absolutely gorgeous afternoon, the kind of day that lured Wetmore here from New Jersey in 1991. "You make less money here and you pay a lot of rent," he says, "but all those people in Connecticut, making all that money, you can't buy them this."

Despite his ills, Goucher rolls along, and by the fifth 300 he is already about to pass a pack of freshmen women. "Here's Goucher," Wetmore says as Goucher passes, "about to devour this group." Despite the heady results from around the country this weekend, Goucher still looks so strong it seems inconceivable that he will get a race at Pre-Nationals. Of this, Wetmore is confident. He says unequivocably, "Nobody will be near him. He'll win by 30 seconds." On Goucher's next time around Wetmore calls out to him, using a phrase that will be oft repeated in the coming weeks. "Make a movie in your mind," he says, "make a movie in your mind." He needs Goucher to visualize winning now, in practice, for his proclamation to bear fruit.

The main pack rolls behind Goucher. Penciled to run 50–52, they drop 48's. To no one's surprise, Sev and Friedburg push the recovery jog and start each interval a few steps early in order to gain an advantage on the group's kickers.

Despite the Varsity pack's brisk recovery pace, Ruhl, Slattery, and the Mooch, the three Jersey boys, have moved ahead of their hapless Colorado counterparts to join the front pack. Slattery and Elmuccio have been dueling it out on each 300 with Ruhl right behind them. The Mooch is definitely making a statement. Seeing Elmuccio run well, Wetmore again justifies his decision to bring Berkshire. He says, "Wes busted his ass to make that team. He's been running 100-mile weeks and he had one bad race. I said to Mooch, 'Look, you beat him again and it's an easy decision. You've beat him once, ever.'"

Mooch and Slattery waste no time taking charge of the first group. Slattery busts to the front on the ninth interval, tearing down the straight. After a moment's hesitation, the Mooch weaves through the pack and gets up on his shoulder. It is a full-scale pissing match, and neither of them are about to concede any turf. The pack hangs onto the dueling duo, knowing they have fourteen repeats while the Jersey boys are only assigned twelve.

On the twelfth interval, Napier decides he has had enough of the young bucks' antics. Napier runs right on Slattery's shoulder and starts screaming at him, turning his head and looking him right in the face. "COME ON SLATTERY, COME ON SLATTERY!" Napier is visibly pissed, and Slattery does not respond; he only inches up the pace. The verbal jousting leaves the door open for the Mooch, who tears by on the left of the duo to cross the finish ahead of Napier and Slattery.

The coaches do nothing to discourage the competition, and the three runners insist it is all in good fun. "I was just messing with him," Napier says. "Usually freshman year you try to go after it on the last one. But I talked to him, and it's all in good fun."

The Mooch denies that he tried to make a statement out here this afternoon. "I just feel good right now. Tuesday is the day I like to run hard, more than any other day." Then he adds with a straight face, "I'm not racing for two weeks anyway."

Slattery has his own rationale: he is sick of getting killed all the time in practice. "This is the only thing nobody can beat me in, this workout." The Mooch may have something to say about that.

Old J-Bird Johnson, meanwhile, looks smooth in the third pack. He is visibly leaner than in late August, and he confirms that he is down from 155 pounds to 142. Despite his good performance on Saturday, when he was CU's 10th man, he remains nonchalant about his expectations; he has none, for cross country. "If I run three PR's this year, I'll be super psyched." He has a desire not necessarily to win, but to better himself. To be better than he ever has in his last year of competition.

Tessman finishes in the middle of the lead pack. He is anxious about Saturday's race, and he is not happy about a workout he feels has spiraled out of control. "It wasn't a good workout today. We ran 48 seconds. We took the workout in our own hands and somehow decided 50–52 seconds was not fast enough. It would have been easy, but I think it was supposed to be that way. But, whatever, I did the workout. I could have gone slower, I guess no one wanted to go slower today."

Reese also thinks they ran too hard. He says, "I was dragging ass at 48.2. But I was alright. We have an easy day tomorrow: Mesa Trail to Eldorado Springs." This will be the first easy Wednesday this season. It was not originally planned, but Wetmore has taken stock of his men, and he knows they are hurting. Wetmore says, "Sev's got something sore, Gouch has got something sore, maybe we ought to read the handwriting on the wall."

As they wrap up the workout, less than a week from Pre-Nationals, Wetmore reflects on their chances. "When we lost Bat," he says, "that was a big blow. But I gotta feeling the Big Three [Stanford, Arkansas, and Oregon] are all missing somebody. I haven't seen [Michael] Power of Arkansas, or [Jonathan] Riley of Stanford. We'll know where we stand in five days." He catches Reese's attention before he jogs off, "All right, Captain Reese, make sure they don't overeat tonight."

It's in God's Hands

Slattery and Tessman dropped by Wetmore's office to bullshit with him last night after practice. Once there, Wetmore offered Tessman some good advice for Saturday's race. "If you can get to four miles feeling good, then people will be doing the skeleton dance there." But how can Tessman ascertain if he is feeling good? "Do it by sensory data," Wetmore tells him. "It's never wrong . . . Respiration tells you everything."

The team has yet to do any anaerobic work this season, so chances are they will not be running as fast this weekend as they will at season's end. Without any anaerobic work, the runners have to be more careful about getting into oxygen debt early than other teams that may have done some anaerobic work in order to be sharper for this race. They will also be running at a faster clip at sea level then they are used to running here, which makes it even more imperative that they go out cautiously. Knowing this, Wetmore always instructs his runners at this point in the season to go out slowly, and attack from behind. Because many runners go out too fast, regardless of their conditioning, it has proven to be a very successful style of racing. "We want to be holding back, holding back, holding back." Wetmore instructs Tessman. "Then when we get to the ponds [at four miles], we start moving."

The meet will offer CU a good chance to test some of their primary competition at Nationals, but neither Oklahoma State nor Arkansas will be there. But, there are two other teams besides Stanford that concern Wetmore. The Matt Davis–led University of Oregon Ducks and the Abdul Aldinzani–led NC State Wolfpack. The storied Oregon program is in the midst of a coaching change with Bill Dellinger retiring at the end of the year. Martin Smith, the former Wisconsin coach, is replacing Dellinger. Wetmore comments: "Sadistically, I hope there's turmoil over there [Oregon] and that Stanford and Arkansas have lost a guy so that we'll be on even ground again." As for the Wolfpack, "They're good, and they'll show it this weekend. They're the hot team in the country."

Even without Bat, Tessman does not think CU is in a position to need someone to go down on another squad for them to pull out a victory this weekend. "I think we're gonna win. I really do. We might not this week, but that doesn't matter." Already, Tessman understands the beauty of Wetmore's system. It is designed to make you run well at a specific time. It is a system built on faith, because you cannot panic if you are not racing as fast as you can during the season. But Wetmore has the results from each cross country season he has been in Boulder to prove that it works. In years past they have always made a significant improvement from Pre-Nationals to NCAA's . . .

Wetmore wears new Nike Zoom Air Lites this afternoon. All of the gear he receives is a big change from his days at Seton Hall University. "I didn't get shit when I was at the Hall. I got maybe one pair of shoes a year. But that's what it was like before we got the Nike contract here . . . That's the one aspect of our program that's really Rolls Royce now." He pauses, and then adds, "It's amazing, we live in a culture of shoes."

Wetmore needs the psychological boost the new shoes could give him because he is *hurting* from his own training. "I run all out every Sunday. Not this crybaby LSD stuff for this old dinosaur. Given that I ran a twelve-mile race on Sunday, eight 200's Tuesday, and 84 minutes yesterday when I usually do 65, there's a great likelihood I'll be a bag of shit today."

Some of his guys feel like a bag of shit themselves. Thankfully, they are assigned a 70-minute easy run from the school across the Mesa Trail that runs beneath the Flatirons to Eldorado Springs. Everyone is in a group, and the guys are excited because CU alum Alan Culpepper has shown up to run with them.

What Wetmore did not know is that the Boulder Forestry Department lit a fire in the woods east of the Mesa Trail this afternoon. Once on the trail, everyone is forced to run with their T-shirts covering their mouths for a half mile as they run through smoke moving up at them. It is enough to get them riled up.

But that is not the end of it. Wetmore also miscalculated the distance of the run. They reach the Mesa Trailhead in 67 minutes, and Wetmore has instructed Severy, Friedberg, and Goucher to cross the road and run to the end of the Dowdy Draw trail. The easy 70-minute run turns into a 1:52 minute misadventure.

Waiting for them with the van at run's end, JD can tell Goucher is pissed. He explains, "You could tell Goucher was grouchy from a half mile away. He was behind the other two a little bit. He wouldn't be behind if he wasn't grouchy." Goucher climbs into the van wordlessly before letting loose a minute later. "I don't think it's a great fucking idea to run two hours three days before Pre-Nationals," he says angrily.

JD is not overly concerned. "Fuck 'em," he says. "They should've known when they got to the place [Mesa Trailhead] in an hour seven. I tried to cut 'em off but I missed 'em. I don't think they ran that many miles anyway. They were going slow. Ah, it'll keep 'em honest this weekend."

Severy is more lighthearted about the fiasco than Goucher. "Oh well," he says, "I guess it's just in God's hands." An agnostic if not an atheist, Severy was in Wetmore's office this afternoon when Wetmore received a call from a parent wishing them luck over the weekend and reminding them that, no matter the outcome, "It's in God's hands." "Yep," Wetmore replied with a grin, "it's in God's hands." Sitting across from Wetmore, Severy started cracking up. Like Wetmore, Severy has faith— in hard work.

Wetmore is a little less cavalier about the goof than JD, but he, too, is not overly concerned. Again, he will have to make a slight adjustment in their training. "So we go to Pre-Nationals a little less rested than I intended. We'll do a little less today, a little less tomorrow. We'll be a little less rested than I intended, it's okay now."

Biding Time

With the exception of Arkansas and Oklahoma State, all the perennial-players for Nationals are here. The course looks fabulous, with gigantic ten-foot statues of former Kansas running legends like Olympic 10k champ Billy Mills and miler Wes Santee perched around the course. As CU arrived in their van yesterday, the first visible statue they saw was that of Jim Ryun. Seeing the immortalized champions was enough to get them all jacked about today.

The women's race went off first this morning with blue skies overhead and balmy 70 degree weather, and CU finished a disappointing tenth. Wetmore has but a few minutes to get their impressions of the race before transferring any knowledge he has gained to the men. The men have finished their warm-up jog and are gathering by the van in the makeshift parking lot behind the course. Wetmore addresses his runners while they stretch in silence. "The women's team felt like they went out too slow, so you might want to push it *a little bit* at about two and a quarter, two and a half miles. But don't forget, the women only had three miles to solve their problems, and you have five."

The course is narrow at points, only a couple feet wide, especially mid-race. This will test their patience, and their race tactics. Batliner takes pictures of his teammates while they stretch. He has made the trip to view the course so he can "make a movie in his mind" before Nationals. He will not run today, but he plans on toeing the starting line on November 23rd.

Tessman talks to a teammate as Wetmore gives Severy some last-minute counsel.

There is no look of worry or tension on the runners' faces as they pin the numbers onto their jerseys, and only the loquacious Berkshire breaks the silence. But as they switch into their spikes, Goucher has a funny look on his face. His spikes feel tight, and he asks Roybal to check his spikes to see if they have not mistakenly switched pairs. Sure enough, Roybal is wearing Goucher's spikes that are a half size larger than his size ten's. Wetmore just shakes his head and laughs at the snafu. He sarcastically tells Goucher, "Why don't you wear a ten and a ten and a half? That'll be good."

Wetmore returns to offering some last-minute counsel to his guys. He is concerned about Berkshire keeping a calm mind out there. "Relax and release on the back hills," he tells him. "You've never been in a race like this. They're gonna go out in 4:35, so be cool." Berkshire nods his approval, and his brow tightens in concentration as he listens.

"Ronald, 5:05's is about right. You other guys, it's about the same. Five minutes to 5:05. Gouch, 4:48's. Ponce, 5:05's. Brock 5 to 5:05's." Severy chats with Batliner while Wetmore gives his instructions, and Wetmore is annoyed by his inattentiveness. He turns to him and says, "We got about five minutes to go till we race, let's get to business please."

"Reese, about 5 to 5:05's and just respond to the race. Maybe work a little harder up here around mile two, you can get pinched off down there [around mile three when the course narrows]."

The men head to the starting line for a couple of strides before the gun. They are in a box on the left side of the starting line—as good a place as any on the line. The University of Montana huddles a couple of boxes down to the left in front of the starting line, and offers a scary cheer. "Motivate! Motivate! Oh, ah, gonna kill somebody! Oh, ah, gonna kill somebody!" Wetmore looks at them and says, "Good, good, that oughta do it." Batliner laughs and adds, "Man, I didn't know we were gonna have to contend with that!"

Wetmore catches Friedburg's eye as he walks back to the starting line, laughing with Berkshire. "You stay comfortable. You've never been in a race like this. Be calm minded, Iceberg. Let's go. It's a skill you gotta learn. There's 300 guys. You stay calm and do what you gotta do."

He raises his voice a notch so they can all hear him as he stands behind them on the line. They are facing the course now, and the starter has marched out into the middle of the fairway. Arizona is the closest contender to them on the line. "Keep an eye on those in red and blue [Arizona]. Keep them at a comfortable distance, but let them go."

The gun sounds. As the runners head out of sight a half mile from the start, CU lags in last, as is their custom. In the mayhem, a runner falls in front of Friedberg and tucks himself into a fetal position to protect himself from the onslaught. The Iceberg sees him catch a spike in the head. The runner does not get up.

Goucher is the exception. He heads out with the lead pack, which has already dropped eleven seconds behind Butler's Julius Mwangi at the mile. Wasting no time putting his mark on the race, Mwangi hits the mile in 4:27. Lagat of Washington State, Arizona's Abdirahman and Utah's Simonich race alongside Goucher as Stanford's Hauser twins lead the chase pack.

Goucher did not want to go out so fast, but he was afraid to let Mwangi get too far ahead. Two and half miles into the race, Goucher rolls hard to catch him. Behind him, Oregon's Matt Davis moves up along with Stanford's Hauser twins. Back in the pack, the CU guys' fears are being realized—the course is too tight for them to pass. Ponce and the Iceberg accept the dilemma and settle in, hoping to start moving up in a mile.

When Ponce and Friedberg move, they pass people in packs. They are forced to run unevenly, sprinting around groups on the course's edge before passing them so they do not get forced off the course with a well-placed elbow in one of the narrower sections.

Severy runs ahead of Ponce and Friedberg. He employs the same tactics to move up, but he is biding time until Billy Mills Hill, the steep climb that challenges the competitors at mile four. He knows that no one can climb quite like he can.

A large crowd awaits the leaders at Billy Mills Hill. When the runners had disappeared into the back of the course for several miles, Mwangi

A straining Mwangi leads in mid-race.

led comfortably. Now, when Mwangi arrives, Goucher runs with him, stride for stride. No one else is in sight; it is a two-man race. The crowd responds to their arrival, and everyone, it seems, is pulling for Goucher. "Come on, Goucher! Let's go, Goucher!" The cheers energize him. Goucher rides the crowd's cheers into the lead, putting ten feet between him and Mwangi as they crest the hill.

All fall in practice, Goucher has been indomitable once in the lead. He relishes putting the hurt on his competitors when he is in control. Batliner, watching at Billy Mills Hill, says as Goucher passes, "It's over." But Mwangi has other plans. As the spectators dash madly to the finish line, Goucher and Mwangi again become visible. With only a half mile left, Mwangi retakes the lead and improbably gaps Gouch. He extends his lead to the finish, and he raises his hands in delirious exultation and looks towards the heavens just moments after crossing the line. He celebrates like this through the chute, and Goucher does not miss a thing. It is a display he is unaccustomed to seeing.

Soon after Goucher crosses the line, the rest of the field starts to stream in, and Stanford looks great. Oregon's Davis finishes between the Hauser twins in sixth. Soon thereafter, Jason Balkman crosses the line in fifteenth place. He is the third Stanford finisher. Colorado has yet to get in their second. Severy chugs in in twentieth to stop the bleeding. But behind him, Stanford's four and five battle Ponce and Friedberg down the finishing stretch, and the Cardinal's Jennings and Weldon prevail to round out the Cardinal's scoring with an impressive 80 points. Ten seconds and eight places behind Friedberg, Reese completes a valiant race in 40th place to round out CU's scoring. Tessman finishes 54th in the sixth position, with Roybal right behind him in 57th.

CU's five-man score is 120, good enough on this day to earn them third behind the

Mwangi and Goucher battle up Billy Mills Hill.

Cardinal and Oregon. Scoring only 80 points, Stanford looks dominant, but Oregon finishes only seventeen points ahead of CU with a score of 103. Immediately following the race, the emotions of the CU runners are wide-ranging. No one is thrilled with his performance, but while Goucher is at times irate at his second-place finish, Berkshire is crushed by his second consecutive poor showing and his first poor showing in a race of this magnitude. He finishes out of sight in 170th and Valenti is even further back in 210th. They do not need Wetmore to tell them that they have run themselves off the Varsity squad today.

Wetmore is more encouraged by their third place showing than his guys. "They're alright for now. They've got to understand how unready we are to mix it up on this day. We've done no anaerobic work, we're really race rusty, and we're tired. We raced Saturday, ran Mags Sunday, and ran 90 minutes on Wednesday. They're not well rested at all. But if they're going to panic, I'll have to remember that and give up that rate of training in the future."

Goucher does not panic. He ran 23:54, or 4:48 a mile, just as Wetmore planned. He is not upset with how he competed; he is more displeased with Mwangi's glee. "That guy was celebrating," he says through pursed lips, "a little too much." Regardless, Goucher felt "like trash" the whole way. "It sucked," he says. "I didn't have it. I don't have any anaerobic capacity right now. When I'm usually at my best, in the last mile, I didn't have shit. My legs were tired and they felt heavy."

His heavy training load has affected his legs and his mind. He continues, "My head was working against me. I was already condemning myself before the end. I'm training so hard right now, it's hard to get motivated. I mean, I doubt that guy did what I did last week."

Like the spectators, Goucher thought he had the race won when he passed Mwangi at the top of the climb. When Mwangi came back at him, he had nothing. "At the top of the hill, I was tired, and I thought, 'This is it.' But I just didn't gap him enough. When he came up it was like, 'Oh, hello,' you know. I thought I'd get him there, but up here [he points to his head] my legs were yelling at me, 'You're sore, you're weak.'"

Goucher feels their meeting at NCAA's will be a different story. "I had a bad race today and I was second. When it comes to that point in the race later on, then we'll have some fun. We got six weeks. See what happens then. He was jumping around like he's the national champ." "I'm not worried," he continues, "I'll destroy him when I'm ready. I'm a little worried because I'm not too worried about it [losing], but that's because I'm training so hard. The fire's a little low right now, you know."

He does not plan on running the NCAA's much differently than he ran today. He says, "I may push the hills a little more. I ran conservatively up the hills and I may need to run a little harder. But I probably won't change anything. The main change is just a matter of being ready to run. I did everything right, I just didn't feel well enough to continue on with that. We got six weeks."

His supporting cast passed their first big test as well. Wetmore is particularly pleased with the performances of Friedberg and Ponce, who were racing against a national-caliber field for the first time. Like Goucher, Ponce knows how unprepared they were to race today. Next time, the battle with Stanford may turn out a little differently. Of his race he says, "I followed Sev for a while and we were running on the outside of the course. I just wanted to go with Stanford's four and five. They out-kicked me, but next time it will be a 10k so . . ." His voice trails off into the distance. With another mile and a quarter, Ponce will look for his strength to give him the edge against Stanford's middle-distance runners.

As they board the van to head back to the hotel, the men are sub-dued. They lost to Stanford and Oregon, but they managed to beat Ari-zona and NC State, among others. Next time they come here, they will have more time to catch people in the extra mile and a quarter who made too many mistakes early on. Ponce alone passed an estimated fif-teen people in the last 1000 meters today. He hopes to double that fig-ure in the last mile six weeks from Monday.

Certainly, other teams are training as hard as CU is now. Georgetown finished in seventh place behind a strong eleventh place showing by senior Justin McCarthy. Wet-more's college coach and longtime Hoya mentor Frank "Gags" Gagliano thinks the ante has been upped in re-cent years, and that all teams are training more like they used to in the seventies and in Georgetown's case, the early nineties. "In the last couple of years," Gags says afterwards, "some of the Old Timers, some of us may have stopped working them hard.

Severy charges up Billy Mills Hill.

But I tell you what, I'm going back to it. You can't do that [train with low volume and be successful]. Back with [Pete] Sherry, [John] Trautman, and [Steve] Holman, we were busting it every day. Hey, I'm going back to that."

McCarthy's result is an example of the dividends such training can produce. Says Gags, "He was a 9:18 high school two miler. He got eleventh today. All summer he was devoted to running 100 mile weeks. He was completely devoted to running, you know what I'm saying?"

Sev ices his knee before boarding the van. As expected, he passed about a dozen guys in the last mile, but he wanted more. "I was 21st," he says [he was actually 20th]. "Man that's awful." Sev, too, figures to benefit tremendously from the added distance in six weeks. His face brightens as he sees Wetmore. Sev says to him, "Mark, there's more evidence that God's in control. There was an icepack in the van." He laughs about the aches and pains now plaguing him. He turns to his good friend Batliner, "Bat, get healthy, I need someone to take my place." He does not know it now, but Batliner will remember these words for the rest of his life.

BOB TIMMONS INVITATIONAL

PLACE	NAME	UNIVERSITY	CLASS	TIME
1.	Julius Mwangi	Butler	Sr.	23:47.5 CR
2.	Adam Goucher	Colorado	Sr.	23:54.37
3.	Abdi Abdirahman	Arizona	Sr.	24:33.53
4.	Bernard Lagat	Washington State	Jr.	24:42.55
5.	Brad Hauser	Stanford	Sr.	24:46.11
6.	Matt Davis	Oregon	Sr.	24:47.65
7.	Brent Hauser	Stanford	Sr.	24:49.70
8.	Jeff Simonich	Utah	Sr.	24:56.85
9.	Ricardo Santos	Iona	Sr.	25:01
10.	Steve Fein	Oregon	Jr.	25:03.03
20.	Chris Severy	Colorado	Sr.	25:24.42
30.	Oscar Ponce	Colorado	Jr.	25:37.49
32.	Mike Friedberg	Colorado	So.	25:38.32
40.	Tom Reese	Colorado	Sr.	25:48
54.	Brock Tessman	Colorado	Sr.	25:56.56
57.	Ron Roybal	Colorado	Jr.	25:59.04
170.	Wes Berkshire	Colorado	Jr.	27:07.63
210.	Chris Valenti	Colorado	So.	27:40.26

A Day of Rest—for Some

The team arrived late last evening from Kansas City. They were exhausted, yet more excited about their performance at Pre-Nationals than they had been directly following the race. There are six weeks until Nationals, and they like their prospects of upsetting Stanford and winning it all when they are sharp and rested. Wetmore is giving the team a welcome day of repose—between an hour and an hour thirty on their own. The long run will not be forgotten, however; it is simply postponed until tomorrow.

Despite Wetmore's instructions, not all the runners run easy today. Friedberg joins Severy for an "easy" eighty-minute run up the road from Sev's cabin at Walker Ranch. Nearing the final climb on a relentlessly hilly run, they spot a mountain biker ahead. Sev starts hammering, and they motor wordlessly until they catch and pass the biker. When they finish, Severy apologizes for the brisk pace. "Sorry about that, I just had to show him how you climb this hill. I thought we should pass him."

This is typical Severy: determined, unassuming, and unfailingly polite. His demeanor would suggest that he is placid and mellow. But underneath that exterior burns the fire of a fierce competitor. Zeke Tiernan, his former Aspen High and Colorado teammate, likes to recount how in high school, when someone biked past them as they biked to school, Sev would hammer. Characteristic of Sev, he would deny he was racing. He would tell Tiernan, "I just wanted to ride."

Later this evening, while relaxing at his sister Robin's apartment in Boulder, Sev calls Reese to see if he wants to go grab dinner and catch a flick. Reese cannot make it, and Sev decides that he had better go to his cabin anyway to get some work done. They talk about the rest of the season, and Sev tells Reese that he is going to do everything to the "T" to be as fit as can be on November 23rd: extra strides, extra morning runs, and no second helpings of dessert (the biggest challenge of the three). In addition, he pledges to start bicycling down to school from his cabin instead of riding his motorcycle. He has been riding his motorcycle without a license or registration, so he promised his mother that he would commute to school in some other way.

Only Sev would even consider riding his bike to and from school every day. The ride from school to his cabin is an extremely arduous 2500 foot climb that switchbacks relentlessly to the top of Flagstaff

Mountain. Pedaling hard, an elite cyclist can scale the mountain in thirty minutes. The thought, however, of doing this each day, *after practice*, with a backpack full of books, in the dark, is absurd. Reese questions the wisdom of doing this, but Sev reasons, "It'll get me extra fit, and it won't be hard because I'll be pedaling easy." While cycling up Flagstaff would undoubtedly be physically taxing after a hard training session, Sev is certainly capable of doing it. For as good of a runner as Severy is, he is perhaps an even more talented cyclist.

In high school, Severy spent his summers cycling competitively in open races in the western United States. He sheepishly admits winning over $2,000 on the roads from his sophomore through senior years against more seasoned competitors. His success as a cyclist prompted Mark Barbour, his high school cross country coach, to suggest he quit running to further his cycling. Sev almost did, but the camaraderie of cross country running and the dirty tactics often employed in bike racing kept him on track.

On one occasion, in a cycling race the summer before his senior year at Aspen High, a competitor sprayed Cytomax into his spokes in a race, making it difficult to switch gears. Incidents like this dampened his enthusiasm for the sport. Yet, such occurrences were counterbalanced by astonishing successes; perhaps none greater than his victory in the amateur portion of the Mt. Evans Hill Climb in Idaho Springs as a 15-year-old high school sophomore.

He raced the Mt. Evans Hill Climb, a ride that starts at over 7000 feet and finishes at over 14,000 feet, clad in a T-shirt and shorts. He was then, and still is, "anti-gear," and he loved "how all the other cyclists would be pissed when some kid in a T-shirt and shorts beat them." He was there, he said, "to race, not to win a fashion contest." Nobody thought much of his chances there, yet he recounts with a grin how as he reached the summit in the lead, spectators shouted to one another, "Hey! Look! It's a munchkin on a Merlin beating Mark Allen!" He beat legendary triathlete Mark Allen by two minutes, and his time would have placed him 20th among the pros. The following year he finished third in 1:55, a performance that would have placed him ninth among the pros.

His climbing ability translated to another arena as well—snowshoe racing. He started snowshoe racing his sophomore year in high school, and by his junior year, "I was up there with all the top guys. I never beat [renowned altitude runner and snowshoer Matt] Carpenter, but I got a reputation as a hill runner in the state; that's how Mark [Wetmore] knew me."

Be it snowshoeing, cycling, or running, Severy has the temperament and the aerobic capacity to make him a climber non-pareil. He says, "When people are running uphill breathing hard, I can rest. I don't know why." He cannot wait to run at NCAA's when he is rested. Such a hilly, inconsistent, up-and-down course throws many runners for a loop. The course is similar in this respect to the 1996 NCAA course in Tucson, Arizona, where he finished a career-high seventeenth. He says, "No one liked it because it was so ridiculous, but I loved it because I am a fan of all things ridiculous."

Climbing, however, is only half the story. Sev, as Wetmore aptly surmises, "doesn't comprehend the concept of moderation." Everything Sev does, from studying to dumping mammoth quantities of ketchup over his eggs and hash browns, he does full bore. There is little doubt that he descends all hills, no matter the mode of transportation, with reckless abandon. It is a skill he has learned from cycling and yet another of his athletic pursuits—downhill skiing. He learned to ski at an early age from his geologist-turned-ski instructor father. While he did not ski much with his father, who "was always teaching," he mastered downhill skiing on Aspen's renowned slopes. Whether cycling, skiing, or running, Severy knows only one way to descend a mountain—as fast as possible. And if someone gets down in ten minutes, he will be damned if he is not getting down in nine.

Sev's competitiveness and recklessness are famed among his teammates. Last fall, while at preseason camp in Winter Park, some of his teammates went to an attraction called an Alpine slide—a concave, concrete track that winds down a mountain like the bobsled track in the Winter Olympics. A rider lies down on the sled feet first, and a lever that lies between the legs is used to brake. As Reese explains it:

> We were up at cross camp in Frazier, right outside of Winter Park at the YMCA of the Rockies. We spent a day hanging out in Winter Park, and at a ski resort there there is this alpine slide. We all said we were going to time ourselves from the top to the bottom. Afterwards, we go and compare times, and mine was a second faster than the Dog's. He was like, "Oh, [grumbling] I was too careful, this time I'm not using a brake at all." So, we're waiting for him at the bottom, when we see him running down with the sled without any skin. He'd been going so fast that he just went out of control and fell off. So then he got cleaned up, barely, I mean his skin was just gone, and he went up and did it again and beat the record.

Before leaving his sister Robin's apartment, Severy gives his mother a quick call, and tells her about the race and how proud he is of the team. They were beaten by Stanford and Oregon, but he tells her that CU will be prepared to give them a run for their money at Nationals. The last thing he says to her is that Goucher, "got beat by some fuzzy, freaking foreigner," but that he is going to get him at Nationals.

Soon thereafter, JD spots Sev and Robin eating dinner at The Sink, a popular student eatery on the Hill. JD is there getting dinner with Cate Guiney, a stellar distance recruit from New Jersey, and Robin and Sev invite JD and Cate to join them. JD later laughs when he recalls that the newly svelte Sev was drinking a beer with his pizza. "JD," Sev said, "I just *had* to have this beer. Besides, it's twenty percent off here on Sunday night. How could you *not* come here!"

After dinner, Sev said goodbye to JD and departed to his cabin. No one could have possibly fathomed that on Monday morning, Christopher Severy would be dead.

Black Monday

Goucher ran seventeen miles in 1:40 early this morning so that he could go give a speech to the high school team that his best friend Tim Catalano coaches in Denver. Giving these speeches is something Goucher does several times a year, and he gets a kick out of it.

He is scheduled to leave from his apartment around 3:30. But when it is time to leave, Goucher sits slouched on his sofa barechested and in jean shorts. He covers his eyes with his left hand and his body heaves as he bawls quietly. He composes himself before looking up a minute later. "Sev," he says, choking up with emotion, "is dead. He died in a bike crash this morning coming down Flagstaff."

Wetmore called him a quarter hour earlier to tell him the news that he had received from the police earlier this afternoon. He tells Goucher moments before telling the team at a team meeting that had been previously arranged to discuss other matters. Unaware of the meeting, Batliner wandered into the field house a few minutes late, but he will never forget what he saw:

> *I came late, and they were all walking down the stairs. I'm walking towards the track office and I turned around. My first thought was, "Fuck, we had a team meeting and I didn't know about it." But then I see Lindsay Arendt, and her face is all red, and then five other girls look the same. Then I see Oscar and Ronald, arm in arm, holding on for dear life. I didn't even move. I just watched everyone go past me, then Ronald told me.*

All the team knows is that while Sev was coming down the mountain this morning from his cabin, he lost control of his mountain bike, and crashed into a tree. The force of the impact killed him. A police officer discovered Sev's body earlier this morning when he stopped to investigate a stranded bike on the side of the road. As he approached the bike, he saw Sev, already dead, lying amid the trees.

After telling the team what happened, Wetmore dismissed them, and everyone split off into different directions, unsure what to do next. Some, like Reese, went for a run. He went out to the Tank, and he alternately sprinted, walked, and jogged while crying, screaming, and cursing. Then he went to the Hotel Boulderado where Sev and Reese's good friend Clint Wells works to tell him the news.

This evening, the men's and women's teams, along with Wetmore and JD, convene at Robbie, Batliner, and Roybal's place to comfort and console one another. People bring photos of Sev, and everyone shares stories, laughs, and cries. The gathering serves a different purpose for everyone there, but the underlying sentiment is one of love—for Sev, and each other. It is an unspoken agreement; we are here for each other. Afterwards, Batliner, for one, feels a little better. He says, "Everyone who showed up left in a little better shape. It was helpful to talk about the good stuff, laugh, and celebrate his life even though he just passed. It helped me a lot. I was really pissed that he was gone."

It is hard to believe that just seven weeks ago the world was there for the taking. At that moment, everyone, says Batliner, "realized we had a lot of potential. For the first three weeks, it seemed like everyone was getting better. Tommy was getting better, Friedberg was coming out of nowhere, Brock was coming out of nowhere. Everyone was clicking from day to day." Then Bat went down with injury, then Blondeau, and now this.

Were it not for Sev's legacy and everyone's unwavering conviction of what Sev would want them to do, ending the season now would be justifiable. In dealing with their loss, the thought of whether or not to continue has crossed each runner's mind, if just for an instance. But to Batliner, the decision to continue is clear. Late last year, there was some strife on the team, and Batliner remembers Severy's words well. He says, "Last year when we had problems we were having a meeting and Sev raised his hand from the back of the room and said, 'Can we all just shut up and run?' Some people took offense, but that's Chris, all business . . ." Batliner continues, "I've thought about it and I'm of a mind that Sev would like nothing better than for us to get back to work and doing our regimen."

But right now, everyone's thoughts are on Sev, his family, and each other. They will deal with running later. Says Batliner, "Whatever synergy we had, now we have to start over. The whole thing with synergy is every component is a key to the wholeness." But the team is no longer whole, and now they must somehow find a way rebuild the web and carry on.

A Struggle to Understand

The men who will race this weekend are running repeat quarters this afternoon, as scheduled. Before the workout, some of the runners gather in small groups to talk. Reese says he went to the crash site today and found pieces of Sev's helmet scattered in all directions as far as fifteen feet from the tree Chris hit.

The mood is quiet and somber as Wetmore emerges from his office. He tells everyone to sit down. In a strong and sure voice that camouflages his intense grief, he begins, "The qualities we admire here are faith, endurance, and courage. We go back to practicing those values today. If we asked Sev if we should race this weekend, Sev would say, 'No doubt about it.' As I told some of you last night, the route past grief is through it. We're going to go on from here, and go ahead with the business at hand."

For the past 36 hours, the men here have experienced a range of emotions: anger, betrayal, agony, despair. Those seniors who have known Severy intimately for five years are especially struggling. As Wetmore speaks, Goucher and Reese sit next to one another, hands grasping knees, heads bowed, silently sobbing along with most everyone in the field house.

Zeke Tiernan is here to address the team, and he speaks next. He tells them a memorial service for Chris will be held in Aspen on Sunday, and a memorial given by the CU athletic department will probably be held on campus next Tuesday.

Wetmore then steps forward again, and tells his team that there are four layers of support available to them as they sort out their grief. One, the coaching staff. Two, each other. Three, a team psychologist. And four, university psychiatrists.

The psychologist is on hand, and he tells the men that grief is a process. It will affect them and become more poignant for each person at different times—at holidays, on runs, listening to certain songs, seeing different sights. Anything can and will trigger Severy's memory. He stresses that they must remember Sev, "as you should remember him. He achieved a remarkable deal in a short time."

Tiernan has put a Buddhist prayer flag up at the crash site, and after practice some of the men and women are going to see it. But first, there is business to attend to. The Varsity men head out for a jog, and the Bluebirds hit the Creek Path for their warmup to Potts.

JD, Wetmore, and Lorie also run to the track on the Creek Path. It occurs to JD while he runs that the creek never stops moving. "My whole world has stopped," he says, "but the creek, it's still running."

Flowers from coaching staffs around the country—including Arkansas, Texas and Iona—pour into Wetmore from around the country. They only serve to make Wetmore grumpy. But it is as if the coaching fraternity is reaching out, saying, "we know the special bond that develops between coach and athlete, we sympathize with your agony."

The condolences make Wetmore grumpy because the last person he is thinking about is himself. He will deal with his grief on his time. His thoughts are on his athletes. JD's thoughts are also with his athletes. "I'm exhausted," he says on the way to Potts. "I'm completely exhausted. I can't even imagine working out today." But the show must go on.

As the men finish warming up Jen Fazioli strides in front of Wetmore, and he is as demonstrative as he has been all year. "All economy begins in the face and shoulders. All economy begins in the face and shoulders. Pick up the heels! OK, let's go! How do you know you're relaxed? How do you know?" Only a freshman, Fazioli is logging upwards of 80 miles a week in an effort to make the Varsity squad. Wetmore is concerned she is overdoing it, and he pulls her aside as she comes around again. Putting a hand on her shoulder he looks down into her eyes and says, "I don't want to spoil you, OK?" She nods. "Sev didn't know moderation. I don't want that to happen to you, so I'm gonna haunt you about that."

The men are running 68 to 70 second quarters, with a 200-meter jog. It is supposed to be an anaerobic effort, and after four intervals, they do not look like they are hurting enough. As they pass, Wetmore admonishes Schafer and the group, "Come on Schaf, you want to be puking over the fence at the end of this one. Let's make it hurt now, boys! It's time to get tired!"

It works. Schafer is an old-school guy who likes being on the receiving end of a verbal tirade in practice; it fires him up. Schafer looks back at the guys, and says, "Let's tighten it up!" Johnson turns to Crandall before the next one, "Let's hit this one, Zach."

Wetmore's enthusiasm is contagious, but it is not enough to keep some of the guys from falling off the back. JD says to Wetmore, "Those men are hurting at the back of the pack." Wetmore replies, "Good, good."

Ruhl falls off the pack, and Wetmore has him sit one out before jumping in the next one. Soon thereafter, Slattery falls behind on the recovery jog. "Come on Slattery, take the pain, take the pain. Get in there!" But all the coaxing in the world will not help him. He falls off the back on the eighth 400, and walks across the infield to catch his teammates before they take off on the penultimate interval. Wetmore yells to him again, "Come on Steve, this is your area, here on the track, this is your forte!"

Johnson, whose appearance is remarkably similar to Severy's, tears up the last quarter with Elmuccio, and Slattery joins them on the breakaway. Jay Johnson (Jay Johnson!) is imposing his will on the workout. Wetmore is ecstatic. He yells to them as they tear down the backstretch, "Control, control, control. Come on Steve, stay in there. Johnson's back! Jay Johnson's back! He looks like a 3:49 guy," he says to JD, "doesn't he?"

Hair bobbing up and down, Johnson's stride loses some of its bounce as he moves at a quicker clip. Wetmore gets more excited with every step Johnson takes. "You saw him in August, it's incomprehensible!" And yes, in the aftermath of one of the worst days of his life, Jay Johnson, the runner, appears resurrected. Afterwards, Johnson does not talk about his turnaround or his workout today. After all, it is only a workout, and he is too preoccupied with the tragedy to gloat over his improvement.

As the men finish their last interval, Goucher comes around towards the finish line to do some strides starting on the backstretch. Eyes red, he has had to stop intermittently throughout the run to shed some tears. As he passes, Wetmore calls out to him, "Good, good. It's time to start feeling good again. It's time." Teresa Dean, a walk-on from Alaska, starts a stride on the curve and blows by Goucher. As she passes him, Wetmore yells, "Right by, TD, right by, no mercy!" For the first time since everyone learned of Sev's death, people laugh.

The guys head back to campus on their cooldown, and Wetmore also runs back to his office. When he arrives, he collapses into his chair. He takes a deep breath, and, eyes closed, slowly runs his fingers back through his long black hair. For the first time, the only time, Wetmore is a shell of himself. It has taken every ounce of his energy to maintain his spirit on the track. Now, in the seclusion of his office, he looks completely defeated . . .

After practice, JD and Lorie take vans up to the crash site with the men's and women's teams. For many it is their first visit to the fateful turn. Everyone makes their way to the side of the road where Sev crashed. Some stand together, and others sit, silently staring at the tree. The only reminder of Sev are the prayer flags dancing in the subtle breeze.

The crash site itself is not what one would imagine. It is not a hairpin turn that proved too tough to negotiate. Instead, it is a gentle curve that slopes mildly to the left. Here? How could that be? How could that happen? It seems incomprehensible that it happened here; Chris was an expert cyclist, and the turn is quite manageable.

There are skid marks in the dirt in front of the tree. Before he crashed, Sev was most likely riding towards the middle of the road. Then,

The turn.

something must have caused him to quickly change direction, forcing him to skid off the road. Perhaps a car was coming in the other direction and forced him to jerk his bike to avoid a collision. Perhaps there was some gravel on the road and he simply lost control. Perhaps a bug flew into his eye. Perhaps. Perhaps. Perhaps. It is a futile game to play.

Hours pass. The sun goes down, and the evening's chill descends upon the runners. There are over twenty men and women here, and no one is willing to move. The silence—the void—is too much for some. But as they break down the others reach out to comfort them, to hold them, to remind them that, yes, they are not alone.

A memorial to Severy.

In the coming days many people unknown to the team who have cultivated relationships with Chris in other arenas also visit the site. Earlier today, a young bike racer came to the site and just sat there, legs crossed, completely beside himself. Perhaps he had ridden against Chris in a race, or perhaps he had imagined racing Chris in a training ride up Mt. Evans, just him and the munchkin on the Merlin, side by side, attacking the hill.

Some of Severy's professors also make the journey, themselves struggling. As they stand watching where Severy died, many describe how Severy was the best student in class. Oh, to see a student with such a thirst for knowledge! So young, so much potential.

Goucher, makes his way up to the site with his mother to leave some flowers in Sev's memory. By chance, Sev's mother and sister Robin are there when he arrives. Robin and Mrs. Severy recall the message Chris left on the machine about the race, and they laugh. They remember him saying, "Some freaking fuzzy foreigner beat Goucher, but he'll kill that guy next time they race." Mrs. Severy tells Adam's mother, "Just keep Adam running." It is what Sev would have wanted.

Progress

Wetmore gathers the team again before practice and says:

> *We're making progress with the ceremonies for Chris. There will be a cere-*
> *mony on top of Buttermilk Mountain on Sunday. We hope it's a nice day.*
> *On Tuesday at 10 a.m. there will be a ceremony here for Chris. We'll cer-*
> *tainly know Monday. Most of you will be asked to consider the Tuesday*
> *ceremony adequate. Those of you who have known Chris for four years . . .*
> *and want to be there, that's understandable. We'll meet in the morning and*
> *drive up. But, out of respect for Robin and her mother, who over the course*
> *of a year have had to cope with the death of a father and a son, an inti-*
> *mate ceremony in Aspen would be best. Chris's mother is at her last piece*
> *of energy. Please, send no flowers. She's so devastated, she can't even an-*
> *swer the door. If you do plan to go up there [to Aspen], please keep a low*
> *profile. Every hug is agony for her.*

That said, the Varsity runners not competing at Ft. Hays jog the two and a half miles to the Buffalo Ranch for another "Dam" workout. Wetmore knows they are hurting—physically and emotionally—so he asks them only for a hard effort, no watches.

With little fanfare, the runners get to work. Wetmore is quiet today, and the course seems more desolate than usual. For some, the running intensifies the pain, every step a quiet torture. For others, there is solace in performing the endeavor that Sev was so passionate about. And for some, running simply serves as a reminder that Sev is gone.

Goucher runs the dam in 53:00—over a minute better than his previous effort. In his log he writes, *"legs tired/body tired, mind tired, not really in running mood. Run felt pretty easy, didn't feel like I was running hard. Ran 1:15 faster than last time. Thought about him every step (easier today than yesterday)."*

Behind Goucher, Reese runs the course in 54 minutes—a two-minute improvement for him—followed closely by Valenti in 54:30, also a two-minute improvement. Friedberg runs 55 minutes and Berkshire finishes a minute later.

Others are not as successful. Tessman and Roybal slog around the course, gaining nothing from the workout. Each abandons the run with two miles to go. Recognizing all they have been through, Wetmore lets them be. He knows that now is not the time to try to squeeze more out of his athletes.

The men nonchalantly go about their business. As they put on their sweats, they give each other "the shake," a clasp of hands and a knock of fists that says simply, "you are one of us." The shake never meant as much as it does now. As they hold each other's hands and look into each other's eyes, the shake communicates what words cannot.

Impressions from Afar

Batliner is hurting. While his teammates have been able to lean on each other for solace every day in practice, he has had to go at it alone. It has been four weeks since Bat was diagnosed with a stress fracture. On Sunday, he ran for the first time since the injury: 25 minutes around Kitt. He ran with his shirt off in the 80 degree weather, and for the first time since he was condemned with the diagnosis, he again felt . . . free.

As with seemingly every cross-training regimen, his ambition to get after it cycling or swimming has faded with each subsequent day. At first he figured that since he was running roughly eleven hours a week, he would cross-train that much and then some for good measure. But then he got the flu. That triggered his sinuses, so his nose bled when he went swimming. That curtailed his swimming for a week, and then he was finally able to get in a pretty good week of training. Now, having reexperienced the joy of running, his desire to cross-train has diminished even further.

Bat is embarking on an ambitious running schedule to get back. After returning from a stress fracture, a runner normally begins running with some light jogging. But Bat has only five weeks to get ready for Nationals, so he must push the envelope. Tuesday, his second day back, he ran 35 minutes around Kitt with 8 x 300 in the middle. He ran the 300's in 55–57 seconds, or as he terms it, "slow, out-of-shape cross country pace." The good news is that his leg felt good. The bad news is he still had to run in the pool for 45 minutes—"putting my time in." Today he added another ten minutes, running 45 minutes easy with Schafer, again around Kitt.

It is an aggressive plan to get well, but "the doctor understands the urgency better than most. Either I push now, or I don't even bother and rest for indoors." Before Sev's death, he was planning on running again this season. Now, even knowing Sev would want him to compete, he is not sure.

His emotions are constantly changing. Says Batliner, "Every hour, it's completely different." And while he wants to run for Sev, for the most part, "I get this numbness you get when you feel empty. That's how I feel about this whole thing. It's empty, just not quite there." It does not help that while he has been cross-training, he is not nearly as fit as he was before he got injured. Like the others, his training is what gives him confidence, or as he puts it, "my training and fitness govern my mind. My mind is completely reactive to my physical strength and my fitness."

His comeback starts this weekend in Ft. Hays. Earlier this week, Wetmore told him he is going to run three miles at 5:30 pace, but Batliner talked him into rethinking it and letting him run the full five miles. "I'm sure I can handle five miles, real slow like an AT." The key words here for Bat are "real slow." He admits it would be tempting to race all out if he feels good, "but I don't want to get carried away and end up with another injury, even if it doesn't bother my leg. I want to run 5:30 miles, really back-of-the-packing it. Running with the bluebirds and the hack squad, the puppy dogs."

On Tuesday after practice, the seniors had a seniors-only meeting in the gym with Wetmore. They debated whether or not to honor Sev with a symbol of some sort on their uniform. They discussed wearing a patch, and Reese and Goucher suggested wearing armbands with Sev's initials embroidered in them. Reese and Goucher were adamant about doing something, but others, like Jay Johnson, were not so sure.

Wetmore let them debate the issue among themselves before putting in his two cents. "I have 49 percent of the vote," he said, "and you have 51 percent. My feeling is, we don't advertise here at the University of Colorado." He stressed that everyone in the country knows what happened, and he does not feel wearing an armband to commemorate Sev's memory will serve any purpose but to satisfy the expectations of those outside the team.

Goucher was the first to disagree with Wetmore when Wetmore left the field house. He stressed to his teammates not to be swayed by Wetmore. "It's *our* decision," he said, "not Mark's." The seniors could not come to a consensus on the issue, and it remains unresolved.

Batliner has been thinking about it since then, and he concurs with Wetmore. "This whole business about the armband makes me think of what Chris would appreciate, and it's just kick ass, you know, get it done. That's what he was all about."

Sev attacked his activities with a blinding devotion. Says Bat, "He had this ferocity, this tenacity. He threw himself into so many directions at the same time. I don't know anyone whose been able to do that, and so modestly, so quietly."

Bat recalls meeting him for the first time as a freshman when they ran up the highest peak in Colorado, Mt. Elbert. "I met him at Mt. Elbert when we were freshmen. He set the record by eleven minutes, untrained. It was unbelievable. Afterwards, he strides up to me because he's so cordial and soft-spoken. It was almost weird, like 'Whoa, what's his deal, where's he come from?'

"I remember the second run we ever did in Boulder. Me, Goucher, Tommy, Jay Johnson, Sev, and [former teammate] Colby Cohn were talking ourselves up. We were saying, if we just do the work and get the job done for four years, we'll win the national championship when we're seniors. It's funny how it ended up, we've all had such different experiences. Sev would run 120 miles a week, and Tommy would be lucky to get 95. Everyone had different plans going, but we thought . . ." His voice trails off. No one could have imagined it would unfold like this, "It's just what happens, I guess."

Fortunately, Batliner has other passions besides running to turn his energy towards and help him cope with the loss—mainly his paintings and his writing. He is a double-major in English and Fine Arts—an accomplishment in itself considering he was, by his own admission, "a very shitty student in high school." He is excelling in both, with a 3.87 GPA in his majors. He credits not his professors, but Wetmore for transforming him into a diligent student. "I don't know if he knows how much of an effect he's had on me. Most of my accomplishments are in some way inspired by him. Running for sure, but good grades and things like that as well. Somehow he managed to get the idea of being a renaissance man into my brain. You get your run done, then you go get the job done doing something else. He's made me realize my potential."

For him to realize his running potential this season—whatever that may now be—he will have to outsmart his competition. This means biding time, and running a typically conservative CU race at NCAA's like he has seen his teammates run so often. If executed well, Batliner can run a race that transcends itself, that becomes a work of art. He says, "a well-crafted race is one of the most beautiful things you can watch. I've been completely moved by races. [For instance] Alan [Culpepper] winning the 5k [at NCAA's two years ago] was completely unbelievable. We watched it on TV, and he was not a factor until he decided to make himself one with 500 to go. All of a sudden, out of nowhere, he took off. He ran 1:08 for the last 500. It was unreal."

In many ways, a race is analogous to life itself. Once it is over, it can not be re-created. All that is left are impressions in the heart, and in the mind. Two weeks ago Sev had talked to Bat, telling him, "I can't wait for you to get back. It was so good when it was me, you, Zeke [Tiernan], and Clint [Wells]." "He wanted it like it was two years ago," Bat says, reminiscing about the lunch-pail starless crew that exceeded everyone's expectations and took third at NCAA's in Tucson in 1996 without Goucher. "Those were the glory days," says Bat. "We didn't realize it then. We knew something cool was going on, but we couldn't put a finger on it. It takes a couple years to realize how cool it was."

Memories

Goucher is recovering from his 6:30 a.m. run: sixteen repeat quarters in 63–64 seconds with 200 jog. It was a good anaerobic workout, the first one of the year, and despite some pain in his upper left quad, Goucher feels good. "Today," he says, "I felt the speed coming back." Ideally, he would like another two weeks in the 90's. "From there," he says, "I want to concentrate on just feeling good. I want to let Mark know I don't need 90 miles a week until the week before Nationals. I want to go for a good taper. Wetmore usually has a slight taper. For me, I want to make sure my legs are sharp. That's most important, that my legs feel good."

At Pre-Nationals, he didn't have the sharpness "to just boom! Explode! So to some extent, I'm really excited. I'm gonna drop to 75, 80 and really start feeling good."

But with Severy's death, it is hard to get too excited. Goucher is leaning on his teammates to help him work through his grief. "Since it happened," he says, "I think the team has become closer, more of a family. You have us all sitting there emotionally drained together, hurting and crying and holding on to each other. It's as if we've created what we assumed was there, but we didn't realize how much we love one another." On Tuesday night, "Tom, Roybal, Oscar, Johnson, and me just held on for 20–25 minutes, crying, talking . . . More than teammates we have a friendship. It's like Mark says, when you spend three to four hours together every day with blood, tears, and pain, you become inconceivably close. A lot of people don't realize that. We didn't to some extent, but now we do."

Goucher is convinced his teammates will run better than ever now at Nationals. "In many ways," he says, "it'll be spectacular. Every step we'll have Sev with us in our memory. That's why many of us want armbands. But no matter what, he's gonna be there, if nothing else whispering in our ear, 'Kick that guy down! Get him!' That's what he'd be saying. That's what he'd be doing."

Goucher thinks often about his last conversation with Severy, when they landed at DIA after Pre-Nationals last weekend. "Hey," Sev told him, looking straight into his eyes and clenching his fist, "I'm proud of you, man. You ran awesome today." Sensing doubt in Goucher's eyes, Sev reassured him, "You'll destroy that guy when the time comes." Goucher then told Sev not to be discouraged about his performance, telling Sev that he, too, would rise at Nationals. "We'll all be ready," he said, to which Sev responded, "Yep. No doubt about it."

For Goucher, winning the national crown has never been so important.

Tornado Coming—PFB's!

At 7:30 a.m. yesterday morning, right after the Varsity had finished their quarters, Batliner and the junior Varsity runners boarded a couple vans for the long monotonous trip east through the plains of eastern Colorado and western Kansas to Ft. Hays—smack in the heart of Tornado Alley in Western Kansas. As they headed east out of Boulder the sunny blue skies turned dark and gloomy. A storm was heading west across the plains, and at 2 p.m., a fierce hailstorm broke over Denver and swept its way into Boulder. Fortunately, the Varsity was already done for the day, and the Bluebirds rode through the storm en route to Kansas, but a solitary figure had to endure the onslaught. Slattery, staying in Boulder because he is redshirting, got nailed while running an eight-and-a-half-mile tempo run at the Buffalo Ranch. Said Slattery, "That's the worst shit I've ever run in in my life." And he was the lucky one . . .

After checking their bags into the Ft. Hays Days Inn, the team drove over and checked out the flat, fast course before heading back to the hotel for some R&R. While some stayed and relaxed in their rooms, most went to the movie theatre down the road.

Lorie Roch was in the theatre, and just after the movie started, sirens started blaring. She did not think much of it, but then a shrieking woman ran into the theatre screaming for her kids. Roch then knew this was not a joke. It was not a warning, *it was an actual tornado alert!*

She calmly went back to the ticket window to get a refund for her ticket when a woman told her, "Don't worry—the mayor is here." Lorie thought incredulously, "What difference does it make if the mayor is here?" before she gathered the team to head outside.

Back at the hotel, Wetmore was standing on the balcony outside his room, watching the chaotic scene unfold. He could see an ominous looking black cumulus cloud approaching, but he did not see the funnel cloud itself. Nevertheless, cops were racing up and down the boulevard, and a cop shouted at him through his megaphone to get the hell down off the balcony!

The tornado touched down five miles outside of town with enough force to pull several houses off their foundations. Fortunately, that was the extent of the damage, but whistling winds throughout the evening suggested the race conditions would be anything but peaceful . . .

The runners woke up to 20 mph winds and a 50-degree morning. While unusual, inclement weather at this meet is not unprecedented. Two years ago, Wetmore says, "the wind was roaring." Last year calm conditions prevailed and current redshirt Matt Napier ran a 24:40. He later earned All-American honors, so Wetmore knows that anyone who approaches that time today is pretty fit.

The wind could slow things down but the grass on the course is manicured like a golf course fairway, and the course is flat as a pancake. The men's race will not lack for a squad to get out and push the pace. The Dodge City Kansas Community College Squad is here, and their contingent of African all-stars has been tearing up the cross country circuit all fall. Two weeks ago when they raced at the Cowboy Jamboree in Stillwater, Oklahoma, they beat Oklahoma State and gave Arkansas a run for their money. Their top man, Eliad Njuhi, defeated Arkansas's Sean Kaley by seven seconds to win the 8k race in 24:21.

There is much at stake today for the CU men. The hard fact is that Severy's death has opened a spot on the Varsity for Big 12's next weekend. Matt Elmuccio and Jay Johnson appear to have the best chance of earning that spot today. The Mooch beat Johnson by two seconds at the Shootout, but Johnson has vastly improved since that race. And if Batliner cannot go next week, there will be two open spots.

The men take off their winter caps and sweats and head towards the line with a few minutes to spare. They appear relaxed, and Batliner has experienced no pain in his calf while warming up. Nevertheless, there is something about Bat's appearance that draws Wetmore's ire. From the looks of him, he has spent more time at the Village than in the pool. He is significantly larger than he used to be. The striation that was once visible in his upper body has disappeared. The additional weight will do nothing to help relieve the pressure on his shin.

The five Kenyans, a South African, and the token American that make

Dodge City, moments
before the start.

  CHRIS LEAR

up the Dodge City Squad put their hands together in a little huddle and jump up and down before the start. They laugh as they do so, and by the looks of their chattering teeth and ceaseless movement they want to get the race going so they can simply warm up.

A pack of four Dodge City runners head right to the front from the gun; they will not wait for others to dictate the race. They pass two miles in 10:05, and Jay Johnson follows close behind their fifth man in about 10:10. The Mooch lurks behind Johnson, and he seems to be running effortlessly. Behind him, a pack of CU runners comes through two miles in 10:33 with Batliner, the out-of-shape monster, in their midst.

The lead pack passes four miles in 19:56—well clear of the rest of the field. Boniface Ndungu is alone in fifth, with Johnson 25 meters back.

Johnson passes four miles in 20:26. More significant, Johnson has now extended his lead over Elmuccio to 50 meters.

In the fifth mile, the action heats up. The lead pack starts rolling, racing each other for the first time. Each puts in surges to drop the other guys in the pack, and eventually Eliad Njuhi prevails in 24:21, having run 4:25 for the last mile. His teammates follow closely behind in second, third, and fourth, but the competition for the fifth spot is hotly contested.

Johnson races all out to catch Boniface Ndungu, Dodge City's fifth man, and as they round the turn down the long finishing stretch with less than a half mile to go, Johnson improbably passes him. Ndungu has another

Coming soon to a Big 12 school near you.

gear yet in him, however, and with 300 meters to go, he blows by Johnson towards the line. As spectators cheer them in down the finishing stretch, a frustrated Johnson yells at those rooting for his foreign competitor, "YOU AMERICANS SHOULD BE ASHAMED!"

Wetmore is not pleased when he hears of Johnson's comment, and a distraught Johnson seeks out the meet director to apologize for his outrageous outburst. His inexplicable comments put a damper on an otherwise breakthrough performance. He covered the last mile in 4:40, and Wetmore is clearly pleased with his performance. He says afterwards, "It's been a long time since I saw Jay Johnson running fast and passing people, being competitive and moving through the race. He was rolling that last mile."

In light of what Ndungu says after the race, it is not surprising he kicked so hard at the end. He and his teammates saw photos of Sev on the Internet this week, and when he saw Johnson coming after him with his long blond hair and blue eyes, he says, "I thought I was running against a ghost."

Elmuccio is the next Buff across the line, in eighth place in 25:29. Despite missing his opportunity to make the Varsity squad, Wetmore is pleased that the miler's great finishing kick brought him home past several competitors. Says Wetmore, "Matt had a real nice kick—his last quarter must have been 55. It was good to see him and hear him repeat

The ghost charges.

that he's gaining confidence at 8000 meters, and that he's starting to think like a Varsity guy for us next year."

Next year. It appears that Elmuccio will not run Varsity for the Buffaloes this season, because Batliner finishes fourteenth in 25:53. It is a remarkable run considering he has run *three days* since developing the stress fracture in his lower leg. After the race, Bat has mixed feelings about his performance. He says, "I felt pretty good. My body just doesn't want to do what my brain and legs are telling it to do. I felt almost there, I just have to get everything together on the same page. I definitely have to get my running legs back. It felt pretty good until the last mile, where my calf started to get tight. That was the symptom I had before. For the longest time I thought it was muscular, because my body's response to a stress fracture is to tighten up the muscles around it to protect it and take the shock off the bone. So that kind of worries me. I won't do a lot tomorrow. It's a precarious position I'm in now. I have to be careful."

His concern heightens twenty minutes later when his calf and hamstring tighten considerably. If the race ends up impeding his development, he will think back to today's third mile (when he got excited and ran a 5:03) as the cause of his setback. But you cannot fault him for taking the risk. NCAA's are only 5 weeks away . . .

The out-of-shape monster.

FT. HAYS TIGER INVITATIONAL

PLACE	NAME	SCHOOL	AVG. MILE	TIME
1.	Eliad Njuhi	Dodge City CC	4:53	24:21
2.	James Karanu	Dodge City CC	4:54	24:25
3.	Likhaya Dayile	Dodge City CC	4:55	24:28
4.	Herbert Mwangi	Dodge City CC	5:01	25:01
5.	Boniface Ndungu	Dodge City CC	5:01	25:01
6.	Jay Johnson	Colorado	5:02	25:06
7.	Richard Jones	Dodge City CC	5:06	25:23
8.	Matt Elmuccio	Colorado	5:07	25:29
9.	Jason McCullough	Fort Hays State	5:07	25:31
10.	Jeth Fouts	Fort Hays State	5:08	25:35
14.	Adam Batliner	Colorado	5:12	25:53
17.	Sean Smith	Colorado	5:14	26:02
18.	Chris Schafer	Colorado	5:14	26:04
19.	Cameron Harrison	Colorado	5:15	26:06
21.	Adam Loomis	Colorado	5:16	26:15
23.	Zach Crandall	Colorado	5:17	26:20

CHRIS LEAR

Into the Sun

It is a quiet run on the trail this morning. Conversation is kept to a minimum as the upperclassmen run together in a pack that includes Goucher. Most of the runners present are heading to Buttermilk Mountain after the run to attend Sev's memorial service.

Goucher runs with a bit of a limp, but he mentions nothing of any pain that he is feeling. One suspects that maybe he is thinking of Sev, and how he would run through a brick wall before admitting he was hurt.

Sev relished Sunday runs. They were his proving ground. After his superb run at Mags on September 20th, when he ran 20 miles in 2:03, Severy, in his unassuming but slightly mischievous way, talked about how he had been crushing Sundays ever since he was a freshman:

> *I was a stupid freshman, but I didn't care. [Jay] Cleckler was my biggest influence. I'd see him hammering and say, OK, I'm gonna hammer too. I was so tired from training, but I'd always kill myself. I loved Mags. I once ran 1:24 for 14, and I still haven't gone as fast. Without fail, I'd see Mark at eight miles and he'd say, "Sev, are you going out over your head?" I'd say, "no," even though I was dying. I lived on Advil freshman year.*

He trained himself through exhaustion his freshman year. Eventually, he was forced to call it a year because of severe patella tendonitis—he went so far as to take "twenty Advil a day" to make it through. But his biggest disappointment that first fall—not making the Varsity for NCAA's—laid the foundation for his biggest success:

> *Not going to Nationals fired me up, and I trained harder than ever for Jr. Nationals. Me, Tom, and Bat went up there. I hung back, and by mile two I was fifteenth. I kept hammering saying, "there's no way this guy is beating me." I ran out of distance, and finished seventh. But [Stanford's Greg] Jimmerson was too old, and so was another guy, so I was fifth for World's qualifying purposes . . . Thus began my intense training.*

But watching NCAA's served a purpose of its own. It was a watershed moment not only for Goucher, who would finish second, but for Sev as well.

I watched the race go off, and the Arkansas guys were way out ahead. The CU guys were in the back of the pack. Clint [Wells] was 50 to 100 meters off the back of the pack. We all said we hope he's feeling alright. Then they disappeared into the woods, and when they came out, Goucher was in the twenties, Al was 30th, Cleckler, Coop, and Clint were in there. And at mile three or four, Goucher was just rolling people up. He used to hate foreigners, so we'd yell, "Go! Foreigner up ahead!" He was tenth by mile four and a half, and picking off people one by one. With less than a mile to go, he was in second. That was by far the best, gutsiest, most emotional race I've ever seen him run. Al was eleventh, Cleckler was 25th—which was amazing since he had exercise-induced asthma. Wells went from last to 33rd and Coop was 34th. But Gouch, that's when he proved to us, he's for real. No doubt about it, he showed us he was something unique. That race set the tone for our collegiate careers. Every year, we want to match that performance.

Sev was as tenacious in his other endeavors as he was in training. A double major in biochemistry and molecular biology with a 4.0 GPA, he embraced, more than anyone, Wetmore's dictum to be a renaissance man and attack all your endeavors with vigor. He embodied Mahler's saying, *Res Severa Verum Gaudia;* the greatest joy is being serious. When asked about his study habits, he said:

I study a lot. Freshman and sophomore year, I would run, study, and that's it. I'd go on eight hour bus rides and study orgo the whole way. I couldn't live with myself unless I knew to the core the explanation of something. I'd get 100's on orgo tests because I knew everything to a T. Through my sophomore year, I never got less than a 98 on a test... My junior year, I got my first girlfriend; she says I was always studying when I was with her.

[He was not exaggerating. The time the guys caught him out on a date with her is now a part of team lore. He was with her in a restaurant waiting for a table. Seeing that he had some time on his hands, he thought nothing of opening up his texts and doing some studying while they waited...]

That second semester we broke up and I went back to doing nothing but run, study, and ski on weekends. I hated to study, but I did it so much that now I love it. I love knowledge. I now regret not studying more that first semester. I would study so much that I figured out what the questions were going to be on the test... Biochem Two was really hard for me, but I learned more than ever. Last year I managed to get an A even though I had all the problems with my father during his long and ultimately fatal battle with cancer. In the lab, I started research the end of my junior year using

atomic force microscopy—AFM—to image DNA and protein interac-
tions—really cutting-edge stuff. I'm in lab twenty to thirty hours a week
trying to get things to work . . .

Tessman puts in a surge with three miles to go, dropping Schafer, who is also running fifteen miles this morning. Sev would have liked that move. Tessman pushes the pace until he reaches the top of the long steep climb that terminates along a mesa overlooking Broadway to run's end. After having already run twelve miles, the thought of attacking this climb seems absurd. Sev would have loved it.

Watching the men fight through this run, only hours before the memorial service, it is hard not to envision Severy charging up one final climb westward, blue eyes alight, an impish grin on his face, shaggy blond locks bouncing to and fro, legs churning impossibly forward, into the distance.

Slattery, I Think You're Full of Shit

As everyone files into Balch to stretch before running an easy hour and strides, a crowd gathers around the board. Tomorrow's workout will be 300's around Kitt. Tessman shakes his head as he sees tomorrow's assignment. "I'm scared for Tuesday," he says. "If it's like Friday, man, I thought I was gonna die. I wanted someone to shoot my face off. I did maybe one or two workouts last year that felt that hard."

On the bottom of the document, Wetmore has posted the names of those who are competing at Big 12's in two weeks. Johnson's name is on the list. He has made the top nine along with Goucher, Friedberg, Reese, Roybal, Ponce, Tessman, Valenti, and Batliner. At Big 12's, Johnson will have a chance to stretch his season even further as the team shrinks to seven men.

After taking yesterday off, Batliner is going to run down on Kitt Field, the home of the injured and recuperating. Wetmore is still marveling at what he was able to achieve at Ft. Hays. "I was pretty sure what Bat could do. We'd talked about running splits for 26:00, but still, I was holding my breath the whole way. I wondered if someone could really take 5 weeks off, train for 2 days, and run 25:50—that was good."

Goucher, wearing jeans, heads straight for Wetmore. "I'm taking a day off," he tells him. "My leg's sore, I don't know what it is, it's going up my back and stuff, so I'm taking a day off." His left thigh aches. "It's just really tight," he says as he massages it with his hand, "I don't know what the deal is." Wetmore says nothing, but he looks like he is trying to hide his concern, like he is thinking, "What's next?"

Slattery joins Batliner for a jog around Kitt, and they debate the efficacy of creatine for long-distance runners as they jog. Wetmore thinks it is "utterly useless, a waste of money." Nevertheless, Slattery tells Bat that he has been taking creatine for two years now, and that the strength gains he attributes to the creatine definitely outweigh the potential decrease in performance due to the weight gain creatine causes. Bat asks him for more evidence that it works, and Slattery says his bench press increased from 185 to 215 while on creatine. "But how does that help your running?" "Trust me," Slattery says flatly, "it does." They run on around the field wordlessly for a few minutes before Batliner chimes in his verdict, "Slattery, I think you're full of shit."

No Doubt About It

In the foyer of Mackey auditorium, people file past pictures of Severy. In most he is active—running or skiing; clearly, he was a man on the go. "Try," Wetmore later remarks, "to find one where he's not smiling." It is not possible.

Inside the auditorium, over a thousand people have packed themselves in for Severy's memorial service. A program for the service has been distributed, with a picture of Chris on the front in full stride on the cross country course. Above the picture it reads, "A CELEBRATION OF THE LIFE OF CHRISTOPHER SEVERY." There is much to celebrate, for he packed in more in his 22 years than most people do in a lifetime.

A group of Severy's teammates sit on stage waiting their turn to speak. Rich Cardillo, the associate athletic director, opens the service, calling Severy "the epitome of the student athlete."

His chemistry and biochemistry professors speak next. Kathy Rowlen, his Chemistry professor, speaks about Severy's efforts to synthesize a DNA molecule. She calls Severy a "talented experimentalist . . . disciplined, yet free." His loss, she sincerely says, "is a loss *for humanity.*"

Regent Robert Sievers dedicates a sculpture to Severy called "The Chemist's Book." Earlier, when Batliner heard a sculpture would be dedicated to Severy, he struggled with the idea. How, he wondered, can you capture all that Severy is in a work of art without pigeonholing him as one thing or another? While the beautiful marble sculpture of a chemist's book on a dais does not capture all that Chris was, it does symbolize, in Sievers' words, "Chris's love of knowledge. Chris spoke the language of science and those whose lives he touched will never be the same."

Severy's sister Robin, who has lost both a father and a brother in the past six months, speaks next. Through tears she speaks fondly of "my best friend." She says, "His life's mission was to defeat cancer. He offered the world so much hope . . . He was so unassuming and nonjudgmental. He worried about Bat's stress fracture, Goucher's training regimen . . . He worked so hard at everything." She laughs when recalling how skiing was his biggest passion, and how he always said "he would marry the first woman who can pull a 360."

Wetmore introduces Severy's teammates, noting that "few can understand how close distance runners are, the brotherhood."

Goucher speaks of how Chris was "the hardest-working guy . . . he taught me how to push the limits ... We became brothers through blood, sweat, and pain ... I loved him. His memory is with us, and he'll finish the season with us, just as he would want us to do."

Batliner talks of how "nothing was superfluous or hidden" with Sev, and how, "he loved to work. He loved all of us. He spent every day wearing himself out doing that." He compares Chris to a brilliant color, "in its complex simplicity. It's the essence of Chris."

Jay Johnson recalls how after Chris's best ever race—his seventeenth place finish at NCAA's two years ago—his thoughts were not on his performance, but on his teammates. He was concerned about Batliner, who dropped out, and Johnson recalls Sev telling his father how he wished Zeke Tiernan could have finished ahead of him. Johnson then mentions Sev's courage "to snub society, and move up to a mountain." Through his achievements Chris made it higher than most even dare to dream. "Try," Johnson says, referring to the legendary Chinese philosopher Han-Shan "to make it to Cold Mountain."

Tom Reese reads Housman's poem "To an Athlete Dying Young" before recounting how when he was rehabbing over the summer, "Sev would kayak in the pool while I was doing pool workouts, just to keep me company."

Wetmore then introduces Sev's good friend, ex-Buff and Aspen High teammate Zeke Tiernan. Tiernan is the last of Severy's teammates to speak. "They've shared innumerable runs, road trips and adventures," says Wetmore. Tiernan plays a slide show of pictures of Chris set to music, and he narrates it as it goes along. Smiling images of Chris running, skiing, and relaxing with friends beautifully convey his openness and joie de vivre.

Mark Wetmore speaks last. He wears a tan western suit with a bolo tie, and he strides purposefully to the podium. He looks straight into the crowd, and begins:

> No doubt about it, Chris was a special young man. Remember, however, our task is to let him go, and find a way to keep him. 'No doubt about it.' He used to say that a lot in my presence, and it says a lot about him. Special? Perseverance, endurance, and courage. No doubt, no one better exemplifies those qualities of character. There is no one better in our program.

Wetmore describes how he told Chris to be patient when he resumed training in June, not to do 105 miles the first week. But by the end of August, Chris *was* doing 105 miles a week—fifteen miles a day. "He was in the best shape of his life, no doubt about it." Wetmore asked him then, "If you, Tommy, Bat, Gouch, our guys click [at Nationals], we can do it, can't we?" "Oh, sure," Chris replied, "No doubt about it." "That no-doubt attitude," Wetmore says, "is what made him so special."

Wetmore recalls how two days after his father died, Chris was back in the stretching circle, "hair unkempt, shirt crooked." Wetmore asked him, "Chris, are you sure you're ready?" "Oh yeah," he replied, "no doubt about it."

He characterizes Chris as a man "without a theology and maybe without a God." "Without a doubt he loved life," he says, "and he embraced the uniqueness of his gifts. That must be the definition of faith. He had complete faith that life is good, and that his gifts were valuable."

Wetmore closes his remarks by urging those in attendance to strive to embrace the qualities that made Chris special: perseverance, endurance, and courage. "Practice," he challenges the audience, "his embrace of our gifts . . . Practice his embrace of life as good. If we do that," he concludes, "we can remember and honor Chris, we can let him go, and we can keep him, no doubt about it."

No doubt about it.

Welcome to Anaerobia

Goucher's leg still aches, and Wetmore tells him to test it jogging to Kitt. They will decide there whether or not he will run the workout. Goucher *wants to run*. The pain in his thigh has not subsided, but, he says, "I don't want to think of taking any more time off. I can feel it from my groin right through my hip flexor. I think its muscular, but it hurts when I grab it right through the middle." Wetmore drives to Kitt with JD, and while waiting for everyone to arrive, he confesses his conern to JD. "Now I'm paranoid about Goucher's leg. It's terrifying . . . It sounds lke a femural stress fracture."

Goucher's presence does nothing to ease his concern. He limps to Kitt. It is obvious that he is in considerable distress, and the sight of him hobbling along is all Wetmore needs to know; Goucher is not running the workout. Goucher approaches Wetmore, and Wetmore immediately calms his mind. "Hopefully tomorrow, you'll feel 100%. What's the big deal, we lose one workout." "Just jog back then?" Goucher asks. "Yeah, we're not going to advance your fitness, so just jog back. You're in monster shape. You're in great shape and you can get in better shape, but not if you half-ass it."

Goucher does not object. JD and Wetmore blankly stare at Goucher as he jogs off with a pronounced limp.

But the show must go on. Batliner *is* doing the workout. Amazingly, he hangs with the leaders for the entire workout. JD stands at the finish line of the uphill 300. As they get ready to start the downhill 300's he encourages them to make it hurt. "Let's get into debt, now, let's get into debt."

The pack is solid up front, and Berkshire is also hanging in there. Berkshire is not running Big 12's though; Valenti is. Valenti has beaten him in three of four races, so for Wetmore, it is an easy call. As usual, Valenti looks like a stallion out here, running casually and powerfully with the leaders.

There is a surprising leader on the fourteenth 300: Tommy Reese. On the fifteenth Reese again pulls ahead slightly with Napier on his shoulder. With one to go, Tessman walks while the others mill around jogging. He has his hands on his hips, and he struggles to regain his breath. He falls off the back on the last interval.

Wetmore and JD talk afterwards, and Wetmore is concerned that maybe they did not get into enough debt. "Ah," JD says, "wait till the 30-30's." The 30-30's, otherwise known as the "Master Blaster," is 30-second 200's with 30 seconds rest *till you can go no more.* It is scheduled for November tenth. "Yeah," says Wetmore, "that'll be a whole different lifestyle."

Changing of the Guard

A CU bus awaits the men after they finish stretching to head to the Tank for their medium-distance run. On the ride over, the bus is decidedly quiet. After a quick glance around the bus, it is readily apparent *why* it is so silent. Goucher, Batliner, Johnson, Napier, Reese, and yes, Severy are not here. The only upperclassman here is Tessman, the Brown transfer. The heart and soul of the team is missing, and their absence is palpable.

Everyone quietly goes about their business when they get to the Tank. The pace is controlled on the way out, and the first group of freshmen turn back after 32 minutes. Roybal, Berkshire, Tessman, and Valenti do the full Tank–Berkshire rolling all the way back. Ten minutes later, Ponce and Friedberg run in side by side while everyone finishes stretching outside the bus.

The void the seniors have left is evident today, but even without these characters, in fact, *because* of their absence, Wetmore expects CU to be a contender next year. He says, "I can see everyone rising up when Goucher is gone. He inhibits their testosterone or something. People can begin to believe there is a little piece of territory for themselves. Now, there's this alpha male haunting. It can be pretty discouraging."

The bus is silent again on the way home. People stare off into the distance, absorbed in their thoughts. A year from now, which of these men will rise to the challenge?

Who is Friedberg?

As usual, Goucher is the last to roll in as Reese directs the stretching circle. He is dressed to run. He says he is OK, so Wetmore has decided to "let him go at it, be smart and communicate with me what's going on." The team takes a couple of vans out to the course. They will run a two-mile warmup once they have arrived.

As the men get ready to go after their warmup, Wetmore gives them some instructions: "You men are semi-autonomous today. Goucher, you're alone, and the rest of you guys are in one big group." He turns to Sean Smith, the walk-on who has been impressive as of late. "You hang in the back, do 5:10's, OK?" Smith nods his approval.

Bat asks Goucher if his leg is good, and Gouch shrugs. "All right." "Good or alright?" "Alright enough." Batliner has been through the ringer enough, so he gives Goucher some advice he hopes Goucher will heed, "Be brave enough to call it early."

Despite the rash of injuries, Wetmore is not backing off his program at all. He is taking Goucher at his word, so he has assigned him six miles averaging 4:42 with 2:30 rest. That is three seconds per mile faster than when he last ran this on September 29th. The others are expected to make similar improvements, running, on average, five seconds faster per mile. While the rest of the men put on their spikes, Goucher takes off alone, shirtless with black Adidas shorts on, into the distance.

Seeing Goucher take off spurs Captain Reese. "Two minutes!" he shouts. Reese appoints Berkshire and Valenti as the designated "time-in-betweeners." Wetmore then offers them some final counsel: "Hey now, listen. Let's go! It's time to get in debt. I want you vomiting after this. Hey, actually, I want you to vomit after three." He then turns to Smith, who looks petrified. "Sean, you don't have to vomit, you can just dry-retch."

The big climb is on the first mile, so it is no surprise that Friedberg leads the men in only 5:09. The pack finishes six seconds later, while Bat runs 5:25 and Johnson is way off the back at 5:45. Johnson's performance is inexplicable since he is healthy. Only after the interval does Johnson reveal that he is having trouble because he cannot see anything. He forgot his contacts. He does not finish the workout.

Down the hill into the second mile, Friedberg starts gapping the pack, to Wetmore's chagrin. "Wouldn't you think these guys would go with Friedberg? You'd think that they'd say, 'Who the fuck is Friedberg?'"

Friedberg runs past Wetmore as he speaks. "Friedberg's drilling these guys!" Friedberg runs the second mile in 4:44. Elmuccio mixes it up with the main pack. "Yeah," says Wetmore as he sees the Mooch move, "he's decided to be good now."

He speaks too soon, for Mooch is off the back on the third mile, running 5:37. He skips the fourth. "I just feel like poop," he says after the others take off. "My last one was 5:37 and I didn't think it would do me any good to run 6:00, so I'm skipping one."

Some of the men started out with shirts, but by the third mile, everyone is bare-chested as the action heats up. Reese is right on Friedberg's tail on the fourth mile. This is by far his best workout of the season. Roybal encourages Smith before as they ready for the fifth one. "Let's go Sean," he says. The walk-on is hanging tough. He has yet to be dropped on a single interval.

On the sixth and final mile, they fly. Roybal and Reese lead the charge, and no one holds back. When they finish, Roybal turns and tells Reese what they ran. He stares at him after hearing the time and says, "Are you fucking with me?" They have run the last mile in a blazing 4:21. Tessman runs 4:30, and Friedberg run 4:32. Friedberg jokes that his time almost equals his PR in the mile.

All alone, Goucher ran his last mile in 4:23. It was the capper to a brilliant workout. He exceeded Wetmore's projection by eight seconds—running a cumulative time of 28:04. If anything, the days off appear to have him energized.

Batliner quit after the fifth mile, and running two uphill miles slows his average, so he is not disappointed that he did not meet his goal for the workout. If he ran the last downhill mile instead of the uphill mile, he would easily have averaged 5:10 a mile. He has run a fantastic workout, and he feels every step of it afterwards. As he stretches before cooling down he says, "I am without a doubt more muscularly sore than I have ever been in my entire life. There's no decipherable pain beyond the muscle soreness, but every once in a while I feel a pain on the inside of my shin. It scares the shit out of me but"—he pauses—"even if it hurts me, what the hell am I going to do at this point? Take two weeks off?"

Wetmore yells at Batliner and Mooch to get moving and catch the guys who have already begun their cooldown. "Come on Mooch, you fell off, let's get back on!" You are either on the bus . . .

Name	9/29 Pace	10/23 Goal	Actual
Elmuccio	5:08		DNF
Johnson	5:17	5:10/31:00	DNF
Smith	5:16		No watch
Valenti	5:06	5:00/30:00	NT (watch prob.)
Schafer	5:08		30:49
Roybal	5:12	5:00/30:00	29:44
Tessman	5:06	5:00/30:00	29:51
Reese	5:10	5:00/30:00	29:30
Ponce	5:06	5:00/30:00	30:02
Berkshire	5:06	5:00/30:00	30:15
Friedberg	5:00	4:55/29:30	29:27
Goucher	4:45	4:42/28:12	28:04
Batliner	Did Not Run	5:10/25:50	26:24 (uphill)

One More Victim

Old Man Mags is a greedy old bastard, and he is hungry for more—but Wetmore sits on a hilltop of his own. Wanting a little extra rest before Big 12's this weekend, Wetmore steps off the gas and decreases the distance the men normally run on Sunday. Six men, including Goucher and Reese, are assigned fifteen miles while the others are assigned twelve. There is another reason why Wetmore is easing today's assignment. The results of Big 12's will largely determine his roster for regionals and Nationals, and "the people who are on the bubble, numbers five through nine, two of whom are going to be whittled down, need to be on the same page as far as rest is concerned." Tessman, Valenti, Johnson, and Bat cannot afford to be too tired to race well this weekend.

It is bitterly cold on Mags this morning. Everyone is bundled up to protect against the chill. Two miles in, a small car flies by and parks along the road. It is Reese. His alarm did not go off due to a power outage last night. He jumps out of his car and joins the guys.

Goucher appreciates the extra rest he will get before Big 12's, and he "only" runs 1:31 for 15 this morning. He is unusually subdued this morning and he does not speak to anybody after his run. Physically, he is hanging on, but emotionally, he is suffering. Two weeks ago he lost one of his best friends. Yesterday, he split with his fiancée. His far-off stare is enough to know that he is lost in his thoughts, and does not want to be disturbed.

Valenti and Tessman crank twelve miles. Everyone is seemingly in one piece, but Tessman felt a shooting pain in his foot towards the end of the run. He dismisses it and mentions it to no one. Only later would he learn the heartbreaking severity of his injury.

It is the last the men will see of Old Man Mags this fall. When they leave, no one sheds a tear.

Musings

Conference week. Around the nation, teams are running for local bragging rights, and those teams on the bubble for NCAA's will be trying to establish themselves as worthy of an at-large selection to the Big Dance in Lawrence. There is a lot at stake.

For Colorado, ranked fourth in the nation in the last coaches poll released on October 20th, the Big 12 conference meet does not have the significance that it does for lesser teams unsure of their post-season chances. But even if it did matter, Wetmore would not alter his preparation. Some squads will peak for the race, but Wetmore will only rest his runners a little more than usual (as he did yesterday) to give him a better read on how they are progressing for Nationals.

The race should be competitive. Says Wetmore, "Oklahoma State is a good team, and you can't overlook your conference meet." A victory by the Buffs is by no means assured. The Cowboys are led by steeplechaser Chuck Sloan, a senior whom Reese and Batliner have battled frequently. They are a talented, veteran squad that the pollsters have ranked ninth in the country. If they have done a lot of anaerobic work in preparation for the Big 12's, they will be even tougher to beat.

Nevertheless, Wetmore has made his preparations to peak for one meet: NCAA's. He says, "I have never adjusted the preparation throughout a season for the Big 12's, and I'm still not. We're resting this week because in preparation for NCAA's we need to run well. We need a good race."

Batliner will have his second test this weekend on the road back from his stress fracture, and depending on how he responds, it could well be his last. Despite their fourth-place ranking in the latest polls, Wetmore says, "At this point we're not contending for the national championship. If his leg hurts, I'm not gonna risk his outdoor season. We're certainly not going to push the envelope in this case."

Tomorrow Batliner will run a full workout of repeat 800's with the others. The workout is designed to induce anaerobic debt with "some sub-race pace work. But I don't want 8000 meters of anaerobic stimulus in their legs. It's gonna be faster than race pace without much recovery."

One man Wetmore is expecting a lot out of this weekend given his recent training is Mike Friedberg. Wetmore is impressed with his progress.

"Two years ago he didn't know shit. He was a total rube. But he learned it so fast. He sounds like a 29:30 10k runner now. He could be the guy, like [CU alum and national class marathoner] Scotty Larson, who two years out, in the Olympic Trials, people will say 'Who is this guy?' We expect him to be top 40 at NCAA's."

Wetmore says Friedberg's success is due, interestingly, to attendance. He says, "Seventy percent of the best [high school] runners in the last ten years disappear. They're all gone, sitting on a hillside. In the top 25 at NCAA's, many of the big Foot Locker stars from '94 to '96 will be gone. They'll be back in the 30's and 40's." He laughs thinking of the diligence it has taken Friedberg to climb past those who excelled in high school. "If you want to be successful in college, don't go to Foot Locker or run 8:55 [for two miles in high school]."

Friedberg and his mates are facing another challenge this weekend: the first race since Severy's death. Wetmore is not sure how they will respond. He talks about the feel he had for this team, and what may lie ahead: "Each team has its own character and style. Five years ago, they were hungry. There was an esprit de corps of the underdog. Even though they were fourth that year, and second the next year, they still felt like the underdog. Now that we're on the top level, the fourths and fifths don't thrill us. I have to sit down and say, 'Stay hungry. It's all brand new. Stay hungry like a new team. The '98 Colorado team ain't done shit, keep thinking that way.'"

"I have to sit with them and tell them, 'Don't presume you're good because you got the uniform on.' The irony is I felt best about this team's dynamic. It was a great group dynamic. Now they're back on their heels. Now I don't know."

And while Wetmore never counts on his athletes running out of their heads, he admits that "once in a while, you get a group of guys. You can feel the synergy moving. I felt that about this group."

That said, he was and is preparing them to approach NCAA's as just another race. After all, "How many people go to NC's and run better than they have all year? Ten percent? I don't want to go in having to run better than ever. I want them to think business as usual. If five of us run business as usual, we'll be alright."

For this reason, there will be no fire and brimstone speeches about winning one for Sev this weekend—or ever. Wetmore believes "the more cranked up you are on rhetoric, the less likely you are to run well. You go out too hard the first mile, mile and a half, and run worse than you would have."

The armbands the guys got, on which to embroider Sev's initials, lie in a pile in the corner of Reese's living room.

Let It Rain

It is an overcast Tuesday afternoon in Boulder. The sky is portentously gray. Snow is forecasted for later in the week. Regardless, there is business to be done. By the time the runners have finished their warmup, the sky has opened, dropping a light steady rain on the harriers. Wetmore welcomes the discomfort. "Messner," he says in a booming voice so all can hear as they change into their spikes, "it's gloomy. What's good about that?" He answers his own question: "Right now, our opponents would say, 'It's a crummy day, I feel crummy.' This is our day to get an advantage! The worse, the better!"

Then, Wetmore explains the goal of today's endeavor. "Today, we want to simulate what we want to do in November. We're doing seven 800's for the men, five for the women. Men, on the first five, I want you getting out that first 100. Then settle in to your race pace and go." On the last two, the men will kick home the last two hundred meters as they would at the end of a race. Of the last two, Wetmore says, "You are gonna be ooh, aah. Oh, man, I don't even want to think about it! I hope you didn't eat lunch today. But if you did, no puking in lane one."

Seeing the runners duly intimidated, Wetmore injects some levity, offering a tale of a former Bernards runner. "Michael Hinson at Bernards High puked in lane one. It was so acidic, it left a hole in the track that was there for *five* years. That's what he was famous for. That, and for running *1:58* as a frosh and 2:17 as a senior."

Roybal flies past JD.

The runners continue lacing up their shoes, and make their way to the starting line. Wetmore turns his attention to JD. "You're in charge of getting them tired. The mistake I've made in the past is that they've gone out too fast, and didn't settle in. That's what you have to solve in the beginning."

Batliner sprints onto the track as the men are finishing their strides. Wetmore screams, "Bat where are you, you're holding us up, slowing up the whole operation!" "I'm skipping the first one," says Batliner, "remember?" One other runner is absent: Brock Tessman. He met with Wetmore this morning and, while reticent about what transpired, Wetmore makes it known that it did not go well.

Bat needs to get in the work to be ready to go in Lawrence, and Wetmore is continuing to cautiously test Batliner's limitations. Today's experiment is another success. He nails the workout, staying with the pack for all six intervals.

Wetmore turns to the men as they toe the line, "Now, the first part of the workout is mental. The first three, I could do the workout you're doing. Feel good."

Fifty meters out, Goucher is in front. The rest of the Varsity squad competing at Big 12's battles behind him. "14, 15, 16," they fly through the first 100. They settle in, and Goucher rolls through the first interval in 2:14. The rest is brutally short—a 200-meter jog around the bend to the pole vault pit and back. They will toe the starting line for the first five, JD giving a starter's call on each one.

Behind Goucher, a surprising leader has emerged in the second pack: Ronald Roybal. The man who saved their ass at NCAA's last year has turned the corner. Not only has he assumed command of the pack, he is making it look easy. For the first time, Roybal is demonstrating the form of the Big 12 indoor 5000 meter champion from two years ago.

Wetmore and JD could not be happier. On the second interval, Wetmore lets out a spirited "ROYYYBBBAAALLL!" Wetmore says to JD, "You know, I don't think Ronald thinks of himself as a runner. Some guys sit there all day and think about it, wondering what they're gonna run that afternoon. I honestly don't think practice even occurs to Ronald until he gets to Balch. I don't know if that's good or bad." Clad in Kiwi black with the sleeves rolled up and black gloves, Roybal looks lean and mean. As they line up for the third interval, JD says, "Roybal, you're looking buff!" He sarcastically adds, "You're spending too much time in the weight room!"

Lean Jay Johnson hangs onto the back of the pack. He has quietly made remarkable strides the last few weeks, and now he is fighting for a top seven spot. At 5'10" and a buck forty-two, he is a different runner from the 158-pound object of Wetmore's sympathy in early September.

Ironically, the seeds of the both Johnson and Roybal's growth were born on August 18th, when the two discouraged athletes splashed and chatted in the Boulder Creek. On that day Johnson told Roybal, "You know what, we have experience, we have to be calm, and we'll run better, even if it takes to indoors." They have both made the jump. Reese also started his comeback at the same time as Roybal and Johnson, "but whereas he [Reese] made jumps right away, it took me time," says Johnson. Part of the reason it has taken Johnson so long to round into form is that he did nothing but rest when he had mono this summer. "When I got mono," he says, "I quit everything. Job, everything. I'd get up, read two hours, get lunch, read, then fish in the evening. For two weeks all I did was chill out." He started running August 1st, and did not hit 50 miles a week until camp.

Johnson's progress has come in part because of a hectic schedule that does not allow him time to celebrate or dwell on his running. He says, "I'm super busy scholastically, and I'm super busy socially. So, [running] is a choice now. I've never felt trapped by running but I feel . . . I go to practice, run the workout, then forget about it. Like Friday, I was horrible. I came back, relaxed with [girlfriend] Laura [Sturges]—it was cool."

And as he has progressed, his level of expectation has risen. "In August, I thought if I PR'ed in every race on the track, I'd be satisfied. Now I don't think I'd be satisfied with that." Johnson now wants to be on the squad in Lawrence. But even if he does not make it, "this weekend, just being there, I'm completely psyched. There's a big likelihood this is my last race, and I'm glad it's with these guys."

Johnson aspires to compete beyond Big 12's, and it is a situation he has been in twice before. The experience is impacting his strategy this weekend. "My sophomore year, I didn't make the team [to Nationals] and my junior year, I did. I need to give myself a shot to be fifth or sixth [man]. Seventh doesn't matter. If I get fifth, I can make a case to be on that team. I would hope our team's seventh guy is fitter than I am," he says earnestly, "but I don't know. Who knows, I guarantee if Sev was on the team I wouldn't even have the chance to be on the team. Valenti and I are a long way back from Brock and Ronald. I have to run 20 or 30 seconds faster for me to feel like I deserve to be on that team."

Roybal also believes that first dip with Johnson set the tone for him. "That day . . . we talked about the season and put it into perspective. I could see the season as one big long road." He has made a breakthrough today, and he credits "that patience and faith in training and in doing little things. It finally paid off. Plus, I've been doing it for so long, I know when to back off and when to go."

Roybal is ecstatic to be running Big 12's with Johnson. "With Sev dying," he says, "when Johnson ran good it was the perfect thing because

Jay and Sev were best friends. It makes it a little more balanced that he ran good. It feels awesome to have Jay running with us."

But Roybal wants to run well for himself. He says of racing, "It's understanding that that's the beauty of it. It's for you, not like buying something, but for your own growth, maturity, understanding and walk through life, basically." He thinks of how hard he works in races that receive scant media attention or coverage. "How many people work so hard, then pour it in a river? Whether or not people see it, or it's a big deal to anyone, or it makes any difference in the world, it's something big that happened. That's what's happening. Within each runner something's going on, a person's growing."

Roybal thinks back to when he turned the corner, and he points to the quarters the morning of October 16th. "Ever since that day, I don't know what happened. I just ran good, an awesome workout. I can run pretty good workouts [now]. I can't stay with the pack yet on Sunday cause my recovery is slower, I'm not used to all those miles."

Roybal wisely picks and chooses his moments. He says, "Sunday and Wednesday runs kill me. It looks like I'm not trying, but I am. To run faster on Sunday, I'd have to be digging in the well. It's better for me to run 70 a week, with good workouts, being patient, than pushing the envelope, risking being hurt. Sometimes, other people look at Sundays like I ran weak, but that's where I am. I gotta do what I gotta do, and that's the point."

Now Roybal feels that he is on the precipice of a breakthrough, and he feels slightly . . . guilty. "In a way," he sheepishly admits, "I feel embarrassed. I don't want to pass Oscar and Friedberg because they worked harder than me over the summer." But, embarrassment is not enough to make him relent any at Big 12's. He is prepared to stick his nose in it. "I need to make a jump, and if it kills me, it kills me. In workouts, I feel like I can be top five [on the team]. I think, 'Fuck, this is it.' I find a pace, feel the pace, and it's comfortable. That pain feels good. That's when you know you find pace."

More than anything, this weekend, Roybal wants to really compete. He says, "You could say my goal is top ten, top five, but I feel like I don't know what's going to come of it. Mentally, I'm going to be in that race, but it's hard to say because we're running so close now, all of us. I have no idea what spot I am on the team, but I know for sure I'm gonna go out and really go after it. Last year, it wasn't until NC's. It was good at the time, but I need to shape up now because I can't be 45th if we are going to be good. I imagine myself getting second [at Big 12's]. Those fantasies are ultimately what take you to second, behind Gouch—being brave enough to live it. On the other hand, I can just suck, get eighth and not emerge to Nationals, but I don't think that's going to happen."

Roybal will run the race thinking of Severy. "You can feel Severy being gone," his says sadly. "Every day at practice, someone says, 'Hey, who's missing?' I wonder if the other guys say, 'Hey, it's Sev.' In workouts, I wonder where Sev would be. I wonder if Sev could do that 4:21 mile [that he ran at the end of last week's mile repeats]. It's hard to say. People gave him shit about not having speed, but he could bust it out. You don't necessarily need quickness. He was as strong as a fucking mule." In four days, Roybal and Johnson, with Severy in their thoughts, will have a chance to show how far they have come.

Out front, Goucher continues to impress. While still sore, his groin troubles him little today. The others run the first five 800's in 2:25 to 2:22, but Goucher consistently runs 2:14 to 2:12 while running the first 200 in 31 seconds and then settling in to race pace.

For the last two Goucher is allowed a rare luxury—the opportunity to come from behind and kick people down. He bounces up and down in place from toe to toe as the rain keeps its steady patter. He eyes Wetmore and takes a couple forceful exhales as he waits for Wetmore's signal. Three . . . four . . . five seconds pass before Wetmore barks, "OK, Adam, go!" With that, Goucher is off, and as he tears after the others Wetmore yells, "Control, Adam!" He gains ground on the pack as he passes the quarter in 65. Down the backstretch his enormous stride continues to eat track, and he continues to gain. Around the turn he passes Johnson and Ponce, who have fallen off the back of the pack. Eyes set on the rest, he charges down the homestretch, passing them all before the line. Closing in 30, Goucher has run 2:06.

They jog around the turn and back, and yes, the rest is too short to be rightfully referred to as rest. They set off for one last go, and again, Goucher waits for the word to go from Wetmore. Sore groin and all, he repeats the feat, again charging by all his mates, closing in 30, for a half in 2:07. The rain continues.

How Good Are We?

Wetmore's pessimism about their chances of winning NCAA's has sub-sided. The guys are running 40 to 60 minutes easy, and he is holding out hope they do well enough to merit more optimistic projections about their chances. He says, "We gotta find out how good we really are. Ok-lahoma State ran against [number two ranked] Arkansas twice and Ore-gon once. I want to run what we are capable of, and see how we com-pare. Is [winning Nationals] it in reach? Is it believable or not? I want to go to NC's and if we get fourth, I want to say it's a good job if it is a good job. We have a lot to do this weekend and we need to take it more seri-ously than we usually do; not to mention the fact that we're defending champs and we want to defend our championship."

Wetmore is also mulling over Roybal's reaction to some comments he made to him before yesterday's workout. "Just as a joke I said, 'I'm sick of your shit, hiding out in the back.' Maybe I accidentally found a way to motivate him, I don't know. His eyes lit up like I hugged him." He laughs. "Maybe I'll tell that to Valenti and all the guys! Friedberg will be in a race with six CU guys around him going 'What the fuck!'"

A lot goes through the mind when there is nothing to do but wait . . .

Friday, October 30, 1998
Lincoln, Nebraska
Airport Inn Best Western
10 p.m.

Remember, We're Buffaloes

Big 12's are thirteen hours away. The men's and women's teams are crammed into Wetmore and JD's room for some final instructions. With all the bodies piled on the beds and on any open space on the floor, the heat quickly rises. Everyone has just returned from a team dinner at Giordano's. A large CU contingent including parents of some of the athletes were there, and although the food was unspectacular, everyone enjoyed watching if Goucher was going to get "gouchered" with his meal (he did not). Good thing, for Wetmore says, "He's being especially grouchy this weekend." Despite massages, treatment and easy running, his left leg is still sore. It irritates him to no end. His competition had better watch out, for when he is grouchy, he is usually at his best.

The big question mark right now is the status of Brock Tessman. Last Saturday, on an easy ten mile run, he began experiencing acute pain in the ball of his left foot. "Something," he says, "flipped out—out of nowhere." Running a hard twelve miles on Magnolia on Sunday worsened the pain. The pain continued to worsen on Monday, and he began debating whether he ought to take a day off to rest his foot. However, he ruled against taking a day off and on Tuesday morning he met Wetmore at the track to run the 800-meter repeats the others were running that afternoon. "It was," he says, "a bad idea." He never finished the workout. "I just couldn't do it anymore. It went from sore to something I've never felt in my life." A visit to the doctor on Wednesday confirmed the worst—a neuroma in his foot.

While not commonplace, the injury does occur to runners training at a high level; particularly those who, like Tessman, are forefoot strikers. A neuroma is an inflammation of the nerve between the third and fourth metatarsals on the foot, and there is no cure besides surgery to cut off the inflamed nerve ending, or rest. Neither option is feasible three weekends before Nationals.

Tessman needed an alternative, one that would alleviate the pain and allow him an opportunity to finish out the season. With no guarantees, Tessman elected to have a cortisone shot in his foot yesterday—something that appalls him—but he saw no other options.

He was conspicuously absent from practice on Wednesday and Thursday. Only today do his teammates hear the news. He is planning on giving it a go tomorrow but only then will he know if he is capable of running.

Goucher is late, and they are delaying the meeting for him. When Wetmore remarks that he is late, Jen Gruia sarcastically says, "No!" and everyone busts up. He arrives momentarily and everyone passes out the loot from the race sponsors — water bottles, towels, and PowerBars.

Wetmore goes over some administrative details and instructs Captains Reese and Burroughs to make sure everyone is in compliance. Then, he gives the men his final race instructions:

If you run 3:10 a kilo, that's 25:20. That's a pretty good day. As a rule of thumb, that's what you're looking for as you click forward . . . but remember that's just a tool as we're really here to run our opponents. Tonight you should make your plan. Plan on beating people.

We're in box twelve, and that's a good piece of luck. I like to be on the edges. Instead of being boxed in, not able to move, we're smashing into trees. Remember, we're buffaloes, we like that.

The main thing we're looking to do here is see our opponents. We probably want to practice getting out faster than we're used to. Staying calm when you're stuck, it's a good plan when we're at Rim Rock. A team that keeps its head through that is going to do pretty good.

The men's race is a dual meet vs. Oklahoma State. They're a top-ten team as far as I can tell. I met with you all individually, so you know what I expect. Men, from 7k on in, take advantage of people being stupid. Stay calm, we don't need any rah-rah. That's how we win, taking advantage of other people's unnecessary enthusiasm.

Now the only thing left to do is celebrate the great occasion of Jen Fazioli's birth. Eighteen years ago we were blessed with her and we're very happy about that.

With that there is some cake, and everyone sings her happy birthday. Everyone starts filing out, and several people linger around to chat with Wetmore, including Tessman.

Wetmore has had some experience with neuromas because he has one himself. He tells Tessman that years ago he was diagnosed with a neuroma, and he scheduled the surgery so as not to put his consecutive days running streak in jeopardy. At midnight he ran a two-mile run, and he figured he would have 47 hours until he had to run again. But when the doc informed him that even if they performed the surgery that morning there would not be time enough time to recuperate and get a run in that next day, Wetmore decided against the surgery.

Tessman is dumbfounded. "What!" he says. "How do you run?" Wetmore chuckles and tells him, "You gotta understand, you're dealing with a person with a whole different pain tolerance than normal people. I just can't sprint or run on really rocky ground. That day I ran on the Mesa Trail, I must have dinged it ten times." Tessman stares at Wetmore incredulously. "This is not gonna be fun. This is gonna be the worst day of my life."

The course record at Pioneer's Park was set way back in 1992. Kenyan Richard Kosgei, then of Barton County Community College, ran the 8k course in 23:54. Goucher wants the record. The course record is listed in the race program, but no one sees it, because Wetmore does not distribute it at the meeting.

He does not distribute copies of the program because there is a prominent tribute to Severy in it, and he feels giving this to them will do nothing but engender unreasonable expectations and unnecessary enthusiasm as they try to win one for Sev. It is his best decision of the evening.

The 1998 Big 12
Cross Country Championship

It is an hour until race time and the men stretch in their black CU sweats and chat on the grass next to the van. JD blasts some techno music from the van and the guys enjoy this very uncharacteristically Colorado move.

It is a perfect day for racing—50 degrees and overcast. With these conditions and Goucher on the prowl, the course record of 23:54 is in jeopardy. Tessman only hopes he can compete.

Tessman stretches with the knowledge that he has had the cortisone shot, along with enough Advil this morning to numb an elephant. He does not divulge just how many Advil he has taken, but he later remarks, "I only took what anybody in my situation would take." He cannot believe how fast his fortunes have changed: just a week ago he was the "X Factor," and now his season, and his collegiate career, are in jeopardy.

He heads out with the team ten minutes later on the warm-up. He has not run since getting the cortisone shot, and he is apprehensive as they start moving. Three minutes later, his worst fears are realized. The pain is too great; he cannot go on. "Guys, I can't do it," he tells them as

Ponce prepares for battle.

CHRIS LEAR

he stops. "Good luck." Reese turns and says, "OK, Brockford, nice try." The team jogs on. Tessman puts his hands on his hips and walks away in the opposite direction. He is inconsolable.

The team has no time to waste. Tessman lets Wetmore know he cannot run. In his place, the team has an option. Berkshire has made the trip out here to watch and he could go on a moment's notice. Wetmore would have to file an emergency declaration for him to run, but seeing as they probably will not need him, Wetmore elects to go with the eight men he has left.

When the runners return from their warm-up, Goucher heads to the training tent to get a last minute massage from Tammy on his sore leg. Her massage seems to help, because when the gun goes off, he heads right to the front of the pack—running *hard*. It probably would have been harder if the meet directors had their way. They approached Wetmore before the race to tell him they planned on having a moment of silence for Sev on the starting line. Wetmore quickly nixed that plan.

Goucher hits 1k in 2:45, with Andrew Hennessy, a freshman at Oklahoma State, right with him. Brian Jansen, a junior at Kansas, is also right there. At 2k, Hennessy has faded some, but Jansen is still there, challenging Goucher. More important, Oklahoma State is dominating the race. At 2k they have five runners in the top ten. But 6k remain.

At about 2.5k, Goucher starts putting some ground on Jansen, and at 3k, Goucher is all alone, 50 meters in front of the field. "I didn't know who was with me," he would say later, "but I lost him in a matter of seconds. One second I could hear him, then five seconds later, I couldn't. He was out the back door pretty quick."

Behind Goucher, CU runs a typically conservative race. At two miles, Friedberg is the second Buffalo, in eighth place, and Roybal and Reese run together in the twenties. Just then, Roybal looks over at Reese and Reese slaps him across the face—*hard!* It takes Roybal by surprise for he had forgotten that he had told Reese to do it. He would laugh about it later, saying, "I didn't know he was gonna do it, but I was glad. I *needed* it!"

Goucher passes 5k all alone, running through a throng of supporters who have lined the area by the top of the course. Wetmore waits for his guys here, and Goucher looks positively effortless as he passes in 14:50— ten seconds ahead of pace. "Let's get that record!" he yells to Goucher. "Let's go!" His teammates have started to move up, and Friedberg is now in fifth, surrounded by three athletes from Oklahoma State.

Ponce has moved up to eighth, and he can see Friedberg up ahead. He would say later, "I saw Friedberg surrounded by all these orange jerseys and I thought, 'I gotta get those motherfuckers!'"

Meanwhile, farther back, Johnson has moved up to twentieth and

Batliner is right on his heels. Johnson is following through on his pledge to get into it. But at this point, they have work to do, because Oklahoma State is threatening to run away with it.

Goucher cruises up the course's most challenging feature—a gradual 400-meter climb followed by a steep 200 meter hill that crests about a half mile from the finish—with ease. He is on course record pace, and as he makes his way down the finishing stretch, he sees the clock and knows the course record now belongs to him. He shakes his fist in the air as he crosses the line in 23:45, over eight seconds ahead of the old mark, and a whopping 50 seconds ahead of runner-up Chuck Sloan of Oklahoma State.

Goucher is nonchalant about his win. He says, "I feel sharper. My legs are still tired for some reason, and I got a little complacent, I was looking around, but I definitely felt better than at Pre-Nationals. I had a lot left at the end. I felt like I was doing an AT, it really wasn't bad."

With Goucher in first and OSU's Sloan in second, the battle for team honors is on. Finishing five seconds behind Chuck Sloan is none other than the Iceberg himself. Mike Friedberg has gone from the Junior Varsity a year ago to third at conference. He is ecstatic about the race: "I felt better than I ever have, *ever*. I didn't even feel bad until the last 2k, and I was just, like, rolling the whole time, feeling good."

One of Iowa State's Kenyans finishes fourth while Kansas's Jansen impressively hangs on for fifth. OSU gets their second man across in sixth, but Oscar Ponce finishes right behind him in seventh to keep CU a step ahead in the team competition. Right behind Ponce, Roybal battles Oklahoma's Rene Carlsen down the finishing stretch and neither is giving an inch. But thirty meters from the finish, Roybal stumbles, almost falling, and that gives Carlsen the extra step he needs to finish eighth.

Reese finishes two places and four seconds back in eleventh to round out the scoring for the Buffs, and seal another conference championship. Roybal is psyched with his performance, but Reese is not. "I didn't take any chances," Reese says. "I didn't take any chance on switching gears, ever." But nonetheless, he likes his chances in the season's final races: "It usually happens like this with me. I need one race where I don't take a chance, and the next race, I know I'll be OK. I know I can be up there the next few races, if I just take a chance."

Johnson and Batliner finish 20th and 21st for the sixth and seventh positions—in 25:19 and 25:23. Last night Wetmore had said running 25:20 would be, "a pretty good day." Well, as their fifth man, Reese ran 24:57. Wetmore is pleased. He says afterwards, "I'm happy with the men. It's their first race in three weeks. I thought they did a good job." He is particularly delighted with Friedberg. On his third-place finish he says,

"That's cool. It's a great race for him, people gotta be scratching their heads over him, [saying] 'Who is that guy?'"

For Batliner, the good news comes *after* the race, when his calf feels healthy. He says, "I finally got my running legs back. At 5k, I picked it up, and I felt like there was this little angry man trapped in me, somewhere, and I haven't quite managed to dig him out yet. But I finally got my running legs back. It's my first hard race and my calf's handling the work now, so that's good news." He will continue to evaluate his progress from day to day, but he does not plan on missing any more hard workouts.

There are only a few hard ones left, anyhow. Says Wetmore, "We'll run ten or twelve more hard days." And then, well, it is like Goucher says, "Then I'm gonna get ready to kill people."

It is a joyous squad on the victory stand as the CU men are presented with the conference trophy. Wetmore does not join them, and neither does Tessman. Tessman stands alone off to the side watching his teammates. The twenty feet that separates him from his teammates feels like a mile. He cannot bear to even crack a smile.

THE 1998 BIG 12 CROSS COUNTRY CHAMPIONSHIPS

PLACE	NAME	UNIVERSITY	CLASS	TIME
1.	Adam Goucher	Colorado	Sr.	23:45.7 CR
2.	Charles Sloan	Oklahoma State	Jr.	24:35.5
3.	Mike Friedberg	Colorado	So.	24:40.5
4.	Philemon Too	Iowa State	Jr.	24:42.6
5.	Brain Jansen	Kansas	Jr.	24:43.8
6.	Nathaniel Lane	Oklahoma State	Sr.	24:50.4
7.	Oscar Ponce	Colorado	Jr.	24:52.8
8.	Rene Carlsen	Oklahoma State	Sr.	24:53.1
9.	Ronald Roybal	Colorado	Jr.	24:53.4
10.	Brandon Jessup	Kansas State	So.	24:55.9
11.	Tom Reese	Colorado	Sr.	24:57.0
12.	Brian Young	Oklahoma State	Sr.	25:01.5
13.	Chris Wells	Texas	Jr.	25:03.0
14.	Ryan Pirtle	Missouri	Sr.	25:05.1
15.	Nick Smith	Missouri	So.	25:06.1
16.	Joe McCune	Missouri	Jr.	25:06.4
17.	David Lichoro	Iowa State	Jr.	25:07.5
18.	Andrew Hennessy	Oklahoma State	Fr.	25:13.8
19.	Ben Dawson	Texas	Fr.	25:14.8
20.	Jay Johnson	Colorado	Sr.	25:19.4
21.	Adam Batliner	Colorado	Sr.	25:23.5
36.	Chris Valenti	Colorado	So.	25:50.8

Back to Work

Everyone is exhausted from the race and from a Halloween party that lasted late into the night at Robbie, Roybal, and Bat's place. Robbie DJ'ed, and everyone dressed up in costumes and danced through the night. Goucher and Reese had one of the best costumes, dressing as Chippendale dancers, complete with large tufts of chest hair.

But today is Sunday, and the long run is a ritual that must be observed. The pace mercifully stays controlled the entire way, and even the mileage hogs "only" run sixteen or seventeen miles. Everyone silently goes through the exercise, too tired to converse . . .

Master Blaster

Tessman walks into the gym as the team stretches. It is the last anyone will see of him this season. "It was hard enough to watch the race," he says. "I'm getting as far away from running as I can right now. I'm gonna take time off until December first."

Despite the injury, he is still a convert to Wetmore's system. Reflecting on the season he says, "It was going better than I thought it would go. The fact that I didn't race doesn't change the shape I was in. I know what kind of shape I can get into with this type of training. This is definitely encouraging for track."

The seven runners that are competing at regionals and alternate Chris Valenti are running 12 x 400 around Scott Carpenter Park. It is the first time this season that they are running here. The park is just down the Creek Path from the school and it is a grass loop that rises and falls. Running clockwise, there is a gradual ascent followed by a steep downhill. Wetmore will have them alternate directions so that they practice running hard up both short, steep hills and more gradual hills.

The men are paired up with women into teams with names like Slugs, Tapeworms, and Maggots. Goucher is a Maggot, and he is paired with freshman Jen Fazioli, the slowest member of the women's squad. Goucher sees his pairing on the board and says, "I always get my ass kicked in this workout. I might as well give up, I never win." Now, he does not exactly get killed, but to his ire, in five years, his team has never won. Wetmore still likes the Maggots' chances. "She's not out the back as much as he is out front," he says. But this does nothing to calm Faz's fears. "I heard about last year," she tells him, and those in earshot laugh, including Goucher. "Hey," he tells her, "all you gotta do is win."

The little red-headed freshman from New York is still apprehensive. Last year, Goucher brought his teammate to tears. He says, "It just sucked. I was getting pissed because I thought she wasn't being tough. I was being a competitive jerk. I'm a competitive person; I want to win. But shit happens. This workout is not meant for me to win."

The other teams' chances are helped by Goucher's lingering soreness. Running 17.5 miles on Sunday at 5:45 a mile the day after setting a course record at Big 12's does not help. But, in a continuing effort to get healthy, he ran an easy 65 minutes yesterday and then received another hard massage on his left leg last night.

Wetmore addresses the team as they finish stretching: "This is the last hard anaerobic workout significantly above race pace. It's up to you to make it work. Meet me at Scott Carpenter Park in twenty minutes, psyched up and spiked up."

When they arrive at the park, the air is chilly. The sky is threatening snow, and Wetmore greets them brusquely, "Hurry up! If it starts snowing, I'm going home, and you're doing this alone." Everyone laughs, knowing no matter the weather, he is not going anywhere.

As is his custom, Wetmore offers more information on the purpose behind the workout as they change into their spikes. "You can develop your own team strategy. You can tag each other, do any secret strategy, it's entirely up to you. Everyone does twelve. The object is to get a deep anaerobic stimulus. It's easy to do it on the track and have me yell at you, but this is more fun." He emphasizes how much they should be hurting: "Make sure we're getting into debt. If we're feeling good and controlled by six, you better get going."

After the first interval, Goucher looks at Wetmore and says jokingly, "What if you've already achieved the workout?" Wetmore smiles and says, "Then you have eleven more workouts!"

Some of the athletes have stripped down to their shorts, and some are in tights. All jump in place to stay warm while waiting for their teammates. Alan Culpepper jogs by as they are full into it, and Wetmore announces, "Hey, Dung Beetles, here's a former guest champion." Culpepper smiles and waves hello.

The practice is competitive, and Reese is not too happy that his team is falling back. "I'm in debt, dude," he says halfway through, "I just ran three hard." Unhappy with his teammate's effort, he yells after her, "Come on, Gruia! Try!" Batliner is also already whipped, and thinking of his minuscule recovery he says, "I don't know if I want Bri to go faster or slower."

Wetmore is not impressed. "Come on," he yells, "you guys should be barfing by now." He is especially vocal, and he addresses individuals as they get ready to set off. He yells to Reese, "Come on, Tommy, reach down! Time to roll up the sleeves," and to Goucher, "Reach down. Where's Lagat? Look at Lagat! Think of Rim Rock Farm, you gotta sprint when you're tired!"

Despite looking like she ran to the death, Faz is not victorious, but she is relieved not to have finished last. The Maggots actually finish second to the Dung Beetles–Burroughs and Valenti. Ponce was leading into the last one, but, already exhausted, he could not hold his position. After trudging home on the last one, he says, "I didn't have shit."

Tomorrow is another medium distance run, but everyone is already dreading Friday, when they will run their last session of repeat miles this year—on the track.

Skeleton Dreams

Jason Robbie is back at practice. He is recovering from surgery on his IT band and is set to start running in the pool today. Already Captain Skinny before the surgery, he looks positively malnourished now. Every muscle in his left leg is atrophied from his quadriceps down to his ankles. The muscle loss is accentuated because of the swelling in his knee that has yet to subside since the surgery. If ever there is an infomercial for starving Norwegians, Robbie will be a plum candidate.

He grabs Batliner to see if he, too, is going for a pool run. "I don't know," says Bat sarcastically. "Let's just kick each other in the face for ten minutes and go home." Misery loves company, and today they have a crowd; Goucher is joining them.

Not surprisingly, Goucher is fussy about going to the pool, but he sees no other option. Even running around Kitt for 40 minutes is not an option because by doing so he will not be resting his leg. If he is going to run, he figures he might as well go to the Tank with the others. He elects to go to the pool because he thinks that a day off (God forbid) might give his leg the recovery it needs to get well.

At pool's edge, he reconsiders. "Oh man," he says, "I don't know if I want to do this." He jumps in. Bat, Robbie, and Gouch run in the deep end of the diving area. Women on Stairmasters look down at them from behind black tinted glass overlooking the pool, and a high school diving team ignores their presence in the diving area.

After only 30 minutes, Goucher has had enough. "If you're going to advance your fitness, or get any aerobic benefit out of it, you gotta work hard, and I'm just not in the mood." He starts feeling guilty about his abbreviated pool run, but then he reconsiders. "At least I did something. I didn't take the day completely off."

Batliner is out a few minutes later. He had thought of calling it a day, but then he decides to jog for 30 minutes around Kitt. He wanted to run the Tank, but he skipped it fearing he would be doing too much. "What sucks right now is I'm so tentative," he says while jogging around Kitt. "The last time I felt like this, [five weeks ago] I couldn't run without a limp three days later. I feel like a pussy." He should not. It is commendable that he is able to heed his own advice—"Have the courage to rest." Twenty minutes into the run, his leg starts to ache, so he calls it a day. Now is not the time to risk injury.

Batliner hopes to extend his discipline to the dinner table. Wetmore has put him on a 2000-calorie-a-day diet. Batliner is down to 138 pounds—six pounds over his racing weight—but he needs to lose more. He says Wetmore told him, "Don't go eat Village for breakfast and have your 2000 calories 'cause then you're screwed, you can't eat anything all day." Batliner went anyway this morning, getting the number five over medium. After which he says, "I ain't eating shit till dinner." It is only a couple of hours away . . .

In Wetmore's opinion, the emphasis on weight is not overrated. "Leanness is underrated," he says. "I tell people, 'Go look at *Track and Field News*. See what those people look like. You should look like a skeleton with a condom pulled over your skull.'"

While Goucher, Batliner, and Robbie were in the pool, the men quickly get down to business at the Tank. They ran the full Tank—12.5 miles—in a blazing 1:17. For Friedberg, it was a "good steady pace," but Roybal emphatically disagrees. He fell off early and tried in vain to catch them on the way back. He tells Friedberg, "I was running my fastest on the way back and I couldn't catch you assholes. I thought I was catching [you], but it turned out to be a bunch of overweight women training with a personal trainer."

Ponce is not laughing. "My shin is hurting," he says, "really bad." The complaint is alarming considering his pain threshold. He is not one to cry wolf. Against his better judgement, he stayed with the leaders the whole way. "I was trying to take it easy, but it's hard to do that and go faster . . ." Pride, it seems, can cause more pain than any natural obstacle.

Milers on the track are two days away.

Down

Repeat miles on the track. Wetmore's men have been anticipating this workout since August. Each previous session of "milers" has led to this. One final session, in spikes, on the track, *flying!* In years past this workout has served as *the* barometer to demonstrate the progress they have made since the beginning of the season.

The women will start the workout around 3:30 p.m., and the men will start as soon as the women have finished so that each group receives Wetmore's undivided attention. The conditions have hardly been worse all season; it is a brisk, cold afternoon, and the wind is howling. By the time the men arrive at the track at 4 p.m., the women are finishing the last of their four repeat miles. Heather Burroughs, CU's number one runner, is pulled before the fourth interval. With the exception of Carrie Messner and Lesley Higgins, the women are *way* off their projected times.

The sun is beginning its descent behind the Flatirons, increasing the late afternoon chill. As the women finish, a discouraged Wetmore turns to the men, and says, "Men are up in six minutes." At 4:15, they begin the session with their first of six repeat miles with a scant two minutes rest in between. Their target times are as follows:

Goucher	4:26
Friedberg	4:40
Reese	4:40
Roybal	4:40
Ponce	4:44
Batliner	4:44
Johnson	4:46
Valenti	4:46

Batliner is in spikes and shorts on the side of the track as they head around the first turn. He can see his own breath, and he feels the wind rolling westward. "I'm sitting the first one out," he says, "which makes me wonder why I put my spikes on and took my pants off." It is too late to bother with the hassle of dressing and again disrobing. He takes off down the homestretch to keep warm.

"Let's run the first one two seconds slow," Wetmore tells them. "It's a warm-up." Into the first mile, Goucher battles the wind, and himself.

He labors as he passes with a lap to go. Wetmore senses his distress. "Come on Gouch, control, control!"

He finishes five seconds slow, in 4:31. Friedberg, Reese, and Roybal come across in 4:44—four seconds slow. Ponce and his aching shin hit the line three seconds behind them, in 4:47. Valenti and Johnson run 4:50, also four seconds too slow. At least they are consistent.

They jog slowly around the curve past the water pit to the hundred meter mark before turning and shuffling back towards the start line. No words are exchanged, and as they reach the line, they have only twenty seconds longer to recover before the second mile. They set out knowing they are off pace, but despite their best efforts, the second mile is worse than the first. Goucher scratches and claws his way to a 4:30 mile. Valenti is off the back; he trudges home in 5:06. Wetmore has seen enough there. "Chris V," he calls to him, "you're done." He does not object.

The Junior Varsity watch their teammates by the finish line. They catch Wetmore's controlled wrath. He does not yell at them so much as pronounce in a tone of voice that says, "Listen, or else." He glares at them and says, "Don't stand around getting cold, you got a race tomorrow. Get outta here!" They waste no time filing out of the gate at the track's entrance.

The sun has almost completed its inglorious descent. The temperature drops precipitously. Goucher fights the elements, fights Lagat, fights Mwangi, fights time. He cannot get ahead. It is not for lack of effort. He comes through the half in 2:16—three seconds slow. His respiration is audible as he barrels down the homestretch. His lungs are desperately seeking oxygen that simply does not exist in the Rocky Mountain air. With each lap, his respiration is louder. He slows to 4:34. Before today, Goucher had not missed his splits in so much as a single workout. Yet, on this interval, he is eight seconds slow. The other also miss their targets. Loud enough for Wetmore to hear, JD says, "God, that one was a disaster."

JD turns to Wetmore as they head around the turn and asks, "Does Gouch always breathe that loudly? You can hear him from 50 meters away." Wetmore looks straight ahead in silence before acknowledging, "He's hurting today." But Wetmore does not budge. Halfway through a workout where not a person has met their goal on so much as a single mile, Wetmore does not relax the standards he has set.

One hundred and twenty seconds have impossibly passed since the third mile. Wetmore admonishes them as they get ready to go. "Come on, let's get to work, you're slow." The wind has mercifully ceased. There is a dead calm as they round the first turn. Goucher raises his intensity, and it is now possible to hear him breathing an astonishing 100 meters away. Despite his best effort, he hits the half in 2:15. "Come on, stay on it," says Wetmore.

Goucher finishes in 4:34. Friedberg pulls away from the pack and runs a 4:41—only one second off pace. But behind him, Ponce falls farther off the pack and Johnson can only manage a five minute mile. Now, Wetmore has seen enough. He calls to them as they start to head around the first turn, "Change your shoes, you're done everybody. Not a good day." Reese and Friedberg turn around in protest. "Come on!" Friedberg pleads, hands out to his sides, "I was less than one second off!" Wetmore does not entertain his input. "Change your shoes. You're done." Reese starts to speak and is abruptly cut short by Wetmore, "You're done!"

"What's the point in killing ourselves?" he continues to no one in particular, "We got a couple of races to run. If we're not ready, we're not ready. Why put a nail in our coffin?"

Thinking of his gimpy knee, Reese again pleads his case. "I want to do this because I don't think I'll be able to run tomorrow." Friedberg butts in as well. "I'll cruise the fifth in 4:40, hopefully, then go for it." Their words fall on deaf ears. Having skipped the first mile, only Batliner is permitted another four circuits. He hits his target pace: 4:44.

Goucher puts on his trainers. The conditions appall him. "It's so freaking windy out there. There's wind on three sides of the track." His body tenses and his voice increases in volume as he speaks. "I felt like shit out there. I had nothing, nothing at all! How the hell am I supposed to race fast if I can't even run a 4:30 for a goddamn mile! Fuck!"

Ponce appears shell-shocked. He speaks in a hushed, funereal voice. "Man, that was a tough day; a weird day. I had no energy. It was one of those days you feel every step. It kept getting progressively worse, too. I was a second slower every time."

They do not waste time getting away from the track. Ever since Severy's death, the group psychology has slowly been pieced together. Now they have bombed a workout at the most inopportune time. As they leave, any synergy that exists billows like a spiderweb in the wind, threatening to lose its grip and disappear.

Another Casualty

A blanket of snow five inches deep covers the cross country course. Any hope the Junior Varsity guys entertained of getting out there and tearing it up in their last race of the season vanished as Mother Nature worked under the cover of night. It snowed last year, too, and Wetmore cancelled the race, to Berkshire's surprise. "I thought for sure Wet would have us run. There could be six feet of water and he would tell us to swim five miles. [But] it was dumping. It was insane." This year the snow is not as severe, so the race is on.

The men slip and slide their way through the course to the end. Matt Elmuccio runs as well as can be expected in these conditions, taking home first place in 27:25, eight seconds ahead of Slattery. Despite the conditions, Elmuccio has managed to run 43 seconds faster than what he ran on this same course, without snow, on September 5th. Clearly, he is fit.

A year ago Slattery finished fourth at the Foot Locker National High School Cross Country Championship. Sean Smith, on the other hand, was a member of the U.S. Junior Triathlon team. Today, Smith, in his first season of collegiate cross country, finishes just one second behind Slattery. Wetmore may have found his next Friedberg.

The cold, dreary day turns frighteningly gloomy for Wetmore after he talks with Reese. Reese has kept the severity of his injury to himself all season, perhaps coming back before he had fully recuperated from the surgery on his femur. Reese could have allowed it more time to heal and started in October, but he says, "I would've said [to myself] 'What a puss! It's my last cross season ever and I didn't even give it a shot.'"

Yesterday, while doing strides, his knee started throbbing—unbeknownst to Wetmore. Reese was able to run the milers, but by last night Reese's knee had had enough. He says matter-of-factly, "It swelled up like a balloon. Right then, I knew three things. One, there's blood in the joints again. Two, the cracking and clicking tells me there's loose, cracked cartilage. That all hurts and affects the bending of the knee. But the cracked femur is what I can totally feel, and that's what stops me. It doesn't feel at all stable when I land, the pain shoots, and it feels like my leg is going to go backwards."

He knows all the data that this sensation tells him because he felt precisely the same pain before he had surgery last spring. Yesterday's workout almost prematurely ended his season. "It was hurting just like this in the springtime," he says, "then I had a workout and I couldn't run because it locked on me. The workout yesterday felt the exact same way it did then. I think the only reason it didn't lock is because that was a steeple workout and this wasn't."

Despite the pain, he has come too far to call it quits now. Reese told Wetmore the extent of his injury today, and Reese says they are both determined to "do whatever we can to get through the season." For now, Reese will treat the pain symptomatically and tough it out. The first step is getting the blood and excess fluid drained from his knee. Reese will do that next Wednesday. If there is an upside to the injury, it is that it has happened at such a late date. "All the training's done," he says. "I'm in great aerobic shape. If it was a couple of weeks ago, it would be different."

While Reese understands why he is ailing, he does not understand why so many of the other guys are struggling to survive the training intact. "He [Wetmore] believes in training a lot of mileage. Lately, people haven't been able to handle that, so it takes away from his ideal program. What sucks is that we're having injury problems off of low mileage."

Because he did not have the mileage base that his teammates acquired during the summer, Reese has thrown everything he has into the workouts. All season he has endured off days where "It's been a struggle just to bop along. I just go eight minute miles, and it feels like there's nothing in my legs. I've tried to do strides sometimes on Thursdays, and it's just no faster." Until Nationals, Reese will rest completely instead of trotting on his easy days. He hopes this will allow him to coast through the few remaining workouts.

Yesterday, essentially, was his last hard effort. While initially he was, "super-pissed," that Wetmore cut it short, he feels better about it today. Initially, he says, "I didn't like it. I felt I was going to make up the difference on the last two. I think I could've rolled one of 'em in 4:29, 4:30. But I don't think it's necessarily necessary to get all that in, especially since I don't have a base."

As captain, Reese is also concerned about what the team is thinking. Now he thinks Wetmore made the right decision in prematurely ending yesterday's mile repeats, and more important, that the team agrees and that the synergy they have struggled to rebuild is intact. "It is," he admits, "a workout everyone prides themselves on running great and being super-confident going into Nationals." But he says, "I think it's good that Mark looked at the team as a whole. I think he looked at Goucher and Valenti and he forgot, though, that on the last ones, you make up a lot of ground. But there's something to be said that Gouch was getting slower and slower. Jay wasn't feeling good. Roybal wasn't feeling good. Nordberg looked good and he felt he was hitting his splits and he didn't have the confidence to do well [at Nationals] without it. It made him the most distraught, but I think he's OK."

He feels the experience that the others have is what makes them realize they will be OK. "Two guys, Oscar and Nordberg, haven't been hurting, and they don't have experience [running NC's]. But with the seasons they've had, and since the rest of us have experience, we should be fine; it shouldn't affect our confidence. I mean, the only two people that haven't been to Nationals are the two people besides Gouch who have the most training." Besides, he reasons, "I feel that all the training we do should give us justification for cutting it short. The less the better in the last two weeks." Is he worried about Goucher? "No. I think Goucher knows that, and backing off will help him. If he's hurting a little bit and that justifies him backing off, then good, because he runs well when he's rested."

Wetmore is not overly concerned about having to cut it short yesterday. He says, "They were just tired, that's all. It's no tragedy. They had four hard days in six. They raced Saturday, ran long Sunday, hard Tuesday and medium distance Wednesday."

"A lot of the guys told me there were absolutely shot after the Master Blaster." But, he reiterates, "There's no tragedy going on, they're just tired. I pulled them aside after that [at Balch], so they wouldn't go home discouraged. In the long run, they needed the rest more than two more repeat miles. I've never done this workout in the same week as the Master Blaster and I had no idea the Tuesday workout was so hard. I thought of it as an easy workout but it turns out they ran their guts out. Anyway," he concludes, "I'm not worried about that workout at all."

CU HOME OPEN

PLACE	NAME	PACE	TIME
1.	Matt Elmuccio	5:31	27:25
2.	Steve Slattery	5:33	27:33
3.	Sean Smith	5:33	27:34
4.	Jim Robbins*	5:34	27:36
5.	David Romero*	5:37	27:55
6.	Spencer Casey*	5:38	27:57
7.	Zach Crandall	5:38	27:57
8.	Wes Berkshire	5:38	28:00
9.	Cameron Harrison	5:43	28:21
11.	Matt Ruhl	5:52	29:09

* open athletes

Punchdrunk Fighters

It is cold and snowy. Coming out of the van at 8:30 a.m. to run for an hour and a half, the runners look glum. Not everyone in Boulder wants to be them on this day. The runners are doing three-quarters of their normal Sunday, but that is of little solace in the cold. Two miles into the run, the men must cross a small creek that is impossible to avoid. Not only will they be cold after that; their feet will also be freezing.

The Junior Varsity runners have begun their active rest, and Reese is taking the day off, so only six men greet the cold this morning: Goucher, Friedberg, Johnson, Ponce, Roybal, and Batliner.

Goucher finishes ahead of the pack, but he is quiet and despondent. Perhaps he is thinking of Friday's workout, or perhaps he is just mentally and physically fatigued. Perhaps he feels worse today, when he needs to start feeling good, than when he blazed 22 miles here on August 30th. Whatever the reason, he is down. He looks exasperated as he boards the van. "I don't know what's wrong," he says, "I just have no fight in me right now." He has two weeks to get his act together.

The best news today comes not from Boulder, but from Wheeling, Illinois. The Torres twins, despite not getting full scholarships, call Wetmore to tell him that next year, they will be Buffaloes. Jorge just won the state meet with the fastest time in Illinois in 23 years, and Ed finished third.

While this year's team has two weeks left in their quest, the Torres twins' commitment has him thinking of next year's squad. "This was supposed to be our year," Wetmore says, "but with all the disappointments and interruptions it's our worst feeling year ever. It won't be our worst finish, but we'll be pretty good next year."

The downside to the Torres commitment is that after them, the bank is empty. "What it means," Wetmore continues, "is we're pretty much on every kid's list, and we don't have the money to bring them here. It's pretty much been like that since we got Goucher. Six months after we signed him, every kid in the country had Colorado on his list."

With money so scarce, his other option is to only recruit native Coloradans. He has toyed with the idea. "We'd be a full in-state program. We'd offer everybody only in-state tuition. We won't be winning every year, but we'll go just about every year with the Gouchers, Reeses, Severys, and Tiernans."

Wetmore examines his current squad: "Elmo and Slattery are major out-of-state recruits. If I don't get Slattery, I get Crandall, who is only ten seconds behind him. If I gave all my money away to all my assistants, we'd still be a pretty good team, and that's a simpler way of life, isn't it? We'd just be stuck in town, and we'd be good." He reconsiders, though, when he thinks of the potential the Torres brothers have. "Ah, we gotta do this Torres thing."

But there is another advantage to having a full in-state team. He could prove it is his method that makes his guys so good, not their superior genetic talent. Says Wetmore, "I'm not a provincialist or a jingoist. The complaint in distance coaching is that you can't be good unless you buy your team. If we did it this way, we'd be a national program, and it'd be a big blow to that argument that there's no other way to do it." He thinks of the foreign all-star teams at schools like Oklahoma State: "If they take 4:20 and 9:20 kids from all the contiguous states, they could get three a year. That's fifteen kids [over five years]. You show up seven days a week, train their asses hard, and you got a pretty good program. They'd be just as good as they are now."

Hard work is the key to Wetmore's program. But how does he explain his overwhelming success with walk-ons who come from altitude? He thinks they have different physiological characteristics from having been raised in this environment, along with some other intangibles. He says, "Physiologically, they know how to race up here. They have sensory data they use to measure the effort they use while a sea-level kid has to throw it all out. The other thing is that they don't know how good they are; no one does. They're undertrained, they have bad facilities. Every front range kid is about 40 years behind everyone else."

But being undertrained is a characteristic too many high school runners share, even the sea-level guys. "Look at Friedberg and [Jon] Cooper. There's just no telling how many 9:30 two milers are gonna be 29:30 10k runners after a couple years of hard training."

Hard training *works,* not only for the walk-ons, but for all his athletes. It is one thing to sell hard work to a kid who comes in with mediocre credentials. It is another thing altogether to convince the 4:10 guy that hey, if you want be good, start running twenty miles on Sunday. Getting his top athletes to train like his walk-ons is one of Wetmore's most difficult tasks. Only this year did Goucher start training like he is better than the others. For Slattery, seeing Goucher's example, it may come earlier. But, according to Wetmore, Slattery's success on the high school level has almost retarded his early development this season. "Steve has a bit of a handicap," he says. "He still hasn't gotten it through his head that it's not any day now that he'll outkick Goucher. He's got to learn that beating people up in New Jersey is one thing. But every single guy on this team is better than [New Jersey scholastic star] Murad Campbell. It could take him a long time until he realizes, 'Hey, I'm an average guy in Colorado distance running.' Until he out-trains them, he's not gonna be what he can be. The better you are, the harder it is to realize that."

The question is: Without the lure of an athletic scholarship, how many guys will be willing to suffer so much?

Tuesday, November 10, 1998
Potts Field
3:45 p.m.

Call to Arms

"Last year," JD says, his breath visible, "they never had a day colder than today." He is bundled up in a big CU parka. The 30-mph gusts will cut through any lighter clothing. The runners are getting ready for a sharp anaerobic workout of repeat 300's: 8 x 300 with 30 seconds rest in 48 seconds—well below race pace. They will jog 800 meters before doing two more at race pace. Those 300's will be in 56 seconds, or 5:05 a mile for the guys, and 51 seconds for Goucher.

Wetmore addresses his team as they finish stretching. "Gouch," says Wetmore, "I'm gonna embarrass you. I talked to [masseur Al] Kupczak, and he says when he gets into your muscles, you feel like a Kenyan. He says you're the only white guy who has ever felt like that." Gouch just smiles as the guys hoot and holler.

Elmuccio is listening. He is here because he has just been called to action. Yesterday afternoon, Johnson was brought to his hands and knees by the flu, literally, in the UMC. Wetmore called and asked Elmuccio if he is ready to go, and Elmuccio did not hesitate. "I'm in the best shape of my life," he told Wetmore. "I'm ready to toe the line."

While laboring some, he does well today, consistently running mid-pack. In the last couple 300's, his posture straightens, and his head starts to bob back as he inhales. Wetmore knows the sight well. "[W]hen he does that," Wetmore says, "[it]'s the beginning of the end for the Mooch." The head bob also comes out to play when Elmuccio is feeling good. The difference is in his posture. If he is still on his toes leaning slightly forward, his opponents are in trouble. That means he is about to unleash his 48 second 400-meter speed.

Ponce and Friedberg hang on to the back of the pack as they finish the set, for good reason. Speed is not their forte. This workout finally offers milers like Reese and Roybal a long-awaited chance to put the hurt on the 10k guys who have made them suffer every Sunday this season.

Despite not yet having had the fluid drained from his knee, Reese looks great. He stays with Goucher the entire workout, and they separate themselves from the pack. "God," Reese says afterwards, "it feels great to be rested." He does not intend to let Elmuccio grab his spot at regionals any time soon.

And neither does Batliner. He looks comfortable in the middle of the pack. It is a good day for him, but as always, Wetmore must wait until tomorrow to discover if the workout has stressed him too much.

After the workout, Wetmore informs his men of the plan for this weekend's Mountain Regional in Provo, Utah. "I want you guys running 5:05's in Utah. That's 31:37." Then comes the surprise, "Goucher, I may have you do that, too." Reese jumps in: "Yeah, but you gotta beat [Jeff] Simonich." Goucher shoots back, "It doesn't matter what happens at Regionals. What matters is what happens at Nationals."

Edge City Is a Scary Place

Wetmore anxiously awaits word from Batliner and Johnson. He is not sure how they are feeling. On top of that, Ponce's shin aches and Reese is getting fluid drained from his knee. Their status gets Wetmore thinking about the rash of injury and illness plaguing this team. "As usual," he says, "I can't find a thread to it. After consistent solid training for twelve, thirteen weeks, we didn't change anything. Usually stress is related to change in what you're doing." Goucher, too, is feeling it. The reason for that, though, is obvious. Says Wetmore, "He's been doing consistently hard training since July 1st. The fact is he's done really hard workouts. We went out on the edge. It's hard when you're doing that training."

If there is a thread to it, it is one Batliner identified back in September. Wetmore says, "The density of the training may be too much. Most people here are doing something up-tempo four times a week—Tuesday, Wednesday, Friday, and Sunday. In any case, something was too much."

Wetmore will attempt to determine what was too much after the season. Now, just about all the training is done. The question is whether the runners can recover in time for the Mountain Regional, and, more important, NCAA's. If Wetmore rests anyone this weekend, Reese will be first, then Batliner. But Reese does not want to rest. He told Wetmore, "If I'm gonna run Nationals, I need to run hard every three days anyway. I might as well do the race as preparation for NCAA's." Batliner looked superb yesterday, so barring excessive wear and tear he is in, and Johnson "can't do anything about the flu, I don't know if he's ready to go." But, Wetmore concludes, "My guess is we'll probably run the regular squad Saturday."

The Mooch runs 55 minutes steady with the guys . . . just in case.

Friday, November 13, 1998
Provo, Utah
Provo Holiday Inn
10 p.m.

I'm No Wildlife Expert

Berkshire, Slattery, the Mooch have survived the eight-hour drive through barren nothingness to Provo, Utah. The highlight of the trip is undoubtedly Slattery, showcasing why he will not be going to veterinary school after his studies. Slattery spotted some rams beside the highway in Western Colorado. The Jersey boy struggled to define what he saw, calling them cows and moose before saying, "I'm no wildlife expert, but I saw that shit!"

The Mooch has brought his spikes with him, "just in case," but it is doubtful he will be needed. Valenti has also made the flight with the team, but he probably will not run either. The only question mark now is Ponce. After Wednesday's run, his IT band was sore from having altered his stride to avoid putting too much stress on his sore shin. But he ran twenty relatively pain-free minutes on Thursday and he is determined to gut it out.

The team jogged the course this afternoon, but later on, the healthiest man on the team, Friedberg, managed to chip his tooth while horsing around in the hotel parking lot with Roybal and Ponce. As Roybal recalls, "Me and Oscar were wrestling and Friedberg jumped in. Bat was walking with the girls, looking all cool, so Friedberg says, 'Hey let's get Bat.'" Ponce and Roybal grabbed Batliner around his chest, and Friedberg grabbed on to one of his legs. Batliner was hopping on his other leg, and Friedberg said, "Come on, kick me." Bat did, hitting Friedberg right in the chin. His two front teeth cut his tongue. Mixed in with the blood were bits of one of his front teeth. Now that Friedberg, too, has been injured, maybe he will feel more like part of the group. He is still sore about the whole thing this evening, and he does not care to discuss it when Slattery, Berkshire, and Elmuccio arrive.

Friedberg did not go to the mall with the others, and he missed out on the most amazing feat of the weekend. While leaning over a railing on the second story, Roybal spotted "one of those fancy trash cans" below, with only a tiny hole on top and a man leaning against it. Ponce and the guys started egging him on, betting he could not land his cup in the trash can. "I didn't want to be weak," he says, so he stuck his gum in the bottom of the cup to give it a little weight, and flicked it into the air. The cup spiraled around and around and around in the air, revolution after revolution, taking its time, and landed right in the hole. The man leaning against the trash glanced all around while the others laughed above him. They are still reveling about the feat when Berkshire, Elmuccio, and Slattery arrive at the hotel. The guys seem loose and relaxed, just waiting for tomorrow so they can claim their tickets to the Show.

Earning Their Shot

Wetmore and JD get in the van to go for a run at a place Wetmore picked out on a map of Provo. He never knows when he or his team will be back in town wanting a cool run, so it pays to explore. Besides, running this early lets him focus on his team without worrying about getting in a run of his own later on in the day. The chosen destination lies on the outskirts of town and turns out to be a bit too rocky for a good run, but it beats running down the main drag and stopping at every other light . . .

CU gathers at the starting line to begin their warm up. Valenti, Slattery, and Elmuccio are here, and they notice, across the far side of the course, what they missed last night under the cover of darkness: the majestic Wasatch mountains. The breathtaking mountain range is similar to the Flatirons in Boulder in that the mountains rise directly from the plains. The Wasatch range differs in that it appears more massive than the Flatirons, and its snow-capped barrenness makes it appear more inhospitable and foreboding.

Fortunately, the men will not have to scale the mountain in the race today. The East Bay Golf Course lies several miles from the foothills, and the race course circles the perimeter. Despite the proximity to the massive mountains, the course is as flat as the Collindale Golf Course in Ft. Collins. The only natural obstacle appears to be the turf itself. Although

Off and running at the Mountain Regional.

manicured, the course's benevolent appearance disguises its greed. It is saturated with water. The soggy turf sucks up energy with every step, without returning a thing.

There is more pomp and circumstance today than at any other meet thus far. The teams wait in a pen as an emcee introduces each team. Each competitor trots out to the starting line as his name is announced. The introductions do not take long, since there are only fourteen teams in the race chasing the two coveted automatic bids to Nationals. Goucher and CU receive the most laudatory introductions, befitting the man who has won this race every time he has competed in it and the team that has taken home the blue ribbon seven years running.

Roybal runs today with a little extra power in his pocket—literally. His brother Philip and his cousin Michael Bregoine killed a rattlesnake back home in New Mexico and sent the rattle to him to ward off evil spirits. He runs with the rattle in his shorts knowing each step he takes is for his brother as well.

Philip, a senior at New Mexico State University, introduced Ronald to running when Ronald was in high school. Philip was talented enough to earn a track scholarship to college, and the brothers often fantasized about running against each other this year. But, last year, when Ronald was in Guadalajara, Mexico, his mother called him and told him he had to come home immediately, for Philip was sick. When Roybal joined his family at his brother's bedside in a New Mexican hospital, he was informed of the severity of Philip's ailment. Philip had a blood clot that was making its way to his heart. If the medication did not work fast enough to dissolve the clot, the clot would move to his heart, and he would die. Philip was ordered not to move, and all the family could do was wait, and pray.

To the family's relief, Philip survived. But as a result of the ordeal, Philip can no longer run. Now, Ronald runs for them both.

Perhaps the man with the most at stake is Batliner. Wetmore thinks he can improve more relative to his teammates, and he is looking for him to be a top-five guy on the team today. Wetmore is realistic about what Batliner can do, "He's not gonna be a top-twenty guy [at Nationals], but he was twenty seconds off our fifth man last time [at Big 12's], and he'll probably be close to our fifth man this time." On the starting line, Batliner betrays no anxiety.

Neither does Goucher. Wetmore has told him to win as easily as possible. Goucher could just run with the guys and concede the race to Simonich, but Wetmore doubts that will happen. "The possibility is slim that he'll run with the guys. The likelihood is that if he's on the line, he's gonna run to win. There are certain things he doesn't like to do, one of which is deliberately take it easy."

But early on, Goucher takes it easy. Matt Poulson of BYU and Jeff Simonich of Utah assume the early pacing chores with the field bunched closely behind them. Unbeknownst to the Colorado guys, Simonich is ailing, suffering from plantar fasciatis in his right foot. He received a cortisone shot in his foot last week so that he could compete today. Simonich is also content to run as easily as possible today, and so, at the mile, the pace is a controlled five minutes for Goucher and Simonich.

Simonich is compact in build and stride. Standing maybe 5'8", he takes the short, efficient steps characteristic of 10,000-meter runners. His head does not budge and his face looks relaxed. His sunglasses shade any anxiety his eyes may reveal. Behind the duo, all the CU guys except Johnson pass the mile in a tight pack in the twenties, only seconds behind Goucher. Johnson bides his time a little farther back.

Ten minutes in, Simonich and Goucher break from the pack and jump out in front, running stride for stride. Behind them, Northern Arizona has a three-man pack running ahead of Roybal, Ponce, and Friedberg. Reese and Batliner are farther back.

At two and a half miles, Simonich turns to Goucher and says, "You're not even breathing; let's go." Goucher does not respond, to Simonich's disappointment. "It was just dead silence. I was thinking, 'I gotta talk to him a little, try to slow him down.'"

Goucher and Simonich pass three miles together in 14:47, and Goucher appears startled when he hears the time. He takes off, and three quarters of a mile later, he leads Simonich by forty meters. Later he says, "I was like, this is stupid, it's time. He [Simonich] came with me for maybe 100 meters and that was it. That was the last I heard of him."

The speed in which he dropped Simonich—an All-American last spring in the 5000 meters—was astonishing, and it left Simonich in awe. "I don't know how he does it," Simonich says afterwards. "Most guys, you can tell when they move. With him his stride just lengthens out. I thought it [pulling away] would hurt him, especially in this soft stuff, but he just took off." Slowly squeezing it down—that is how Wetmore and Goucher refer to it, and Goucher does it better than anyone.

After his big move, Goucher coasts the rest of the way, winning in 30:43—42 seconds ahead of Simonich. Goucher is unfazed about his dominating performance. "It was OK," he says. "As it is, I still haven't gotten fired up for a race yet. There's no one here who can push me, so I ran smart and still got a decent workout." He is already looking ahead to next week. "I haven't been pushed, even at Pre-Nationals. I caught him at four, he passed me, and I thought, 'You know, I'm in the middle of a 100-mile week.' We'll see at Nationals."

The team battle is much closer. At three miles, NAU was dominating the race, with guys in the fourth through seventh positions. But CU was still holding their hand at that point. CU has been training to run a 10k race all season, and in the last 2000 meters they move up through the field.

Despite panicking and moving a little too soon, Friedberg is the second Buffalo across the line, in fifth place. "I picked it up in miles three, four, and five, running closer to fives [minute miles]. The first two were about 5:08, and mile six I think was a little slow . . . I made a bad gamble. With a mile to go, I thought I could just keep rolling ahead and they would just die, but they didn't die. I moved too early. It ended up coming to a kick anyway, so why did I take the lead?" Friedberg raced Billy Herman and Steve Ozaduik of NAU to the finish, beating out the latter.

Emry Carr of Idaho State finishes seventh before Reese and Batliner cross the line in eighth and ninth—remarkable performances for the two less-than-healthy seniors. Reese is glad he had Bat to run with, and that he survived the race intact. "You know how you need someone to leech off of? It's like I was expending too much energy. Thanks to Bat [running with him], I was getting there, getting there. I'll be happy if I can walk tomorrow." There is a little swelling in his knee, and he immediately gets some ice on it.

Batliner, meanwhile, is cautiously optimistic about the race, knowing what lies ahead of him. "I feel great. I finally ran with the guys. But as good as I feel today, I'm scared for next week. It's just a whole different race. You're hurting the whole way."

Roybal completes the Buffaloes' scoring when he finishes twelfth. Although both Batliner and Reese passed him with 800 meters to go and beat him to the line, he feels good about his race. He says, "I felt bad the whole race, but with 800 meters to go, I could still push it. Tom and Bat passed me, but I still had enough energy to go with them. I had an awesome kick, I just felt really, really strong. Now I need to do all the little things—stretch, drink a lot of water. I felt tight all week."

Johnson was their sixth man at Big 12's, and he is their sixth man again today. Coming off of the flu, he runs conservatively early and finishes a solid 30th. He continues to improve, yet he has yet to have a race that fully meets his expectations. He says, "I thought I'd catch more people, but I didn't. I want to race differently next week. I want to be in it a little more. It's hard to tell how you feel after being sick. If I wasn't sick, I'd be pissed. I'm greedy, so I wish I was just a little more in it."

Ponce is the only Buffalo to have an off day. Seeing his teammates move in front of him, Ponce slowed, finishing as the seventh man, in 35th place. "Today," he says, "after the mile, I was really tight. I picked it up a bit, and my shin was really hurting, so I slowed it down. I said, 'Hey, I better wait till next week.'" Ponce was CU's third man at Big 12's, and with him ailing, the others had no room to slack. But they did their job; and as a result, CU won their eighth consecutive district crown.

Wetmore is pleased that CU has won the race, but he cannot praise his runners' performances until he has had an opportunity to analyze the results. "What does it tell me? Well, how much did Goucher beat Simonich and Herman by at Pre-Nationals? Where were the other guys then, and today?" CU has survived the cut along with thirty other teams, but he knows that this battle of attrition is among themselves as much as it is against their adversaries. "The story of our team," he says, "is we're down to five guys. From fifteen we're down to five. We gotta get one more week out of those five guys. But Bat's getting better, Tommy's OK. Oscar, hopefully next week he can say, 'I can rest all of indoors if I need to.' We got what we needed. We got a good run out of Gouch, a good run outta Bat, and a set of plane tickets."

At the awards ceremony, with CU assembled in front of the crowd, the announcer begins: "It's been a long season, but a good one for CU." He then asks for a moment of silence for Chris Severy. The CU men stand arm in arm with Wetmore in the middle of them. And in that moment, with heads bowed, the members of the squad take the time to reflect on their lost comrade, and the painful, costly, convoluted path each has taken to get to this point, a week away from their destiny. Without one another, one wonders if they would have the strength to stand at all.

NCAA MOUNTAIN REGIONAL CROSS COUNTRY MEET

PLACE	NAME	UNIVERSITY	CLASS	TIME
1.	Adam Goucher	Colorado	Sr.	30:43 CR
2.	Jeff Simonich	Utah	Sr.	31:25
3.	Matt Poulsen	Brigham Young	Jr.	31:41
4.	Billy Herman	Northern Arizona	Jr.	31:45
5.	Mike Friedberg	Colorado	So.	31:46
6.	Steve Ozaduik	Northern Arizona	So.	31:47
7.	Emry Carr	Idaho State	Jr.	31:54
8.	Tom Reese	Colorado	Sr.	31:55
9.	Adam Batliner	Colorado	Sr.	31:56
10.	Zachary James	Southern Utah	So.	31:57
12.	Ron Roybal	Colorado	Jr.	32:10
30.	Jay Johnson	Colorado	Sr.	32:56
35.	Oscar Ponce	Colorado	Jr.	33:00

Fired Up!!

Wetmore is hunched over in his chair, staring at his monitor, scanning the weekend's results. That his computer functions at all is a mystery to him. He took it to get fixed when it crashed on him last year and the technicians told him, "If it was alive it'd be dead." Wetmore explains, "Like Goucher and his meals, something always seems to go wrong with my electronics." But since it is working, "I'm wasting time, seeing who gets to go." "Ha!" says Wetmore. "Look at this: Tennessee-Chattanooga gets to go!" He checks out the Midwest Regional results and sees Oklahoma State has easily captured the title, and that Iowa State finishes way out of contention. He really gets a laugh out of the latter. "I get a kick out of Iowa State. They got four Africans and they suck. Their first African was Philemon Too in 17th. That's cool." So much for buying a championship.

The teams that figure to be the Buffs' greatest competition all ran superbly over the weekend. In the extremely challenging west region, second-ranked Stanford and third-ranked Oregon romped past their competition. Previously unranked Washington State surprised the pollsters, finishing third, four points ahead of the seventh-ranked Arizona squad. Abdi Abdirahman of Arizona established himself as one of the NCAA favorites by winning the individual title by six seconds over Stanford's Brad Hauser. Stanford's team victory, meanwhile, is a tribute to the team's astounding frontrunners and great depth. Their fifth man, sophomore Thomas Murley, was only a minute behind Brad Hauser in fourteenth place.

Unlike the Buffaloes, who face relatively easy competition in their district, the Cardinal cannot afford to have their guys relax and ease up like Ponce did, or they risk not qualifying for Nationals. But any fantasy that Wetmore has about CU gaining an advantage from having an easier path to Nationals is just that: a fantasy. "Every year," he says, "I get deceived into thinking that [the districts] will tire them out. Vinny [Lananna, the Stanford coach] knows what he's doing, he knows what to do to hold them back." The defending champion Stanford Cardinal are one of the three favorites to win the team title.

The primary question on Wetmore's mind as he scans each team's results is: How hard did they have to go to qualify? For the number-one–ranked Razorbacks of Arkansas, the meet had all the drama of an intersquad competition. They are the only team in the South Central region to even be ranked in the top 25, let alone the top ten. Arkansas' Michael Power, Andrew Begley, and Sean Kaley swept the top three spots and

Eric Zack and Murray Link finished in seventh and eighth to lead the Hogs to a dominating 21 to 105 victory over a Tulane squad that received no votes in the last coaches' poll.

The toughest region teamwise was the Great Lakes Region. Going into Saturday's race a remarkable *seven* teams, led by the sixth-ranked Wolverines of Michigan, were represented in the top 25. A strong Michigan State squad upended the Wolverines, but of greater interest to Wetmore was the individual battle. Butler's Julius Mwangi won the crown by ten seconds over Michigan's Todd Snyder. Wetmore is not sure how much that took out of him, but, he says, "If this guy's coach is smart, he said, 'Just win. You gotta race again in a week.'"

James Madison pulled the upset of the weekend by upending the NC State Wolfpack to win the Southeast Region, while a resurgent Princeton program earned their spot at NCAA's by upsetting the thirteenth-ranked Georgetown Hoyas for the second consecutive year to win the Mid-Atlantic Region.

After perusing all of the weekend's results, Wetmore views Arkansas as the favorite, followed by Stanford and Oregon. Then, he says, "There's a big gap. Everyone's racing for fourth, including us." Wetmore knows, though, that his team could place as high as third if they continue to improve. At the conference, there was a 17-second spread from CU's second to fifth man. On Saturday, there was a 24-second spread at 10k. "That's not bad," says Wetmore. "Especially since Oscar shut down and just finished. If he can be where he was, with Bat in there, I guess we're a better team than we were a month ago." But if they are to place better than fourth next week, Ponce has to "swoop up and save our ass." In other words, he has to pull a Roybal.

Will Wetmore rah-rah Ponce and the boys? No. Now more than ever, his biggest concern is getting them to the line feeling good, with a calm mind. He says, "Sometimes the kids get mad at me and say 'You don't inspire us to run out of our gourds,' but I just don't think you can squeeze the juice out of something that isn't there." He knows now what he will tell them: "You're fine, you're gonna be calm and cool. You'll beat people who are better because you'll outsmart them and outcool them."

"Outcooling the competition": If the Buffs have a slogan on race day, and especially at Nationals when even the most seasoned veterans can run like freshmen, this is it. Staying cool is partially why Wetmore was against the idea of having armbands for Severy when they first discussed it, and he is glad that they have no plans to wear them at Nationals. He says, "They generally do what I want them to do. But it's just not who we are—advertising. We don't advertise. The second reason is I didn't want them to say, 'I dedicated this to Chris and I ran like shit.' How would Reese have felt when he said he didn't fight [at Big 12's]? That's why we're definitely not going to dedicate a season to somebody. We'll dedicate ourselves to keeping his memory with us forever." They have had to endure more than any CU team ever has, and now there is one more mountain to climb. "We've gone this far," he says, "and I'd like to summit a little more adversity, one more time."

The task will be made easier if his runners toe the line feeling good. Coaches everywhere are agonizing over how best to taper their athletes right now, and Wetmore's concern is especially magnified, considering the feedback he has received from his guys since districts. "I'm concerned," he says, "with how many people said, 'I'm pleased with my performance but I felt like shit,' because of how much we rested last week. But it's a matter of keeping them from freaking out and treating it like any other race; a race where we take advantage of other people's mistakes."

Taking advantage of others' mistakes will be made more difficult by the narrowness of the course. It bothered Wetmore when his team ran Pre-Nationals, and it haunts him now. "Of all the years to expand the field [to 31 teams] they make it on the narrowest course. This course just doesn't comply with NCAA regulations. It just doesn't."

But Wetmore knows there is no sense in worrying about something that he cannot change. What he can control is the last bit of work before the recipe is complete. He is thinking of running two all-out 800's tomorrow to "get 'em sharpened up, make their legs feel snappy. We'll try to do some snappy things, but nothing that will accumulate in their legs. In a normal year we would do an anaerobic workout tomorrow, but I'll have to see if they're gimping around today."

That includes Goucher. He is a week away from attempting to grab a title that has eluded him three times. Wetmore fears he is not as ready as a year ago, when he finished fourth. "I'd say he was better prepared a year ago. I don't know if he's in better shape, because he's had great workouts in August, September, and October, but he didn't have any complications a year ago until this Friday, when he got a cold."

Despite Goucher's interruptions, Wetmore's confidence is buoyed by the ease with which Goucher won on Saturday. Wetmore recalls when Goucher ran past him with a little over two miles to go. "I was standing at four miles with the Northern Arizona and Air Force coaches. They said, 'Is he taking it easy today?' I'm killing that story and I'm telling them he hasn't run anything really hard since the conference meet, so he's going to run the first five miles with this guy. Then he comes by four miles all alone and I say, 'Don't forget to run that last mile,' and he says, 'Oh yeah, sure, okay,' like he was running to get a loaf of bread, and those two guys just rolled their eyes. But there's a lot of good guys out there." But is anyone out there as good as Goucher?

At 3:15, the Varsity runners are still slipping through the door in an effort to get to the stretching circle on time. As if on cue, just as Wetmore is inquiring about their whereabouts, Johnson, Friedberg, and Batliner burst through the door. As Goucher stretches, he looks at some photos from Pre-Nationals of him, Abdi Abdirahman of Arizona, and Julius Mwangi of Butler running together.

"These," Goucher says, turning to Batliner, "these are the guys I gotta beat. Abdi whatever from Arizona, and Mwangi." He holds up a photo taken of Mwangi coming down the final stretch. The strain of the effort is etched on Mwangi's face. "Man," he says to Batliner, "*look* at that guy. He is *hurting*." Rather than being impressed or intimidated, Goucher draws strength from the fact that it took every last bit of effort Mwangi had to beat Goucher on a day when he was less than ready to roll. After staring at the photos for a while, Goucher says, "I like to get a mental image of my opponents in my head before I race 'em."

Then, he turns to Batliner. "See, when I raced him, I'd done 97 miles the day before." Within earshot of Goucher as he walks around the stretching circle, Wetmore chimes in incredulously, "The *day* before? Ninety-seven miles in *one* day! That's like when you told the guy from *the Harrier* that you ran twenty miles at sub five minutes a mile at 9000 feet."

Everyone seated around Goucher laughs freely, and Goucher corrects his gaffe. "Hey, I meant that week, and I can't help it if that guy interpreted what I said like that." He turns back to Batliner, "Anyway, I was in a 100-mile week, and now I'm gonna be rested, *and*, for the first time this season, I'm gonna be fired up!" Wetmore interjects sternly, "Adam, do your talking with your legs."

Good advice to heed, for just as he says this, local reporter Mike Sandrock of the *Boulder Daily Camera* enters the gym. He has an article that he has written for *Runner's World Online* about Goucher that he wants Goucher to peruse before he posts it online. There will be no shortage of hype on Goucher or the Buffaloes as the meet nears.

Wetmore would prefer not to have any of the distractions of the media. In fact, Wetmore never posts articles or press clippings of the team on the bulletin board. He views the media as little more than an annoyance, and he does his part to ensure that the runners do not get caught up in the hype. As Sandrock chats with Goucher and Batliner, Wetmore leads the way to the door, announcing, "OK! Let's go! We're leaving!" without ever losing stride.

The team exits the van at the South Boulder Creek Path for the last aerobic effort of the season: 65 minutes steady. Wetmore quickly briefs them: "We're not trying to build any fitness at this point, but we *are* trying to maintain, so 65 minutes, at Sunday effort. We're doing Sunday pace, with 2/3 distance. OK, let's go."

Valenti is again training with the team. It is a precautionary measure Wetmore feels compelled to make, since Batliner, Reese, and Ponce are all battling injuries. Elmuccio is officially done. "Valenti beat Mooch every time they ran," says Wetmore, but even Valenti is running on borrowed time. Today's run and tomorrow's anaerobic effort will reveal whether or not the wounded soldiers are ready to storm the palace one last time. On Wednesday, if everyone has a clean bill of health, Valenti will finally start his active rest before again ascending to full volume as the team enters the indoor track season.

The weather could not be any better: 48 degrees and sunny. Everyone is dressed in shorts and T-shirts. The ferocious winds that rolled off the eastern plains the Wednesday before Big 12's are back in hiding.

Just one minute into the run, Goucher pulls away from the others. While on occasion he relaxes once he is 100 meters ahead, essentially running the same pace as the pack, today he disappears into the distance. A year ago at this time, he came down with a cold. Today, for the first time in over a month, his glute problem is at bay. He runs without a trace of the limp that has hounded him since he first experienced pain in his IT band almost seven weeks ago, on October 1st.

The pack rolls on behind Gouch up the flat Creek Path, before heading onto the cross country course to kill some time before returning back on the Creek Path. The pace is surprisingly conversational as Valenti, Batliner, Roybal, and Johnson near the halfway point of the run. The pace is more leisurely than Wetmore wanted. Nevertheless, if successful, this will be Batliner's longest run since he was diagnosed with a stress fracture in September. While the fracture has healed, the bone bruise remains, and today, it is causes him some discomfort. It is tight for the first half of the run, and he is very cognizant that he is precariously balancing on the tightrope of good health—pushing it *just a little too much* will cause the bone to fracture. Not only would that ruin what is left of a somewhat salvageable cross country season, but it would also incalculably set back his preparations for indoor and outdoor track. With the team's title hopes seemingly dashed, any worsening of his condition would be grounds for ending the season now.

The pressure in Batliner's calf mercifully subsides as the runners head onto the course from Marshall Road. A few minutes later, Assistant Coach Drake, out on a run of his own, rolls 'em up—evidence of the guy's exertion, or lack thereof. Roybal spots JD and laughs out loud, "Oh no! We got rolled up by JD!" "Not really," JD responds. "Every time you guys got to a gate, I put in a surge to catch you." Nevertheless, JD's arrival lights a fire under the guys, and they get down to business. The tempo increases steadily all the way back to the van. Batliner finishes the run feeling great. "Man," he says, "I feel good. I wish we could race today."

He is not alone. Goucher is excited about his pain-free run. "It's gonna be like this all week. Man, I'm *fired up!*"

Showtime, however, is seven long days away.

Anyone Like Duck?

Wetmore has decided to do two hard 800's, and the men and women are paired into teams so that it will be a 4 x 800m relay. The teams are identical to the ones at the Master Blaster, minus Valenti. Batliner paces nervously as he prepares to get going. Right now, he envies Valenti: "Valenti, that lucky son of a bitch, doesn't have to run this. What an asshole." Wetmore informed Valenti that he is officially done for the season when he arrived at practice, so he took off for an easy run with Aaron Blondeau, who showed up for the first time since injuring his back early in the fall. It has been so long since Blondeau had been at practice that it is hard to fathom that going into the season he was seen as a definite Varsity guy.

Wetmore explains the workout to his men: "It's our last real anaerobic stimulus, but we're not doing 8000 meters of work to do it. You're doing the two fastest 800's you can run. That doesn't mean 1:51, 2:10. That means run 1:59, 1:59. It's your two fastest average 800's. Bear in mind the purpose is a deep anaerobic stimulus. Whoever wins is secondary. When we get back, we'll talk about how you race Monday so you can work it out now and fix it in your nightmares until Monday."

It is chilly enough to wear long sleeves, but everyone still does the workout in shorts. Paired once again with Faz, Goucher again fails to taste victory. The honors today go to Roybal and Brianna Stott-Messick. Roybal runs 2:02 and 2:04 and looks easy doing it. Wetmore is impressed. "He looked good, didn't he? He's a talented guy."

Roybal looks good, but not quite as good as Goucher, who manages a 1:58 and a 2:02. He looks great as he does it, lengthening out his powerful stride on each 800. It is

Goucher in full flight.

not spectacular, but Wetmore says, "I'll take it for now. Think, in track season he'd do that with no rest."

The only one who really struggles is Ponce. He runs 2:00 on the first only to trudge home in 2:17 on the second. He is a 10,000-meter runner, and he does not handle the lactic acid quite as well as the others. Ponce says afterwards, "Man, I got bootylock." Wetmore hears him and says, "Good thing you don't got a big booty; you would have died." Friedberg laughs and says, "I got chestlock." He still managed to run both in around 2:05, to Wetmore's amazement. "Friedberg," he says, "you got two 800 PR's in one day!"

The workout is over in less than ten minutes, and the guys are chatty and laughing as they head back to the gym for some advice from the Boss.

Everyone gathers in the waiting area of the track office as Wetmore delivers his "last rational advice": "Whatever I tell you Thursday, Friday, Saturday, or Sunday, agree and smile, but *don't do it*. What I tell you today is the last rational advice I give you. Take what I say, along with your observations of the course, and formulate a plan by Thursday or Friday, recognizing you'll be crazy Saturday and Sunday."

Everyone listens intently as Wetmore speaks, glancing at maps of the course they are holding on their laps. Nothing he says comes as a surprise. Wetmore simply reiterates what he has been telling them all season long,

Roybal hammers.   PR #2

"Our goal is always to go there and run better than our ranking. If the men can run as they did last week and Oscar can go to the well, we can take advantage of some of the mistakes of the teams ahead of us If we do what we're capable of, we'll be OK."

"The word out there is that if you don't get out, you're gonna get buried. That's the experience after running 8k, but it's not 8k. My feeling is that once again you'll take advantage of the people that go barreling out and move past a lot of chumps. There's a lot of room to move if you're patient. Yes, it'll be crowded and at three miles it will be disconcerting, but if you're 15:15, or even 20:20 at four, you can still attack from there. Even when you're out of the woods, you got one and a half miles to move. Look at it this way: 25:25 was top twenty at Pre-Nationals."

No one can argue with his logic. The one wrinkle in his plan is a concession that maybe they should go out a little harder in the first mile so that they are not too buried when they go into the woods. He looks at Roybal as he addresses them all: "You don't want to be 5:05 at the mile. You want to be 4:50, then run 5:05's till you get out of the woods. You can pass fifty people in that last mile." Roybal nods his approval, running the race in his head. "Once more," Wetmore continues, "it's gonna be one of those gut-wrenching things where we wait and wait and wait. But if you come out of the woods in 60th, you can pass thirty people in that last 2k."

Wetmore focuses his attention on the team battle and offers some surprising counsel on the team he thinks may be within their reach: "We can get them. I tell you, they'll come back to us. We can get them. Without us running spectacularly, Oregon is within our reach. To get Stanford or Arkansas, we have to run out of our gourd. But I look at Oregon, and I think they're limping. Of course, we are too."

Goucher makes it hurt.

Priorities

Nationals are just five days away, so today Wetmore assigns the men an easy aerobic run instead of the usual medium-distance Wednesday. For both Goucher and Batliner, today offers a chance to further evaluate their health and fitness. In impromptu journals that they are keeping this week, they share their thoughts.

Adam Batliner

Today was probably my last day in the pool (thank God) and after I finished I started getting neurotic and ended up tying up my shoes and doing fifteen minutes of 5:30's for no particular reason. I can't believe I had myself talked into it before and now it seems so ridiculous. My leg hurts pretty good today but I'm not worried; it would have to get a lot worse to keep me from doing what I have to do. Friedberg told me I'm the toughest guy he knows today and I tried to tell him that I'm no different than him, just a little better at methodically dealing with injuries, maybe. After I did so well last spring in track on a fractured fibula, everybody expects me to hop out and kill everybody on Monday. My roommates, Roybal and Robbie, said they already decided I am at least a top-twenty guy. Top twenty! I honestly don't think I have the fitness, but I guess I'll find out soon enough. This is making me really nervous and I have to get some sleep, so that is it for today.

Adam Goucher

(5 days to go!) 55 min. easy (4 x strides/pickups)
I felt really good today on my run! My leg hardly hurt at all! Actually, I can't really recall noticing it. It was probably just the fact that I was expecting it to hurt a little, so my attention was drawn to it, thereby making me overanalyze. Anyway, I'm very confident that everything is falling into place. I'm feeling very responsive, strong, rested, and tough. School right now is kicking my ass! I have a lot of work and pressure in a few classes right now. I just have to try to not let it bother me until after Nationals. And by no means will I repeat my sophomore year when I decided to become the model student the week before Nationals, and stay up until one and two in the morning studying. I'll have to kick my own ass if I ever think about doing something like that again! Right now, it's about feeling good and preparing mentally with positive self-talk, reinforcing the fact that I've prepared well. I'm fit, I'm strong, I'm fast, I'm tough, and I've never been more prepared!

The Hay's in the Barn

"Well," JD says to Wetmore as the men prepare to get started, "weather-wise we made it through the season OK." The men are in shorts and T-shirts for the season's final workout thanks to a cloudless sunny sky and air so still it seems hushed, in anticipation of what's to come. All season the weather has cooperated. The only really ugly days this fall were on October 16th, when Slattery endured the hailstorm, and the bitter cold and blustery winds during the season's last session of repeat miles on November 6th.

With the exception of Johnson, who worked out in the morning because he was teaching an afternoon kinesiology class, everyone is present for practice, and they are well rested. The mood is giddy, and the runners joke and laugh as they change into their spikes. They know that after this, there is no more work to be done, and Wetmore senses their relief. Wetmore attributes their excess energy to the fact that they are rested for the first time, but he is careful not to read too much into their mood. The women were giddy like this before Big 12's, and they performed poorly.

The runners line up at the beginning of the final straightaway and Wetmore explains the workout: 8 x 300m, alternating between 48 seconds and race pace (55 seconds), with one hundred jog in between. Goucher's assignment is the same as the others, only he will alternate between 46 and 52 seconds.

Everyone has trouble finding the pace early on, and Wetmore yells across the track at Ponce as he starts pulling away on the second 300. "Now you're on *race* pace, cruising, cruising, cruising, OSCAR!!!" He comes through two seconds fast. He can be forgiven since he was keying off of Goucher, who himself was three seconds fast. "That's 4:24 pace," Wetmore informs Goucher. "I hope you can run that."

Wetmore is animated and vocal today, perhaps more than ever. He has the men start the fast ones on the line, like they are starting a race, and as Batliner gets out slowly on the third interval, Wetmore yells to him, "Come on, Bat! You gonna get out like that in a race? You'll get 300th!"

The runners hit the fourth one, and Wetmore is loud and clear as they approach the fifth interval, "Now it's the middle of a race. You're practicing your relaxation skills. Calm mind, you're just floating. Get a picture in your mind, make a movie in your mind."

"Halfway," Wetmore continues, "let's get a little tired now. This is a standing start. Let's get aggressive in the first 30, 40 meters." He turns his attention to Goucher. "Make a movie in your mind, Gouch, a picture in your mind. It's easy! It's easy!" He turns his attention to the pack as Goucher hits the 200-meter mark, "Make a movie in your mind—it's the four-and-a-half-mile mark, you're cruising, passing people."

They approach the season's last interval. Just one more interval at race pace. The guys struggle to catch their breath as they reach the line. The CU ski team is on the infield, and they cheer on Goucher and the others as they run past. Reese leads the pack. Wetmore announces, "One to go! Pop right over there. Come on Tommy, take 'em, let's go!" They pick it up, and Wetmore settles them down, "Just race pace, just race pace. Have that poised feeling, right on the edge, ready to pounce."

The work is done. Everyone jogs two laps, and then single file, they all do two 80-meter accelerations, building up to full speed by 40 meters, then easing back down to the finish. As Goucher reaches full speed in his black shirt and orange shorts, he resembles a flying cheetah. His arms reach forward and rise to the top of his head with each stride. "Pop it, pop it, pop it!" Wetmore says. Wetmore scrutinizes each runner's form as they pass, and when the last runner finishes, he says, "That's it, the hay's in the barn. The hay's in the barn!"

Reese turns to JD as he walks off the track. "I only got two more nights of sleep in my bed." "Then what?" "Then," Reese says, "it's go time."

All that is left is to rest and defeat any negative visions that invade the mind. All week, Wetmore has hardly slept. He is consumed by the meet. He has been waking up with nightmares, and it is always the same one. Goucher is in the lead, all alone, and Wetmore races to the chute to meet him there. He waits for Goucher but Goucher never arrives. Wetmore cannot comprehend what is going on. Goucher was killing everybody! The field was nowhere to be seen! It is then that he spots Goucher, limping across the field.

"It's not that he's more important than anybody else," Wetmore says, but Goucher finished second in 1994, sixth in 1995, redshirted 1996, and finished third in 1997. In 1995 and 1997, Wetmore and Goucher felt Goucher should have won. This race is all that is left for Goucher, and in some ways, for Wetmore, too. If Goucher does not win, he will not attain the goal he set for himself as a prep at Doherty High. Wetmore tells Goucher that it is just a race, but his thoughts and actions reveal that it means more.

Wetmore has doubts about Goucher's current fitness because of the training he has missed since mid-October while nursing his injured leg. "On October 10th," Wetmore says, half hoping he could go back to that point and erase any mistakes that were made since, "he was the best runner in the country. If he was rested, he would have killed him [Mwangi]." But now, Wetmore is not so sure. He says, "Some coaches think it's 90 percent mental and 10 percent physical. Well, let me train them 90 percent and then give me 10 percent mental. You get them as fit as can be, and the mental aspect will take care of itself." Is Goucher even 90 percent?

Winning an individual NCAA cross championship takes a special athlete on a special day. As Wetmore says, "To win this meet, you gotta be ready 100 percent physically, and 100 percent mentally." But the Buffaloes know that as a team, they are nowhere near 100 percent—physically or mentally. They will have to play the hand they are dealt.

Wetmore leaves at 5:30, and JD sits alone in Balch gym contemplating the season. He thinks aloud, "Well, there's not much we can do now. I'm a pessimist. I was worried after last weekend—worried Bat wasn't going to be able to run. And Ponce was grimacing about his leg today, but what's he got to do, suck it up for a 10k?" But aside from Batliner and Ponce, everyone feels rested. JD noticed, "Before districts they all seemed tired and now they're bouncing off the walls. If we're fourth or better, we'll be fired up. Shoot, even with Sev, I don't know how we would've done with the way things turned out. Maybe with him and a healthy Bat, but not with the way things turned out. But shit, if you had asked me this summer about Jay Johnson going to NC's, I would've thought you were on crack."

If they can just put it together ...

Time Crawling

It is another easy day on the Front Range. But the decreasing physical stress is offset by the mounting mental anxiety. Each member of the team is in a very different phase right now. Batliner and Goucher's journals provide us with a glimpse:

Adam Batliner

My shin is really sore today from running the last four days in a row. It hurts every step when I walk through campus and throbs while I sleep at night. Three more days. I just looked up the trash-talking sites on the Internet and found a large amount of idiot babble and over-excited track geeks proclaiming their love for various schools and individuals; a huge archive that only served to jump my heart rate about twenty beats per minute without teaching me anything about Monday's race. That's America, though. Over-analyzed and under-trained.

The last workout of the season wasn't what I had expected. Yesterday, instead of screaming and drooling on our shoes in an elaborate workout to make everyone dead tired, we did a fairly relaxed 8 x 300 workout with every other one race pace, the others more like mile pace. My leg is fine when it gets warmed up—I don't feel a thing—but on the cooldown it's usually a precariously tender pain from my ankle bone to the knee.

This is going to be my last cross race in college. I can't decide yet what exactly that means for me. Barring a horrible injury or a prison sentence, that probably means a new beginning of running cross country for one of those vast oppressive merchandising empires like Nike or Adidas or Asics. This is the last experience of truly being on a united team, though, and that is what I know I'll miss. To some extent I am anticipating nostalgia for all those beautifully miserable Sundays I used to run with Chris—because I know that these are incredible people with the incredible and audacious agenda to discover their own talents. This team knows what it is to be invested in a plan, to be dedicated to a system that simultaneously scares the hell out of you and makes you so excited you can barely hold it in. Running, like Wetmore said once, is like getting up every morning and shooting yourself. You know that you are going to put yourself through something really painful, <u>but</u> you also know how much strength and speed are going to come with it. The passion of the runner is to force forgetfulness on that pain and embrace the benefits that will without fail make you a better person. I think me and all these guys have it down pretty well, too well even, since we keep managing to forget to listen to the despair that scrapes across our nerves and end up injured.

But it's the respect and camaraderie that goes along with experiencing that together, that is priceless. Chris gave me clarity of understanding when he died. I'll never take it for granted or forget how we grew together over four years of sweat and how we came to know each other the way people seldom do. These are some of the greatest moments of our lives. We may not see it yet, we may not even know it, but I think that we will look back as withered elderly men upon these times as some of the most profound of our lives. And if I don't, that's even better, because it would take a hell of a life to cloud over the shining, glistening days of collegiate cross country.

Adam Goucher

(Three days to go!!) 40 min. easy

Feeling great! Everything with school is straightened out. A huge amount of school pressure has been lifted off for the time being. Anyway, I felt great on the run, nothing is hurting! Saw Al Kupczak for about a half hour. I tell you, that guy is a miracle worker, he has really put me back together! I had an awesome steak dinner with Reese, then some people from the team watched a movie. It was actually really funny, it really felt good to just chill out, laugh, and have a good time! Three days to go, and all is well. I can't wait!!

Lawrence, Here We Come

The CU men's and women's teams flew today from Denver to Kansas City. They were on their own today, so everyone put in a couple of easy miles and some strides before heading to Balch to meet the bus to the airport at noon. After picking up their luggage and getting the rental cars, they finally arrived in Lawrence at 5 p.m. They were starving, so they immediately went downtown to dinner at Chili's. Roybal called the dinner a "disaster"—it seems just about everyone's order got Gouchered. The good news is that Goucher's parents and some of the parents of the other runners happened to be eating there, so seeing them was an unexpected treat.

After a long dinner the team made it over to the Eldridge Hotel in downtown Lawrence. It is the oldest building in Lawrence, chock full of legends and ghosts from its less savory days in the 1960s and 1970s. It has been completely renovated, and now it is one of the nicest places in Lawrence. The guys are all impressed by the décor, and when Batliner gets to his room, he is amazed at what he sees. He writes in his journal:

> *The two big rococo rooms separated by French double doors are more than I ever expected, all in an older style that is becoming rare in America. It makes you kind of despise the newer hotels we stay at with all their undifferentiated sameness that has no character or style. I guess I'm a little romantic about the whole thing since I'm reading* The Great Gatsby, *and I feel like I just stepped into the book itself, complete with all its glamorous 1920s wealth.*

As they try to get some sleep, though, their awe turns to dismay as they discover that the remodeling apparently did not include any work to soundproof the walls. Writes Goucher in his journal: *"The walls must be paper thin, because I could hear people down on the street outside and traffic all night—and I'm on the fifth floor!"*

The commotion he heard outside had to do with a tragic hit-and-run at 2 a.m. half a block from the hotel that left three KU students hospitalized. According to newspaper reports, two of the students had to be airlifted to a hospital in Missouri. All of the activity—the whirring of the helicopter, the police sirens, the wailing ambulances—create an electronic cacophony that lasts till dawn.

Roybal and Batliner were treated to a more benevolent disturbance in the wee hours of the morning. Their neighbors, it seems, must have been newlyweds. Roybal says, "It was ridiculous. I had to call them at 5 a.m. to tell them to keep it down."

Nevertheless, when the sleepy runners arrive at Rim Rock Farm to preview the course in the morning, they discover this evening's hustle and bustle is but a prelude to a far more unsettling sound . . .

A Push From Above

As if the course were not challenging enough, Mother Nature has decided to make her presence known. The team gets out of the van by the starting line and sees squads from all over the United States stretching, doing strides, and jogging the course—all in full sweats. The wind is howling, and if it continues like this tomorrow it threatens to dramatically slow the race, something that will not be to Colorado's advantage.

There is a twenty-mile-per-hour headwind off the starting line, and as NC State coach Rollie Geiger surveys the scene, he wonders aloud, "Who the hell's gonna take this thing?" His assistant coach, Jason Vigilante, confidently answers, "Arkansas." As a competitor and an assistant coach, Vigilante has been to the NCAA cross country meet the last five years, and as much as CU likes to race from behind, he has always seen perennial champion Arkansas get to the front in a hurry, and stay there.

After stretching, the CU team jogs quietly over the course. It is firmer than when they ran it at Pre-Nationals. The firm ground might help counterbalance the wind and keep the pace honest if these conditions persist. Goucher leads the way as the runners pay special attention to the new elements that have added an extra two kilometers to the course they ran in October. The team's silence is broken by Goucher, who narrates the course for his teammates. Despite never having run the 10k course, Goucher knows *exactly* where each mile marker is, and he informs his teammates as they approach each one: "The two-mile marker is down here on the left... The three-mile marker is a quarter mile down on the left." Asked how he knows the course so well, he says without hesitation, "Hey man, I know it. I studied it all week. I have to." While his teammates will be biding their time, he knows where he wants to be: right at the front, dictating the race. He practically bounces along the course as they cross the quaint covered bridge that is one of the many elements that make this course so charming—for the fans.

After the team finishes their shake-out run, Goucher and Wetmore leave the course to get to the meet headquarters for some interviews at 1 p.m. By 1:30, none of the men they had asked to attend (Goucher, Mwangi, Abdirahman) have been interviewed yet.

The day ends with a pre-race banquet for all the teams, hosted by the NCAA. The dinner is as disorganized as everything else associated with the meet, and its brevity is its only saving grace. While the standard chicken and pasta offering is OK, the banquet is so crowded that the CU team cannot even sit together.

When the men get back to the hotel, Wetmore addresses them for the final time. Like Geiger, Wetmore thinks the wind could dramatically slow the race in the early going, and if this is the case, he tells them that they need to be toward the front of the pack. Again, though, Wetmore urges them to be patient. Their success or failure will largely be determined in the last 4000 meters of the race.

After listening to Wetmore, Batliner, and Goucher head to their rooms. They each write in their journals before going to bed. Batliner wrote:

> This course, I realized while we jogged around on it, was the last place Severy competed. I hadn't even thought about it until we were there, and then it hit me like a slap in the face. But I wasn't depressed about it. It's a symbolic measure that we get to finish this season the same place that he finished his. We all get to share a return to that course and put a positive stamp on the season. This team is not tragic, this season is not tragic; Chris's death was tragic. We get to pay tribute to what he was about while he was around by finishing, in grand style, what he never got to finish. I know it's on all of our minds, even though we don't want to talk about it— this is for Chris. That doesn't mean we go out harder and run harder than ever (which isn't possible), it doesn't mean we do a chant on the start line. It means we do what we always have done, which is train intelligently and methodically and race as hard as our bodies will let us. It means continuing the legacy that Chris was a part of. Run our asses off and do what we do so well that we defeat all kinds of people that are supposed to be better than us.
>
> Wetmore gave us our last instructions, which are not much different from what we knew before—hit your splits, be calm, and be ready to start breakin' necks from 6000 meters on. Well, the only change is that we need to be conscious of the _wind_, and if everybody goes out in 5:10 we need to be right up front. In other words, we need to listen to our legs, lungs, and pace and not our position in the pack. I'm going to run the fastest race I can on that course tomorrow, and the pack can all go to hell. If I have to lead or be dead last by 50 meters, I need to listen to my own sensory data and run intelligently. The game is on. I'm going to bed.

Goucher is more succinct. He writes, "Now it's just time to focus and rest. Twelve hours from now I'll be done with my collegiate career, hopefully as the 1998 NCAA National Cross Country Champion."

Monday, November 23, 1998
Rim Rock Farm
Lawrence, Kansas
10:30 a.m.

The 1998 Men's NCAA Cross Country Championship

"Last night was another shitty night of sleep. I've come to the conclusion that the Hotel Eldridge SUCKS!!!" Such is Adam Goucher's state of mind this morning after another sleepless night in Lawrence. Surely this is not what Wetmore had envisioned when he selected the hotel. An infuriated Goucher writes in his journal:

> *What the hell, there was some band playing a block away (on a Sunday night) till like 2:00 a.m. I could hear everything clearly, even the singer. It was so frustrating. After about 30 minutes of listening to this, I got up and attempted to make earplugs out of tissue. It worked well enough for me to finally get back to sleep.*

But the damage is done; on the morning of the most important race of his life, he writes, "*I woke up pretty tired.*" He has his traditional pre-race meal of Pop Tarts and Gatorade and then decides to take a walk to vent his frustration and clear his mind.

He steps outside and is immediately struck by the morning's chill and blustery winds. But he has trained with this day in mind for 94 days, and as he walks, he rediscovers an inner voice, the same voice that has been speaking to him all week. It tells him, "*You're ready, you're ready to go. If you just do what you're trained to do, if you just execute everything correctly, no one, no one, no one can beat you.*" Wind? No matter. Cold? No matter. All that matters is the voice inside his head, and as he walks back to his room, he knows, no doubt about it, he is ready to go.

Goucher's peace of mind, and that of his teammates, is tested by, of all things, a massive traffic jam on the way to the course. Numerous

Off and running at the 1998 NCAA Cross Country Championship.

teams sit idling on the one way road to Rim Rock Farm. Driver after driver pokes his head out the window, trying to ascertain the cause for the delay—to no avail. There is no accident; the organizers are simply redemonstrating their incompetence with an inefficient parking system. Perhaps they did not anticipate the thousands of spectators that have come to witness the event. But the reason why there is a delay is of no concern to the guys; the end result is that they arrive just in time to watch the women's race go off—a scant hour before their race.

The delay adds to their anxiety. Warming up, each athlete is hypersensitive to his body. Are my legs heavy? Is that a cramp coming on? Did I eat too much? For Goucher, "Everything felt good. I was a little nervous, which was different for me. All season, I can't think of one time that I was nervous. So coming into this race I was wondering if that nervous adrenaline edge would come back. It did, and I knew I was ready. Now all I needed to do was get the job done."

Every team has its own pre-race rituals. Now, twenty minutes to showtime, each team is busy completing their preparations. The Princeton Tigers gather at their box, number 16, in the middle of the starting line. They do a fast 400-meter stride as they have done before every meet this season. For the Tigers and their competitors, the repetition of a familiar routine helps them to treat the race as just another race. Other teams are also assembling at their boxes, lacing up their spikes, stretching, or simply lying down, collecting their nerves.

Colorado repeats their routine from Pre-Nationals. They gather at their van, talking, stretching, and putting their jerseys on. No one disturbs them. They finish their pre-race preparation and head to the starting line. Goucher is the last one to leave. He finishes tying his spikes, and stands nervously, staring into the distance. Wetmore calms him with some final words: "You're fine, Adam, you're fine. Trust it, Adam; trust all your work." His voice terse, Adam responds, "I know." He turns away from Wetmore, and leaves to meet his teammates at the starting line.

He is only ten minutes from a moment he has worked toward since late November 1994, when as a precocious freshman he finished second to the University of Arizona's Martin Keino at the NCAA championships in Fayetteville, Arkansas—in the process becoming the highest freshman finisher in the NCAA championships since Indiana yearling Bob Kennedy took home the title in 1988. He moves with confidence.

He is not alone. Oscar Ponce, Mike Friedberg, Ronald Roybal, Tom Reese, Adam Batliner, and Jay Johnson—each with aspirations of his own—also ready themselves as they prepare to join Adam in the battle to establish collegiate distance-running supremacy.

On August 18th, 23 men dreamt of standing in their shoes. In the ensuing 94 days, these seven demonstrated that they indeed, possessed *the right stuff.* They emerged after myriad trials, leaner, meaner, wiser, and ready.

The Buffaloes are in box fourteen, right toward the middle. Northern Arizona University, their mountain district rivals, are to their left in box thirteen, and a box of individual qualifiers (including a man familiar to all the Buffaloes after training with them last summer, Columbia's Tom Kloos) are to their right. Oregon, their primary rival, is at the far end of the line on the right.

Roybal stands at ease, snaps his arms backwards, and takes in the sight of the 250 foot soldiers—a battalion awaiting the bugle's call—that surround him. Reese stands in place, shaking out his limbs, staring blankly into space. Batliner, tired and wanting to yawn, legs feeling just a smidge lethargic, knows it is time to go. Goucher stands and adjusts his necklace of shrunken skulls, symbols of his prey, determined to add some more scalps.

As 250 men bounce, fiddle, and stretch, hoping *by God,* just to get this thing started, Wetmore barks final instructions to his runners. "Gentlemen, you'll hear no splits, and you won't see any mile markers. You're running by feel. Pay attention to your sensory data."

No splits? This angers the Buffaloes, particularly Friedberg. "I was pissed," he says. "I just *knew* they weren't going to be able to give splits, because that's the way things were run out there." Hearing this rattles him nonetheless. With only five minutes until the start, Friedberg is losing his shit. Nicknamed "Iceberg" by Wetmore early in the season for his unflappable temperament under pressure, his fears are getting the best of him. Johnson senses his anxiety, and tries to settle his nerves. "Don't worry about this," he says. "This is fake, everyone's full of shit. What's real is Magnolia Road. What's real is milers out on the course." Friedberg internalizes Johnson's counsel, and to a certain extent, it works. But still, doubt lingers. Just a year ago he was a Junior Varsity runner, a walk-on nobody from the Park School in Baltimore, Maryland—hardly a recruiting hotbed. Now he is being counted on to be up at the front, contending for All-American honors.

It's go time. The men nod and slap hands with one another, wordlessly expressing their hopes, their prayers, and their brotherhood. Ninety-four days and thousands of miles since they convened at Kitt Field on an 88-degree afternoon, they await the starter's call. All that remains is 30 minutes to man up and take the pain, one last time. They are not afraid.

The gun sounds. The runners—all 250 of them—take off in a mad dash in order to not get pinched out of position as they head into the sharp left turn less than a half mile into the race. Goucher charges out, determined to establish himself among the leaders. *Get out with the lead-*

ers, he tells himself. *Don't get boxed in. It'll slow after a mile and a half. I'll be alright.* Behind him, the Buffs are uncharacteristically rolling. Perhaps it is their position in the middle of the line, or perhaps they have taken Wetmore's advice to get out a little faster than usual too much to heart. The fast start unnerves Batliner. In races past, his nervous tension has dissipated in a sea of adrenaline and firing neurons. Today, the opposite happens. They are out so quickly that he becomes more nervous with every step. Says Batliner afterwards, "All seven of us took off for the fastest 400 I've ever run in the beginning of a cross race. Usually we would be in the last 30 to 40 people at this point at Nationals, but this time we were in the top 100. That doesn't sound fast, but after five years of going out controlled at a reasonable pace, it felt like we were flying."

Try to fit 250 mad dashing men around a corner with a path fifteen feet wide. The results are predictable; elbows fly, and piercing spikes land not in the ground but in the bony shin of the man *right on your ass.* Boom! A man goes down right in Friedberg's path. Hurdle him? Go around? There is no time to think, and Friedberg's instincts scream "Hurdle!" just as the downed runner rises. Friedberg stops. Bam! Someone slams into him, and Friedberg is eating dirt before he can comprehend what has happened. A singular thought crosses his mind: *If I don't get up as fast as I can, I'm gonna get trampled.* He rises instantly, heart racing, and starts sprinting. He has lost only two spots but he is rattled. He feels the coolness of the blood from the cuts on his knees and a burning sensation from the scrapes on his hands. He sprints to maintain his position. *It's alright,* he thinks, calming himself. *Whatever happened, happened. Now is not the time to panic.* He passes the mile with Batliner and Reese. There are no splits, and they do not know where they stand. Their best guess—in the 80s. Batliner's sensory data tells him it is about 4:50, at slowest 4:55. Friedberg is back into it, into the moment, into the now, and he prepares to hide out here and settle in.

Mark Hauser of UCLA had the early lead. At 1k, Abdirahman puts in a little surge, getting into his rhythm, and the pack follows. A minute later, Abdirahman surges again. Goucher is not surprised; he has raced him before, and he knows this is how Abdirahman runs. "He doesn't surge, surge, surge, [continuously building the pace] and pull away." He knows Abdirahman is coming back.

But it is the NCAA's, and now is not the time to gamble recklessly. So before Abdirahman can get over ten meters on him, Goucher goes after him and reels him in. Only, Goucher does not stop. He catches Abdirahman and goes right past. Now he is in control, he is setting the pace—reminding everyone in that front pack—*I'm here to race.* Goucher appears as relaxed as he did in August on the aqueduct. His face reveals no tension, only a narrowness of the eyes. He hears the crowd around him with every step. "Go, Goucher! Come on, Adam!" The crowd's exhortations fuel his ambition.

Soon after the leaders pass the mile, Abdirahman of Arizona retakes the point. Mwangi is there. Lagat is there. Mixed into the sea of African faces with his pale complexion and black and gold uniform is Adam Goucher. *OK,* Goucher thinks, *now the race begins.*

The lead cart kicks up a cloud of dust as they approach two miles. *This sucks!* The wind blows the billowing dust right to left. Goucher moves to the right-hand side of the plume, right on the edge. The others will bear the brunt of it.

The leaders hit two miles and the pace escalates just a notch. Enough, though, to separate them from the rest of the field. Brad Hauser of Stanford, Jeff Simonich of Utah, Matt Downin of Wisconsin, and Sean Kaley of Arkansas hang on to Goucher and the African trio of Mwangi, Abdirahman, and Lagat. Goucher pays attention to those around him. He does this primarily by listening to their breathing. No one gives any signals of distress; they all seem comfortable. But at this early stage, he expects this, and he is not concerned. *Be patient,* he tells himself. *Good guys take a long time to die. Don't get too excited.*

Goucher feels the grains of dust on his teeth. He is on autopilot, gulping up land with his gargantuan stride. Although only 141 pounds, he looks enormous next to Abdirahman. Goucher powers along, every step a contraction and expansion of swollen muscles that have hardened for this task. With his skeleton-like frame, Abdirahman merely floats. While Goucher's an American SUV, gobbling up fuel from a massive tank, Abdi-

rahman moves with the clean efficiency of a sleek two-door roadster. Abdirahman's engine purrs as his elbows cock back, and his willowy legs glide forward, always forward. He has no backkick, no wasted motion, and looks as if he is out for a Sunday stroll. Only the obvious exertion of those around Abdirahman gives him away.

Goucher, Abdirahman and Kaley.

Goucher eases off the accelerator as they approach three miles. *OK,* he thinks, *your turn, you can lead for a while.* Kaley takes the bait. He flies down a short, steep descent in full stride, but his momentum only carries him through the covered bridge at the base of another steep little climb. Abdirahman flies past Kaley, then Goucher. Kaley holds the lead for less than ten seconds, and as Goucher passes Kaley he *feels* him laboring, hears his rival breathing.

He's had enough.

One down.

Abdirahman pushes up the climb. Lagat goes right with him, and Goucher remembers the cardinal Colorado cross country rule: Take it easy, relax up the climb. *These guys are sprinting!* He relaxes as much as he can, but it is getting a little difficult. Lagat and Abdirahman are flying away up the hill, and doubt starts to seep into his system along with the faintest hints of lactic acid.

The three harriers crest the hill, having gapped the others. Goucher immediately passes Lagat and presses. Lagat struggles to hang on. A minute later, Goucher knows *There's just three of us. This is where we start picking it up.* They shoot down and around a short, steep descent, arms out from their sides like three airplanes as they negotiate the sharp, quick left. They then enter into a corridor of fans. They ride the tube of a human wave, not knowing who will emerge alive. Again, Goucher repeatedly hears his name above the din. Each spectator attempts the impossible task of fixing one eye on the leaders with the other cocked back desperately searching for the faces or jerseys of those individuals they have come to support.

Abdirahman, Lagat, and Goucher fly through this corridor, and whip down a little five-foot dip. Seventeen minutes have expired, and Lagat has quietly slipped ten feet out of the slipstream provided by Abdirahman and Goucher running side by side, stride for stride. Ten feet. The distance from

Goucher and Abdirahman drop Lagat.

gym floor to basketball rim is the same in Kansas as it is in Indiana, but rest assured that to Lagat it is a crevasse as formidable as the Grand Canyon. Goucher need not look back, for now he knows, *It's me and him now. This is where the race begins, this is where it really gets hard.* It is down to two.

Despite the effort, Abdirahman and Goucher look easy and relaxed. Approaching four miles, Abdirahman surges again. As with each previous surge, he repeatedly glances over his shoulder, eyeballing Goucher, searching for signs of distress. Again he gains a stride on Goucher, and again Goucher remains calm. He is tired, but he knows Abdirahman is also tired, so he is not troubled with Abdirahman gaining a stride on him. He takes his time climbing back into Abdirahman's hip pocket.

Two miles remain, and Goucher feels the pain. *Anything can happen. We're pressing, and Billy Mills Hill is coming up. It's gonna be hard.* Abdirahman sustains his push. *Don't let him gain any ground.* It hurts, but Goucher feels confident. The stretch from here to Billy Mills Hill is the loneliest stretch on the course. There are few spectators. They race alone. The chase pack is over 30 seconds back.

With less than two miles to go, Goucher takes control. There is a steep little hill before Billy Mills Hill, and Goucher starts to squeeze the trigger. *I can hear him breathing pretty hard now. I'm pressing all the way to Billy Mills Hill. My legs are burning so bad, but I'm just grinding, grinding. He's right on me the whole way.*

A crowd of spectators—five deep on each side—lines the hill. As he approaches, Goucher hears a pack of CU supporters that includes Berkshire, Schafer, Slattery, and Ruhl wildly chanting, "GOUCHER! GOUCHER! GOUCHER!" But Goucher is already thinking past the climb. *At five miles,*

it's all or nothing. The crowd erupts as Goucher and Abdirahman crest the hill stride for stride. Six weeks ago it was he and Mwangi cresting the hill together. Now only Abdirahman stands in his way of an NCAA championship.

Like at Pre-Nationals, Goucher immediately puts a few paces between himself and his pursuer. Goucher's

Going for broke.

mind conspired against him then. His doubts overwhelmed him. But now he is rested. Will he have enough? Wetmore awaits him at 8k. Goucher flies by, going for broke. Wetmore yells, "There's a lot of running left, a lot of running. Stay cool babe!" Abdirahman fights to hang on as Goucher's stride lengthens. Goucher does not look back. *I know he's behind me; he's not breaking. It's all or nothing now; time to make it a guts race. This mile is for everything, for me, for all the hard work, all the years, for Sev.*

Wetmore waits at 8k for the others. Friedberg is the first to appear, and Roybal is right on his heels. "Come on, Mike, come on, Ronald, you're running GREAT!" Wetmore's excitement would be remarkable to the outsider, considering these are his two and three guys, and right now, they are in no better than 60th place. Ten seconds later, Reese appears with Batliner on his tail. Batliner comes through 8k in 25:25, and now the reason for Wetmore's excitement becomes evident. Sev was CU's second man when they finished third at Pre-Nationals. On that day—only six weeks ago—Severy ran 25:24 for the 8k race. They now have five running as fast or faster *through* 8k, and there are still two kilometers to go. Johnson is further back in the mid–one hundreds as their sixth man, and Ponce, grimacing as the pain in his shin gets the best of him, rounds out the squad. It is now clear that CU's fate rests on the shoulders of Goucher, Friedberg, Roybal, Reese, and Batliner. *This is where it happens.* Wetmore races across the field toward the finish line to see how many men they can pass, hoping his nightmare remains a fantasy.

On Billy Mills ascent, five guys tore past Friedberg and Roybal. "I couldn't believe it," says Friedberg. "They tore up it as hard as they could." But he and Ronald had already passed them when they passed Wetmore. Those men paid a steep price for their foolish exertion. Friedberg had been worried up to now, thinking, *People aren't dying as fast as I thought.* But catching them so effortlessly buoys Friedberg's spirit and gives him an incalculable lift. Wetmore's counsel now replays itself in his mind: *Trust your fitness.* For both Roybal and Friedberg, now is the time. *Finally, they're starting to die. There's less than a mile to go. If I get a hard last mile, I can get ten or fifteen places. Gotta keep going as hard as I can.*

Three quarters of a mile is all that separates Goucher from his first NCAA cross country title. He has not relented since starting his surge to the finish at 8k. As he crests the course's last hill, he feels the lactic acid burn erupt across his shoulders, through his veins, down to his fingertips. *God, are they heavy. Stride out, stride out, take the pain.* He glances back as he rounds the corner at the base of the hill to see he is gapping Abdirahman. He knows that with every stride, his lead increases. He hears a spectator yell, "Do it for Chris!" which removes him from the cocoon of pain enveloping his senses. Goucher remembers Pre-Nationals, Mwangi impossibly flying by him here, his legs unable to respond. The lactic acid coursing its way through his system plants seeds of doubt in every muscle fiber being poisoned by its presence. He tries to relax. *Alright Chris, if you're with me, let's do it.*

At 8k, two Stanford runners, senior Jon Weldon and freshman James Gifford, run with Reese and Batliner. Bat passed one of Oregon's top runners, Micah Davis, at mile four, and running with the duo from Stanford tells him they are in it for the team title. *Gotta push now.* Reese and Batliner pass people, but not nearly as many as they normally do late in a race. Worse, the Stanford runners show no sign of wilting. For every runner they pass, the Stanford duo stay right with them. Says Batliner, "I wanted so bad to lead a surge and have Tommy roll with me, or for him to pick it up so I could latch on, but neither ever happened. We were running all out, there was nothing more to be done."

After passing people in droves, Friedberg is done. But an agonizing half mile remains. He passed two NAU guys, Billy Herman and Steve Osaduik, with a mile to go, and they latched onto him and Roybal. Now, as the fog settles in, he gets complacent, content to maintain his position. He goes without passing anyone for the next 200 meters. Then Roybal gets on Friedberg's shoulder and slaps him on the back, literally jarring him out of his complacency. Only six hundred meters remain and they start kicking together with everything that they have.

Goucher continues his all-out drive to the finish. Since starting his surge, he has not relented for a second. He has never broken stride. The quick glance back lets him know his lead is increasing, but the hysterical crowd around him muddies his thoughts. He does not know how much ground he has. Less than 90 seconds remain, and he shakes his arms out trying to dislodge some of the lactic acid that feels like drying cement from his shoulders down to his fingertips. He sees his best friend Tim Catalano off to his right, screaming and jumping up and down, and he knows, *It's time to roll!*

Here comes the champion.

He shakes his arms again, trying fruitlessly to shake the pain away, but it does not relent. Way back, Abdirahman takes two strides for every one of Goucher's. The announcer starts blasting over the PA just as the massive crowd reaches full volume, "Here he is, let's bring him home, the University of Colorado senior." The banner is less than one hundred meters away; he knows the race is his. He shakes a fist at the crowd. And it all starts to pour out—the exultation, the relief, the redemption, the pride, and the grief. Above all, he feels the immense emotional and physical pain. He knows he has done it. "For something to hurt that bad, and feel so good, it's just inexplicable." Adam Goucher crosses the finish in 29:26. Abdirahman finishes in 29:49.

Goucher waits for his teammates at the end of the chute just as Roybal and Friedberg launch into their final kick. They quickly pass a clump of three runners and keep going. They pass another, then another—they are in the finishing stretch—they are all out. The finishing banner is *right there* as they catch Central Michigan teammates Richard Brinker and Ryan Watson with 50 meters to go. The Central Michigan duo respond to the challenge and hold off Friedberg and Roybal. They will pass no more. Friedberg finishes one half second in front of Roybal as both are timed in 31:10. They finish 34th and 35th.

As he crosses the line, Friedberg worries he has outkicked Roybal for the last All-American certificate. He dreads thinking he beat him out of a certificate when he never would have passed as many men in the last 600 without his help. "Without Ronald, it definitely wouldn't have happened. I would've kicked the last 300, not the last 600, so basically, I owe it to him." It turns out that what he owes Roybal is gratitude for helping them **both** earn their first ever All-American honors. Not bad for a self-described "little Mexican from Pojoaque" and a walk-on nobody who will surprise people no more. All told, they passed 25 guys in the last 2000 meters.

Roybal and the Iceberg, inches from the line.

Fifteen seconds later, Reese and Batliner barrel down the finishing stretch. A smattering of cheers replace the roar that awaited the leaders, but the battles are no less fierce. Reese duels Stanford freshman Gifford. His arms flail wildly, and he turns and stares at Gifford with every other stride. "Don't you dare," his eyes say. Gifford strains, heeding nothing but the tape. Reese would rather eat nails than get outkicked by someone from Stanford. He surges improbably just feet from the line, leans, and beats him out by one tenth of a second. He finishes 60th, in 31:36. That is only 26 seconds, but a whopping 25 places, behind Friedberg. Batliner finishes two and half seconds and two places behind Reese. He is 63rd, in 31:39. The indignity Batliner feels from the losing to *a freshman* from *Stanford,* of all places, is partially offset by the fact that he outran Stanford senior Jon Weldon to the line. But make no mistake, the loss stings on many levels. He later writes:

I finished and stumbled along, and I knew that I ran as hard as I could have. Knowing that I did all I could was actually kind of depressing; if this was all I have, and all I have is 63rd, how the hell am I going to ever make a professional runner out of myself? This season was the first break in my fantasy that I am this great runner who can overcome whatever adversity comes my way and still produce great performances. I placed third in the steeple (at NCAA's last spring) with a broken fibula; why can't I go top

One last glance.

twenty in cross with a broken tibia? I know this sounds stupid, but so does running in general if your aren't obsessed . . . like most of my friends are.

Anyway, I know one thing for sure: I never, ever want to go into a race injured, out of shape, or anything close.

This race was unsatisfying for me. I was really strong neuromuscularly with all the short, fast running we did, but I had no aerobic capacity. As fast as I ran was entirely dependent upon my heart and lungs—I finished and my legs <u>never hurt</u>, I was just tired. If I could have just had a few 20 milers . . .

Jay Johnson finishes 139th, in 32:36, in his last collegiate cross country race. He is the sixth man, so he does not directly affect the scoring. But in a way, he has. Without his help on the starting line, Friedberg would have lost his composure without having run so much as a step. Credit Jay Johnson with stepping up when it counted, in the process contributing as much as Roybal to Friedberg's All-American status.

Ponce finishes 162nd, in 32:51, the pain in his shin too much to ignore. Now he finally gets a well-deserved rest. A first team All-Big 12 runner by virtue of his fine seventh-place performance just three weeks ago on October 31st, he too is left grasping the fumes of a season that has quietly gone up in smoke. He will have one more chance to get that All-American certificate, but right now that is 365 days away.

The Buffaloes stand as one.

The team gathers in the paddock and crowds around Goucher. An exuberant Jay Johnson exclaims, "He won! Goucher won! Yes! Yes!" Huddled as one, they celebrate Goucher's victory and their own. Battered and beaten, they survived, and against the odds, surpassed their ranking, finishing third as a team at the NCAA championships. They will stand on the podium with runner-up Stanford and the champion Razorbacks from Arkansas. A team third is a great performance in any year, yet for them it will forever taste bittersweet. "Hey man, Sev Dog," Roybal says to his teammates. Goucher does not hesitate, "He was there man, he was with me." Clutching Goucher, Roybal finishes the thought each of them already knows. "He was there every step of the way."

1998 NCAA CROSS COUNTRY CHAMPIONSHIPS

PLACE	NAME	UNIVERSITY	CLASS	TIME
1.	Adam Goucher	Colorado	Sr.	29:26.90 CR
2.	Abdi Abdirahman	Arizona	Sr.	29:49.90
3.	Julius Mwangi	Butler	Sr.	30:00.00
4.	Matthew Downin	Wisconsin	Jr.	30:00.10
5.	Sean Kaley	Arkansas	Sr.	30:12.10
6.	Brad Hauser	Stanford	Sr.	30:18.20
7.	Bernard Lagat	Washington State	Jr.	30:20.40
8.	Jeff Simonich	Utah	Sr.	30:22.40
9.	Jonathon Riley	Stanford	So.	30:31.90
10.	Todd Snyder	Michigan	Sr.	30:34.50
34.	Mike Friedberg	Colorado	So.	31:10.10
35.	Ron Roybal	Colorado	Jr.	31:10.60
60.	Tom Reese	Colorado	Sr.	31:36.90
63.	Adam Batliner	Colorado	Sr.	31:39.30
139.	Jay Johnson	Colorado	Sr.	32:36.20
162.	Oscar Ponce	Colorado	Jr.	32:51.10

The Show Is Over

It is a cold and gloomy Boulder morning. As usual, Wetmore is in his office. He has with him a copy of today's *Denver Post*. There is a large picture of Goucher with the pack on his heels in the race's early stages on the front page. It is not often that a picture of a cross country runner appears on the front page of the sports section, let alone the front page of a major newspaper.

Only a day removed from their third-place showing behind Arkansas and Stanford, Wetmore already starts to evaluate the season. On one account, they were successful. They always aim to beat their ranking and they did. They were ranked fourth and they finished third. Another measure he uses to grade his team's success is by comparing each runner's results from Pre-Nationals to Nationals. CU always runs Pre-Nationals, to "get a feel for the course, evaluate that data, and write a plan for NCAA's." If Wetmore's plan was successful, he expects to see marked improvement from one race to the other. Batliner was injured for Pre-Nationals, so he is exempt from the comparison. Johnson also did not run then, but Wetmore does not need that data to judge his season a success. He says, "Jay's improvement curve was better than anybody on the team. From mono in August to the starting line at NCAA's is a very successful story." Ponce is also exempt. He ran poorly at NCAA's, "but we know why. He was running on a stress fracture. He's the only one for whom the formula didn't work, but we know why." The following chart demonstrates how well the plan worked for the others.

NAME	NATIONALS 10K	AVERAGE KILOMETER	8k SPLIT	PRE-NATS 8k
Adam Goucher	29:26.9	2:56.6	23:33	23:54
Mike Friedberg	31:10.1	3:07	24:56	25:37
Ronald Roybal	31:10.6	3:07	24:56	25:59
Tom Reese	31:36.9	3:09.6	25:17	25:48

Each athlete's 8k split at Nationals was *significantly* faster than what he ran for an 8k race on the same course at Pre-Nationals six weeks earlier. Each athlete came through faster, with another 2k yet to run! Again, despite the numerous setbacks each athlete had, they managed to run their best when it counted most.

For these four, "it was a successful story." But Wetmore is not

thrilled. "The other story is why did Bat get a stress fracture? Why di
Oscar get a stress fracture?" He blames Batliner's second stress fracture
in six months and Ponce's injury on the density of the training. For Bat in
particular, "the density of the work will have to be adjusted if he is to get
healthy."

The injuries gnaw at him. He knows as much as anyone, this was CU's
best shot at winning it all. He blames himself. "If we weren't hurt, we
should have won. So I have to look critically at my own work and see
what misjudgments I made." But Wetmore cannot bear all of the responsibility. Batliner, for instance, could have prepared himself better. "The day
we found out he got hurt, I said, 'I'll save a spot for you, but don't get fat,'
and he gained ten to fifteen pounds. When you're a fifth-year senior in
the last-chance saloon, how could you not check? Every day!" He attributes the weight gain simply to carelessness. "He wasn't careful, that's all.
On a macro level, his inattentiveness hurt him. He was 25 to 30 seconds
behind where he could have been just because he had an extra ten to
twelve pounds of weight."

And what about Reese? By an objective measure, he ran well, but
Reese was tremendously disappointed with his result. Wetmore feels for
him, but stresses how difficult it is to really run well without a large base,
which Reese simply did not have.

On a larger scale, the lack of consistency, the number of interruptions that Reese, Batliner, and Johnson had is what Wetmore feels hurt
them the most. He says, "Reese had convinced himself that he was ready
to be top 25 or 30. He was pretty sure he was gonna be top 30, so that
was a big disappointment for him. At some point in the season you get
them to run the best race they have in them. The less time you spend
building up to your peak, the less long you can hold it. Who had the
longest, most consistent buildup? Goucher, Friedberg, and Roybal. Who
had a quick buildup? Batliner, Reese, and Jay Johnson. They all were almost a bridge too far. One more race and it would be obvious."

Goucher also suffered interruptions, particularly in the latter part of
the season, and yet he still dominated the field. If healthy, by how much
would he have won? Wetmore does not care to speculate. He says flatly,
"He lost fitness he could have gained, but it doesn't matter. It's immate-
rial. I don't give a shit. He would have run the same race strategy anyway;
keep the pace steady for 8k, then go. He just set them up, like Ali
working somebody for eight rounds. One by one he took them to their
breaking point, then he took off."

Wetmore feels like he has been in a fight himself. "You take the
blows, it's like a fight. Boom, boom, boom, and then you get moments of
ecstasy. It would be a lot easier if I didn't give a shit." But he does. He lives

es for this team. And through the season's most trying time, the most trying time of his career, he helped steer them through

lay following Severy's death, Wetmore did what he recommended his athlete's do: He ran. The discipline of the distance runner, the same discipline he has adhered to daily for twenty years, is what he credits for helping Sev's teammates and himself move forward. He says of his runners, "They're hard. They're hardened. Every day there's a callusing effect when you head out and you go when you don't want to. You don't see it until they're tapered. They're smiling, happy. These aren't the people I know. They're so tough, callused, and businesslike about that aspect of their life that they came back. I don't think that's something unique to Colorado, I think that's something unique to distance runners. It's hurting every day a little bit, and a little more on Saturday."

"In football, you might get your bell rung, but you go in with the expectation that you might get hurt, and you hope to win and come out unscathed. As a distance runner, you know you're going to get your bell rung. Distance runners are experts at pain, discomfort, and fear. You're not coming away feeling good. It's a matter of how much pain you can deal with on those days. It's not a strategy. It's just a callusing of the mind and body to deal with discomfort. Any serious runner bounces back. That's the nature of their game. Taking pain."

Bouncing back. Rest assured Wetmore will take a long hard look at the faults in this year's program when designing the plan for next year. The season is just over, but already Wetmore is looking ahead. Next year's squad will be dramatically different. The best class he has ever had, along with the most dominant runner in CU history, will have graduated.

Rival coaches need not celebrate. Wetmore feels next year's squad may be the school's best ever. So much for a rebuilding year. He says, "We lost five runners, but we've never gone into a year holding ten better people ever. We have All-Americans in Napier, Roybal, Ponce —who would've been an All-American if he was healthy—and Friedberg. Then there's Valenti, Elmo, Slattery, the two Torreses, and Berkshire. Then you have walk-ons like Zach Crandall and Sean Smith. Zach was only ten seconds behind Sean on November 7th. And who knows who's gonna come out of the woodwork? There are at least ten to twelve really good runners coming back."

Losing Goucher and the others in this year's senior class will hurt. But with Goucher's departure, Wetmore says, "This huge towering redwood that for five years gathered all the sun is gone. All these little sequoias can each grab a little sun."

Epilogue

The 1999 cross country season was a mixed bag for the Colorado cross country team. Despite the graduation of CU's best-ever senior class, the team defended their Big 12 Championship. Ronald Roybal won the individual title, followed by freshman sensation Jorge Torres. Sean Smith not only proved to be another Friedberg, he *beat* Friedberg by one spot to finish fifth and earn First-Team All-Big 12 honors. The Iceberg, though, affirmed his mettle by leading CU with his 42nd place finish at the NCAA championships. Unfortunately, the team had a rare off day at the NCAA's, and "only" finished seventh. Arkansas, again, claimed the team title.

As the 2000 Olympic Trials approach, CU athletes and alums are looking formidable. Adam Goucher is leading the charge. After winning NCAA's last fall, Fila made Goucher one of the U.S.'s highest-paid distance runners by signing him to what was reported to be the most lucrative endorsement contract ever for a distance runner coming out of college. He has proved well worth the investment. He won the U.S. 4k Cross Country title in 1999 and finished 11th in the World Cross Country Championships. He followed that performance with a victory at the U.S. Indoor Track and Field Championships in the 3000 meters before pulling his biggest coup by beating perennial U.S. champion Bob Kennedy for the 5000 meter title at the U.S. Outdoor Track and Field Championships. He subsequently ran 13:11 for 5000 meters in Zurich, Switzerland, making him the third fastest American of all-time. He finished his eventful year with his first trip to the World Track and Field Championships, where he made the final of the 5000 meters and finished 11th.

This fall Goucher not only defended his U.S. 4k Cross Country title, but he also came back the next day to defeat ex-teammate Alan Culpepper to add the 12k title to his collection. Unfortunately, an acute case of Achilles tendonitis sidelined him for both the World Cross Country Championships and the majority of the indoor campaign, and it even threatened his outdoor season. He has apparently righted the problem, and he appears on track to make the team to Sydney at the Olympic Trials in Sacramento in July.

Adam Batliner and Tom Reese hope to join Goucher in Sacramento. Batliner is eking out a living as a professional—he is currently sponsored by Saucony—and is on the verge of qualifying for the Olympic Trials in the 5000 meters. Reese, who parlayed his internship into a position in sports marketing with Saucony, is also trying to qualify for the Trials in the 5000 meters. If Reese and Batliner make it, expect to see them sporting Village Coffee Shop T-shirts along with their Saucony gear, for the Village is sponsoring them as well.

Ronald Roybal will join them on the starting line in Sacramento. At Stanford in May 2000, he ran a PR 13:42 for 5000 meters. The performance qualified Roybal for the Olympic Trials.

Jorge Torres finished right behind Roybal at the Stanford Invite, also clocking 13:42. The time broke Adam Goucher's University of Colorado freshman record. It has been a long year for Jorge, though, so he will skip the Trials to gain strength for next year, when he hopes to lead the Buffaloes with his twin brother Ed.

Brock Tessman may be in Sacramento as well. Innumerable high-mileage weeks in Boulder through the winter and early spring have given him a tremendous base, and his early results indicate he is on pace to be a Trials qualifier in either the 1500 or 5000 meters.

When they have finished racing they will be cheering for Steve Slattery, who will be running the steeplechase at the Olympic Trials. Slattery recently broke Tom Reese's older brother Dan's school record in the steeplechase with an 8:35 at the Penn Relays.

When Slattery finishes and looks into the stands for Wetmore, he is likely to see Jay Johnson, who could be scouting recruits for his *own* program. Johnson was recently named head track coach at Pratt Community College in Pratt, Kansas.

Matt Elmuccio, Slattery's New Jersey nemesis, may be following Slattery's exploits as well—from afar. Elmuccio redshirted this spring and reportedly transferred to Seton Hall University in South Orange, New Jersey.

Oscar Ponce will probably be there as well to cheer on his teammates. Again felled by stress fractures in his shins, he did not get his All-American certificate. But, this spring, he ran 29:35 for 10,000 meters. The mark places him sixth on the all-time CU list. More important, he earned his degree in Spanish literature. He intends to start graduate work toward his masters in the fall.

Back in Colorado, Matt Napier will be getting results on the Internet as he starts an engineering career with Hewlett Packard in Fort Collins. That is, of course, if Napier is not attending to the birth of his third child.

Even if he is not covering the Olympic Trials for a local newspaper, 2000 journalism graduate Wes Berkshire will be closely following his teammates. A member of the all-nobody team coming out of high school,

Wes rebounded from a disastrous fall, where he was just fried after running 130 mile weeks, to run a huge PR of 14:31 for 5000 meters in his final collegiate season.

Aaron Blondeau may also be covering the Olympic Trials, although probably from a Web site of his own. The computer science major will not be running there because he continues to be inexplicably injury-prone. A 13:51 5000 meter performance in the spring of 1999 offered a tantalizing glimpse of how formidable he will be if he can solve his injury woes.

With Wetmore at the helm, and the Torres twins, Friedberg, Blondeau, Slattery, and Smith leading the charge, the future is bright for Colorado. A bumper crop of Colorado-only recruits will join them, and when they line up for the Big 12 Cross Country Championships in Boulder next fall, another Severy may be toeing the line. Chris's brother Jonathan will be a freshman for the Buffaloes in the fall of 2000. But even if Jonathan is not on the line, Chris will be. A tree was planted and dedicated in his memory on the Buffalo Ranch. Now Sev will always be there to watch over the Buffaloes.

Chris Lear
May 2000

Afterword

It's hard to believe it's been almost five years since I moved to Boulder to spend the 1998 cross country season with the Colorado Buffaloes. While so much has happened in the intervening years that it sometimes feels like a lifetime ago, the memories of the unforgettable 1998 campaign remain as vivid as if they happened yesterday.

When I set out to write *Running With The Buffaloes*, I did so without a publisher's contract, and without any certainty the manuscript would ever see the light of day. I suppose you could say that in undertaking the creation of this book I was living in an Edge City of my own, paralleling the journey of the 1988 Buffaloes.

The men in this book were my first critics. They read it when it was nothing more than a rubber-band bound manuscript. I met the guys for breakfast one morning at the Village a short while after they had had a chance to read it. When they uniformly told me that I'd captured the experience, my journey, in a sense, was complete.

Finding a publisher, though, was easier said than done. Fortunately, after an odyssey that included self-publishing the book, it found a home with The Lyons Press. And, to my elation, in the intervening years I've heard from many of you who have been touched by the Buffaloes' tale. I can only hope that the story of Chris Severy, Adam Goucher, and the rest of the men herein will inspire a new generation of readers in years to come.

Inevitably, when readers speak to me about *Running With The Buffaloes,* they ask where the members of the 1998 team are now. It will come as no surprise that while competitive running continues to play a prominent role in the lives of many on that team, it is but a memory for others. Here then, is an update on lives of the central characters of the 1998 team.

Mark Wetmore continues to coach the Buffaloes. Since Goucher won the NCAA crown in 1998 Wetmore has had four other NCAA champions. Kara Grgas-Wheeler (now Kara Goucher) won the 2000 NCAA Cross Country Championship to lead the CU women to their first NCAA title. One year later, the CU men edged Stanford by a point to win their first NCAA title. With that, Wetmore made history as the first coach to capture all four NCAA cross country titles — men's and women's team and individual championships.

Then, this past fall, at the 2002 NCAA Cross Country Champi-onships in Terre Haute, Indiana, Jorge Torres became the first American since Goucher to win the individual title. His twin, Edwardo, finished tenth, making them the best-ever siblings at the NCAA Cross Country Championships.

Steve Slattery concluded a spectacular CU career in Terre Haute. Weakened by mononucleosis, he finished sixty-third, but he departed CU with the school record in the steeplechase — 8:23. He earned that time at the 2002 USA Track and Field Championships, where he finished second. Now engaged to CU standout Sara Gorton and running for Nike, Slattery hopes to represent the United States at the 2004 Olympics in Athens.

Four years ago, it seemed as if Adam Goucher was destined for greatness. When healthy he has been great, but for the past two years that has proved elusive. Though he made the 2000 Olympic final and 2001 World Championship final in the 5000 — the only American to do so — he did so while training sporadically because of a wide variety of ailments. Thankfully, in November 2002, Goucher had surgery for a sports hernia; an injury his doctor believes was at the root of all his ail-ments. He has trained uninterrupted since then, and he's cautiously op-timistic that he'll regain the form that made him such a magnificent world-class prospect just two years ago. "This year may not be as stellar as I'd like it to be," he says, "but it's my stepping-stone heading into the Olympic year. I may not run sub-13 (for 5000 meters) this year, because I haven't had the consistency in my training to back that up, but I think it's going to be a very good year."

Jason Drake is now the head cross country coach and assistant track coach at Washington State University. Assisting JD in Pullman is none other than Mike Friedberg. After concluding his collegiate career as a three-time All-America in cross country, Friedberg decided to hang 'em up. He's now taking dead aim at developing a few Mike Friedbergs of his own in years to come.

JD's departure opened the door for Jay Johnson's return. After two years as the head coach at Pratt Community College in Pratt, Kansas, Johnson returned to his alma mater in the fall of 2002 to serve as assis-tant coach and recruiting coordinator for the Buffaloes.

Upon his return to Boulder, Johnson was pleased to discover that he had some good bloodlines to work with. Among his charges are freshman Payton Batliner, Adam Batliner's cousin, and junior John Severy, Chris Severy's younger brother. Both were varsity members of CU's third-place cross country team at the 2002 NCAA cham-pionships.

While Johnson is no longer competing, Adam Batliner is still getting after it. He's "living the dream," working at a shoe store in Boulder, painting, and running, and he's making a name for himself in all of his endeavors. Batliner's artwork now shows in galleries across Boulder, and last spring he joined Slattery in the final of the USA Championships in the steeplechase, finishing twelfth.

Among Batliner's housemates is Tom Reese. Unfortunately, Reese's knee troubles have only grown more debilitating since his graduation. Though he still harbors running ambitions, he has quickly established a reputation as a top realtor in the Boulder area. He hopes to open a real estate agency of his own in the not-so-distant future.

Brock Tessman is now an instructor in the political science department at CU and on track to earn his PhD in political science in the coming year. He's contined to run, and hopes to lower his 13:58 5000 pr and qualify for the Olympic Trials in 2004.

Wes Berkshire is returning to Colorado after several blissful years as a ski bum in Lake Tahoe and New Zealand.

Oscar Ponce recently returned to Colorado after several years in Oregon. He's pursuing a master's degree in counseling psychology for public education at CU-Denver and assisting the Denver North cross country and track teams. He aspires to coach track and be a guidance counselor at an inner-city school.

Ponce's partner in crime, Ron Roybal, is living in Albuquerque, New Mexico, and working as a homeopathic sales representative. Though chronic foot problems curtailed his running career, he's embarking on the next phase of his life with vigor equal to what he displayed on the track and trails at CU.

One day, these men will have families of their own. No doubt, at that time, they'll seek child-rearing advice from Matt Napier. Napier now works as an engineer at the Sandia National Laboratories and lives in Albuquerque with his wife and four children.

So there you have it. Though they've followed unique and diverse paths since the 1998 season, all are well. Though not as close as they once were, each knows that the brotherhood that binds them will always exist, much like the memory of their brother, Christopher Severy.

Chris Lear
May 2003